GENDER IN

Series editors:
Lynn Abrams, Cordelia Beattie, Pam Sharpe and Penny Summerfield

The expansion of research into the history of women and gender since the 1970s has changed the face of history. Using the insights of feminist theory and of historians of women, gender historians have explored the configuration in the past of gender identities and relations between the sexes. They have also investigated the history of sexuality and family relations, and analysed ideas and ideals of masculinity and femininity. Yet gender history has not abandoned the original, inspirational project of women's history: to recover and reveal the lived experience of women in the past and the present.

The series Gender in History provides a forum for these developments. Its historical coverage extends from the medieval to the modern periods, and its geographical scope encompasses not only Europe and North America but all corners of the globe. The series aims to investigate the social and cultural constructions of gender in historical sources, as well as the gendering of historical discourse itself. It embraces both detailed case studies of specific regions or periods, and broader treatments of major themes. Gender in History titles are designed to meet the needs of both scholars and students working in this dynamic area of historical research.

Love, intimacy and power

MANCHESTER
1824

Manchester University Press

LOVE, INTIMACY AND POWER

MARRIAGE AND PATRIARCHY IN SCOTLAND, 1650–1850

⇒ Katie Barclay ⇐

Manchester University Press
Manchester and New York

distributed in the United States exclusively by
Palgrave Macmillan

Published by Manchester University Press
Oxford Road, Manchester M13 9NR, UK
and Room 400, 175 Fifth Avenue, New York, NY 10010, USA
www.manchesteruniversitypress.co.uk

Distributed in the United States exclusively by
Palgrave Macmillan, 175 Fifth Avenue,
New York, NY 10010, USA

Distributed in Canada exclusively by
UBC Press, University of British Columbia, 2029 West Mall,
Vancouver, BC, Canada V6T 1Z2

British Library Cataloguing-in-Publication Data is available

Library of Congress Cataloging-in-Publication Data is available

ISBN 978 0 7190 9555 9 *paperback*

First published by Manchester University Press in hardback 2011

This paperback edition first published 2014

Printed by Lightning Source

Contents

Acknowledgements

Writing this book took a number of years and was supported by many people along the way. It began as a PhD funded by the Economic and Social Research Council, while the first year of transforming it from PhD to monograph was funded through the receipt of an Economic History Society Anniversary Fellowship. I am grateful to both these institutions for their support. I am also thankful for the assistance of the staff at the National Archives of Scotland, National Library of Scotland, Glasgow City Archives and Glasgow University Special Collections, who helped a new (and latterly not so new) researcher find her way around the sources. Similarly, the staff at Manchester University Press deserve thanks for demystifying the process of academic publishing and supporting me as this book came into its final stages. I would also like to thank Robert Clerk of Penicuik, Archibald Grant of Monymusk, Audrey Mylne and the Mylne family, and Lord Seafield for allowing me to use their papers in this publication. It is the history of their families, and those like them, that this project uncovers.

For their unswerving support throughout the PhD, but also beyond as they read through edits of this book and articles, and provided seemingly never-ending references and friendship, I would like to thank Eleanor Gordon and Lynn Abrams. Similarly, I would like to thank David Hopkin, and Alex Shepard, Valerie Wright and Rosi Carr for reading and commenting on this book in its various stages. Rosi deserves special thanks, not only for the insightful comments, but for the long conversations over lunch that definitely made me think in a more nuanced manner about the shape of the final project. I would also like to thank the anonymous reviewers whose insights made this a stronger work and the series editors for championing its publication.

As well as an intellectual debt, this work is built on the love and support of friends and family. I would like to thank Rosi, Val, Fiona Skillen and Christina Paton for their friendship across what is now several degrees and the years following. The process was definitely aided by the occasional pint or cocktail along the way. My siblings, parents, and in-laws deserve thanks for listening to my endless anecdotes and my need to analyse their marriages like that of my historical subjects. Finally, writing a book on marital relationships was at least in part inspired by my own. I would like to thank my husband Steven for his patience and his love and support. I have no doubt our journey together gave me insight and understanding into the marriages of others. This book is dedicated to you.

List of tables

Introduction: thinking patriarchy

I n 1698 Christian Kilpatrick concluded a letter to her husband, John Clerk, with the words, 'I rest your loving obedient wife'.[1] These words, or a variation on them, were a common subscript for wives during the seventeenth century. The combination of the words loving and obedient could be used through habit or consciously for effect, yet, in most cases, without any sense of incongruity. The relationship between these terms is at the heart of this book. This work explores the nature of power within the marriages of the Scottish elites between 1650 and 1850. It highlights the significance of the patriarchal system in shaping how men and women conceived of marriage and that their every interaction, however benign, was a product of the patriarchal system that gave their behaviour meaning. This study focuses on the conjugal unit, looking at how couples negotiated love, intimacy, the management of the household and, ultimately, the balance of power within their marriage. It demonstrates that the patriarchal system was not static, but recreated in every negotiation, ensuring its continuation across the period.

In the context of Scottish history, research on women's and family history is sparse for the period 1650 to 1850. While there is a growing body of work on women and the family in the medieval period and in the nineteenth and twentieth centuries, until recently the seventeenth and eighteenth centuries have been largely ignored. A collection of essays published in 2008 on the Scottish family contained new research on the early modern period, indicating that this picture is beginning to change.[2] Yet, even this vibrant collection is relatively silent on experiences within marriage and the nature of the conjugal unit. Marital relationships have been included in wider discussions of Scottish families or Scottish women, such as by Lynn Abrams, Keith Brown, Eleanor Gordon and Rosalind Marshall, but have received little attention in their own right. Leah Leneman's research comes closest to discussing marriage in detail, but her work focuses on divorce and illegitimacy, rather than on the everyday functioning of the marital relationship.[3]

Scottish marriage is assumed to be similar to the English experience, despite Scottish marital law taking a different shape from England, the Kirk holding different beliefs from the Anglican Church and having a more significant level of social control than its southern counterpart, and Scotland having a different social, cultural and economic environment. In many ways, Scotland had greater similarities with the northern European states than it did with its southern neighbour.[4] How the unique Scottish context, discussed in Chapter 2, impacted on personal and intimate relationships has not yet been explored. An investigation into how marriage operated within Scotland provides interesting and timely insights into the diversity of experience across Britain and Europe as well as providing the groundwork for a Scottish history of this subject.

While there is little written on the Scottish situation, there is a significant literature on family life in Western Europe. Until very recently, most historians of the family were reacting to a few large surveys written in the 1970s, most notably those by Lawrence Stone, Edward Shorter and Randolph Trumbach.[5] While these authors have different agendas within their writing, they all emphasise long-term changes to family life over the course of the early modern to modern period, closely relating change to theories of modernisation and progress. Stone and Trumbach, although from different perspectives, argue that between 1660 and 1800 in England, choice of mate and motivations for marriage dramatically evolved. Stone argues that the rationale behind selecting a spouse changed from the economic, social or political well-being of the family to more personal considerations such as compatibility, companionship, physical attraction and romantic love, although he acknowledges that motivations could be combined.[6] Stone and Trumbach see the origins of these changes in the seventeenth century. They believe that decline in the social legitimacy of aristocratic paternalism, where landowners had power over and responsibility to their tenants, led to weakened networks of kinship and clientage. When combined with a rise in the power of the state and the spread of Protestantism, this tended to isolate the newly formed nuclear household. This initially resulted in a more patriarchal form of family life, but quickly gave way to affective individualism, where individuals were bound by ties of affection rather than duty to the family, by the beginning of the eighteenth century. The weakening of the paternalistic social system meant community regulation was less viable and that families were more isolated, creating more emotive relationships within the family unit and less need for control over wives and children.

Shorter, and the sociologist William Goode, in their wider studies of European families, attribute these same changes in choice of mate to industrialisation, placing the origins slightly later in the eighteenth century.[7] They argue that industrialisation broke down traditional family structures. Young people became economically independent and older family members no longer controlled economic and political opportunities, leading to less parental control over children. Furthermore, and for Shorter more fundamentally, industrialisation brought with it a change in mentality. He argues that the concept of romantic love became increasingly important and that people were willing to place aside more material considerations and family interest to marry someone they loved and with whom they were compatible.

The findings of these writers inspired the next twenty years of writing on the family and their agendas continue to be the terms on which many historians engage with the family. Much of the literature reacted to the assertion that such sweeping change occurred over this period and particularly the implication that this change was progress. One of the key areas of debate has surrounded the nature of the power within the family, and particularly whether families moved from an authoritarian to a companionate or egalitarian model over the late seventeenth and eighteenth centuries. The place of love within family life and the implications of loving relationships for power is a topic of particular discussion by historians.

The existence of love within patriarchal society has only recently been acknowledged. For many twentieth-century historians, love was almost synonymous with equality, and they had difficulty reconciling the hierarchical relationships of patriarchal society with this understanding of love. Joseph Amato went as far as suggesting that the 'higher emotion' of love was not possible before the 'cultural, social, economic and political revolutions which have transformed human existence in the last two and half centuries' placed 'individuality, personality, feeling, love and friendship … at the center of our private and public lives'.[8] Similarly, Stone and Shorter saw the rise of romantic love in the eighteenth century as commensurate with greater equality and freedom from authoritarian relationships within the family.[9]

As increasing evidence for the existence of love before the eighteenth century appeared, historians attempted to reconcile love with a patriarchal system through positing a divide between theory and practice. When reflecting upon English marriage during the period

1580–1680, Keith Wrightson argued that 'the picture which emerges indicates the private existence of a strong complementary and companionate ethos, side by side with, and often overshadowing, theoretical adherence to the doctrine of male authority and public female subordination'.[10] More recently, influenced by feminist theory, historians of the family recognise that love did not conquer patriarchy, with male dominance being increasingly understood as compatible with loving relationships, even in the seventeenth century.[11] Increasingly feminist historians suspect that love does not remove inequality, but shores up the patriarchal system. Romantic love has come under particular criticism, with Barbara Taylor arguing that love was to compensate women for their lack of power.[12] Viewed through a feminist lens, love no longer appears as a disinterested, equalising force.

Despite the increasing scepticism with which feminists approach love in the past, what a loving, but authoritarian, marriage looked like and what that meant both for the couple and for our understanding of patriarchal systems is a relatively new field. Julie Hardwick explores how patriarchy was played out and negotiated in practice amongst a group of French notaries, while Diana O'Hara and Joanne Bailey, in their respective works, explore the nature of authority within courtship and marriage.[13] These studies provide a deeper understanding of how patriarchy operates within the family, but as David Sabean remarks, 'both power and resistance are always part of marital relations, but there is no straightforward history to tell about improvements for women or men, greater independence or more prestige.'[14]

Since the work of Stone, Shorter and Trumbach in the 1970s, few historians have attempted to study marriage or family relationships over a lengthy period.[15] Indeed, many historians appear to adopt the rather arbitrary division between the early modern and modern periods as a beginning or an end point in their work, rather than question why their research should be constrained by these labels. This is particularly problematic when studying family life because, as Joan Kelly notes, such periodisation is irrelevant to particular social groups, notably women.[16] Furthermore, it tends to leave a gap in the literature on the late eighteenth and early nineteenth centuries as it is no longer early modern, not quite modern enough.[17] This study covers the period 1650 to 1850 in an attempt to readdress this gap in the literature and to explore both the continuities and changes that occurred over the period, in light of thirty years of research written in response to the work of Stone, Shorter and Trumbach. Through focusing on how couples communicated with each other and negotiated the terms of their marriage within correspondence, this book hopes to provide a more in-depth picture of what it meant to be married within a patriarchal culture and provide insight into why a study of love and intimacy ensures there can be 'no straightforward history' of patriarchal systems.

Defining power; defining patriarchy

Studying power and power relationships is complicated by both issues of definition and the nature of human interaction. What does it mean to hold power and what types of power are most powerful? For many, the exercise of power entails some form of domination, or, at least, the opportunity to gain the upper hand in a given instance. Max Weber defines power as the 'probability that one actor within a social relationship will be in a position to carry out his own will despite resistance'. For Weber, when that power is legitimate, it is known as authority.[18] M. G. Smith sees power as 'the ability to act effectively on persons or things, to make or secure favourable decisions which are not of right allocated to the individuals or their roles'.[19] For these thinkers, holding power involves conflict with the rights or wishes of others. It is an inherently antagonistic, if frequently non-violent, process.

Power can be exercised in a myriad of ways, from direct personal interaction, such as forcing your will through violence or the withholding of economic resources, to power that is exercised on an ideological or cultural level, such as control through religious indoctrination, or the removal of freedom through the promotion of wider social values. It can be written into the structures of language itself, so that the very act of communicating is both predicated on and reinforces particular power relationships. The exercise of power is not simply about restricting the rights of others, but can be productive, allowing people to exercise agency and choice, even if those choices are constrained.[20]

This picture is complicated as different manifestations of power cannot be ranked. It is not clear whether a woman is more oppressed by a socio-ideological system that views her as property, or when she is the victim of domestic violence. Lines of power are not transparent or unidirectional, and, even where they are proscribed, resistance can alter their shape. The varying manifestations of power do not operate exclusively of each another, but combine and conflict to create the complexity of human interaction. As a result of this, it can be very difficult to measure when and to what extent an individual exercises power.

Power is given meaning by the context in which it is exercised. In Scotland, from the seventeenth to nineteenth centuries, power within marriage was informed by a patriarchal culture. Definitions of patriarchy are rarely given by historians, possibly because of the difficulty of summarising a complex social experience in a few words. Yet, those who attempt to do so usually agree on certain key issues. The first issue in defining patriarchy is that it is a social *system*. Sylvia Walby, who defines patriarchy as 'a system of social structures and practices in which men dominate, oppress and exploit women', asserts that the words 'social structure' are crucial to her understanding of patriarchy.[21] Judith Bennett, adopting Adrienne Rich's words, offers a definition, which, she believes, incorporates the pervasive and systematic nature of patriarchy. She defines patriarchy as:

> A familial-social, ideological, political system in which men – by force, direct pressure, or through ritual, tradition, law and language, customs, etiquette, education, and the division of labour, determine what part women shall or shall not play, and in which the female is everywhere subsumed under the male.

She emphasises that patriarchy is 'rooted in ideology, culture and society' and that it is wider than male dominance 'rooted in the patriarchal household'.[22]

The second key issue is that patriarchy is a term used to explain gender inequality. It is because women have been consistently disadvantaged across time in comparison to their male counterparts that a single word or phrase is needed to describe this phenomenon. It is to give the social position of women a sense of history and continuity that the term patriarchy is both useful and powerful. Bennett believes that historians are discouraged from using the word patriarchy as it is seen to tend towards the universalism of a complex and changing social experience.[23] She believes the word patriarchy should be used by historians, but that a sophisticated, expanded definition is needed, which recognises patriarchy as a lived experience. Margaret Ezell notes that historians tend to use patriarchy to denote 'authoritarianism rather than sharing of responsibilities, relations between husband and wife expressed in "terms of authority and obedience, not consultation and consent"'. She does not deny that patriarchy creates hierarchies of power, but argues that it should be recognised as a system that was lived in and therefore a system which was constantly negotiated.[24]

Within this system, power is not simply understood as male domination and female exploitation, but recognises the differences between the structural systems that shape the holding and exercise of power and the day-to-day experiences of individuals, which are more complex. As many historians have noted, male power was frequently insecure, threatened and contradictory, while women held authority within the system over their children, servants and those of lower social class.[25] As feminist analyses of power become complicated by the intersection of race, class, and sexuality with gender within historical place, so must definitions of patriarchy integrate more than a sense of male domination and female subordination. Patriarchy was much more than a system of oppression, but a system of life – or, as Michel Foucault puts it, power is productive.[26] The concept of a patriarchal system is not uncontroversial. Bernard Capp argues that between 1558 and 1714 in England, 'there was no patriarchal *system*, rather an interlocking set of beliefs, assumptions, traditions and practices, and the largely informal character of patriarchy enabled each generations to adapt to its changing circumstances'.[27] Pierre Bourdieu, and less explicitly Michel Foucault, suggest that forms of power only become systems over time, when domination is no longer constantly renewed in a direct, personal way, but is integrated into the means of economic and cultural production and reproduced by their functioning.[28] In the context of Scotland during the period 1650 to 1850, patriarchy was embedded in Scottish cultural, economic, social, legal and political institutions, which influenced how people conceived of themselves and their relationships with others. Patriarchy was reinforced through daily interactions between men and women that drew on patriarchal discourses to give them meaning. It was only enforced directly, usually through violence as discussed in Chapter 7, when explicitly challenged. Patriarchy, in this context, can be understood as a system.

A number of historians emphasise the importance of negotiation to the working of the patriarchal system. Capp notes, 'without challenging the general principles of patriarchy, women frequently sought to negotiate the terms on which it operated within the home and neighbourhood, seeking an acceptable personal accommodation that would afford them some measure of autonomy and space, and a limited degree of authority'.[29] Deniz Kandiyoti describes this negotiation as the 'patriarchal bargain'. She argues that:

> systematic analyses of women's strategies and coping mechanisms can help to capture the nature of patriarchal systems in their cultural, class-specific, and temporal concreteness and reveal how men and women resist, accommodate, adapt and conflict with each other over resources, rights and responsibilities … Women's strategies are always played out in the context of identifiable patriarchal bargains that act as implicit scripts that define, limit and inflect their market and domestic options.[30]

For Kandiyoti, it is through these negotiations that patriarchy evolves. Negotiation allows for the questioning of the nature of relationships between men and women, which in turn breaks down the current form of the patriarchal system and allows the development of a new form. Negotiation is key to the functioning of patriarchy, not only because it relieves tensions and limits its impact, but as it is how the system evolves. Michel Foucault argues:

> Power must be understood in the first instance as the multiplicity of force relations immanent in the sphere in which they operate and which constitute their own organisation; *as the process which, through ceaseless struggles and confrontations, transforms, strengthens, or reverses them*; as the support which these force relations find in one another, thus forming a chain or a system, or on the contrary, the disjunctions and contradictions which isolate them from one another; and lastly, as the strategies in which they take effect, whose general design or institutional crystallization is embodied in the state apparatus, in the formal action of the law, in the various social hegemonies. [my italics][31]

By allowing the opportunity for resolution, negotiation allows patriarchy to repair and survive. Resistance and agency by women can reap benefits in the short term by improving their status or conditions, but in the long term, due to patriarchy's ability to adapt, it ensures their oppression. As Judith Bennett notes, the experience of women in the past is marked by 'patriarchal equilibrium', where they experience change in their day-to-day lives, but not in their status in relation to men.[32] Patriarchy can expropriate methods of resistance for its own purposes. As Donald Hall shows for Victorian Britain, male writers appropriated and modified the words of female writers to reinforce patriarchal ideology.[33]

It is integral to the survival of patriarchy that this is the case. Pierre Bourdieu argues that 'any language that can command attention is an authorised language ... the things it designates are not simply expressed but also authorised and legitimised ... they derive their power from their capacity to objectify unformulated experiences to make them public'.[34] An act of resistance may not be legitimate, but it does have power. Patriarchy needs to expropriate any acts of resistance as it cannot afford for authority to rest in any other place. For the patriarchal system to survive, this power has to be subsumed into the system.

Negotiation is a vital part of the patriarchal system, but this should not be understood to imply that there is no room for agency. Negotiation is the space where women and men resist, contest, evade, manoeuvre and limit patriarchy, where they cooperate with other people, and hold power. Women can have victories. Furthermore, the act of negotiation keeps patriarchy in flux. Foucault notes that power relationships are 'modified by their very exercise, entailing and strengthening of some terms and a weakening of others … so that there has never existed one type of stable subjugation, given and for all'.[35] Negotiation ensures the evolution of patriarchy, but also its instability.

Relationships between men and women under patriarchy do not have to be antagonistic.[36] The family is at the heart of the patriarchal system, although its operation is not restricted to it. All members of the family are educated to believe their interests are the family's interest. As a result, it is difficult for women to form a 'class (gender?) consciousness' as they cannot perceive of their interest outside of the family.[37] There are historical exceptions, where women have chosen to work together in the interests of their sex, but these movements are usually short-lived and are usually not directly in conflict with women's identities as part of a family.[38] This sense of shared interest can obscure the exercise of power. As men and women understand the family's interest as their own inter-est, they work together for its benefit, allowing 'all the positive, happy interactions of women and men'.[39]

It has been argued that the rise of individualism, which has been variously located between the thirteenth and eighteenth centuries, helped destroy this sense of family interest. Yet, notably individualism is not seen as conflicting with shared interest between partners. Macfarlane argues that with individualism came the rise of romantic love and the expectation that marriage was a 'blending of two personalities, two psychologies'.[40] If there is any erosion of 'family' interest, then the shared interest of husband and wife ensured that individual interest lay in the home and not with other members of their gender.

For the purposes of this book, drawing on the theory of Kandiyoti and Bennett, patriarchy is understood as a relational and dynamic system of social relations rooted in ideology, culture, and society, which operates to reinforce male power at the expense of women. It is a system that is recreated everyday through relationships between individuals and in the reconciliation of personal experience with wider social, and, in this context, patriarchal, narratives or discourses. It is social practice. As a result, patriarchal systems are constantly in flux and unstable, adapting to the changing needs and experiences of those who live within them. Patriarchy is an evolving system of power that can only be understood in its particular historical context.

Scotland and its elites

Scotland in 1650 was a rapidly changing society. At the beginning of the sixteenth century, it started on a path that would transform it over the next three hundred years from a medieval to a modern society. The one hundred and fifty years before 1650 saw the development of universities, the creation of a formal, unified and nationwide legal system, more centralised government, the introduction of the printing press, the unification of the thrones of Scotland and England in 1603, growing trade and political links with Western Europe and tentative steps into the rest of the world. The Protestant Reformation in 1560 brought more formal schooling and increased literacy as well as a very politically and socially influential church.[41] Between 1560 and 1650, the Scottish population doubled to around one million people with 5–10% of the population living in towns of over 2000 people. Scotland was also cash rich compared to many of its Northern European counterparts.[42]

Elite Scots, especially men, occasionally had continental educations, and many men and women spoke French in addition to Scots and possibly Gaelic and Latin. The elite Scot in 1650 desired to be part of a civilised European state. Yet in other ways, Scotland's medieval heritage had not been completely destroyed. Clan warfare, which was as common in the borders as the highlands; cattle raids on other Scots and the English; the devastation of famine, notably in the 1690s, and disease; kidnapped heiresses and political and legal nepotism were still a part of life, if an increasingly constrained one. Most people continued to work in agriculture and the system of patrimony remained strong.

The Scottish elites before industrialisation were a relatively small, closely connected group, ranging from wealthy, middling sorts to nobility. Unlike in England, where the division between nobility and gentry was clearly demarcated, the Scottish elite, like much of the European upper classes, lacked clear boundaries.[43] This lack of definition arose, in part, due to the relationship between land-owning and status in Scotland. As Leah Leneman and Rosalind Mitchison remark, 'social prestige in Scotland differed in its basis from the English system of values. It was not the absence of a link with trade which made for respectability, but the reality of the link, however slight, with landowning'.[44]

Scottish landowners were known as lairds, but this title disguised a wide range of wealth and power.[45] The highlands and borders of Scotland were dominated by large estates, while 'bonnet lairds', as the owners of single farms were called, were common in Lanarkshire, Galloway, Ayrshire, Banffshire, Bute, Fife, Caithness and the Central Lowlands.[46]

Scotland did not have 'the substantial middling freeholder class that formed the backbone of English rural society'.[47] Instead, they had lairds of greater and lesser degree, creating a system where rank was based on subtle distinctions in wealth and status, rather than allocation to a particular social group.

There was some relationship between size of estate and ranks of the peerage, but some sizeable landowners, with considerable local and national influence, never held titles.[48] Complicating this picture was the legacy of the clan system common in the Highlands and borders, which was still strong in parts of Scotland well into the eighteenth century.[49] Clans were bound together by economic necessity (with lesser landowners holding their lands through their clan chief), political expediency, and strong kin networks based on familial loyalty and bonds of marriage.[50] Clan chiefs were not always members of the peerage, or even the most nationally influential member of their families, but held significant local power. The smooth operation of the clan system was in no small part due to a close working relationship amongst its members, which meant that individuals of different rank and wealth often met for business and pleasure. Sociability was an important part of the clan bond with lairds of different degrees, linked by ties of blood and friendship, meeting regularly for meals and to share gossip. One of the consequences of this system was that status was not simply based on personal rank or influence, but was measured by kin connections.[51] It was the resources that could be mobilised that indicated status, which placed women in positions of particular power.

With only a few exceptions, three ministers and a member of the urban elite, all of the couples who married before 1800 in this study had strong ties to the land, either as owners or children of landowners, although many had additional occupations. There were few bonnet lairds in the sample and those included had strong familial or social ties to those of a higher status. While the Scottish aristocracy often had very large estates compared to its English counterpart, it was poorer. It has been calculated that at the end of the eighteenth century, there were in Scotland 336 large estates worth over £2500 a year, 1100 of middling size, and 6000 worth less than £600 a year.[52] In 1883, fewer than 25% of Scottish landowners had estate revenue of over £10,000.[53] The reality of their economic situation was not lost on the Scottish upper classes. Even the most prestigious families had to look beyond land ownership to supplement their incomes.

Many landed families were involved in business concerns, such as coal mining, trade and, later in the period, banking. Younger sons of peers frequently went into business and the professions. Lower down the spectrum, landowners combined their estate incomes with other occupations. It was the children of this social group who went into law, medicine, the army or navy, government service and university posts. Some did go into the Church, but on the whole the clergy was 'self-sustaining, a hereditary caste'.[54] Before 1780, the vast majority of heads of aristocratic families in this study held positions in the army, sat in parliament and managed large estates.[55] Several gentlemen were lawyers who rose to the judiciary as well as owning small estates, while a few had interests in coal, mineral exploitation and foreign trade.

This situation was also reflected in the Scottish elites' involvement in Scottish industrialisation. From the seventeenth century, the Scottish elites laid the groundwork for economic development, with investments in banking, agriculture and early manufacturing, most notably in coal and textiles. The limited income of many Scottish estates meant that people of all social groups were interested in these events. In turn, Enlightenment thinkers, such as Adam Smith and David Hume, encouraged and informed these developments, linking commercial society to nation-building – a central concern of the elite – as did the growing body of scientists in Scottish universities who provided the technological underpinnings.

With industrialisation came significant population growth and urbanisation at one of the fastest rates in Europe. The population doubled to over two million by 1820. In 1750, there were only four towns with over 10,000 people, holding 9% of the population; by 1820, there were thirteen containing 25% of the population. The geographical composition of Scotland changed as the population growth clustered in the central belt around the new industrial towns. In 1755, half of the population lived north of the line that runs from the Firth of Tay to the Firth of Clyde, by 1820 that had dropped to 20%, with 37% of the population in the central belt. Demographic change was complemented by an increasingly stable society. The repercussions of the 1745 Jacobite rebellion accelerated centralised state control. In 1746/7, landowner's private jurisdictions were abolished, so that all law and punishment were controlled by the State, and military tenures, which were the basis of private armies, were transformed into a form of feuferme.[56] Although private landowners could raise armies until the nineteenth century, they now needed permission from the monarch, had to comply with certain regulations and could claim expenses from the State.

Generally society became less unruly with a decrease in the number of riots and the taming of the clans in the highlands and borders. Political stability and centralised control were influenced in part by the political union of 1707. This removed Scotland's parliamentary independence and created a common market throughout the newly formed Great Britain, although it guaranteed the sovereignty of the Scottish Church and law courts.[57] With it, political power moved in its entirety from Edinburgh to London, where it had in part resided since the union of the crowns. Yet, change should not be overstated. The majority of the population still continued to live rurally and work in traditional agricultural occupations. For those elite families who continued to live on the estate, industrialisation and social change may have had little impact on the operation of their household, beyond widening access to consumer goods.[58]

In the late eighteenth and nineteenth centuries alongside landowning, the elites in this study were involved in the military, customs, trade, law and increasingly professional writing. Most people continued to have some connection with land, either as owners or children of landowners. The exceptions to this rule, however, were not ministers as in the earlier period, but those in trade. James Balfour, the son of a university professor, and Robert Chambers, the son of a manufacturer, were both leading names in the publishing trade. Thomas Carlyle was from a lower-class background, but established himself as a leading member of the Victorian intelligentsia. His wife Jane Welsh was the daughter of a well-respected physician and 'the embodiment of a middle-class hauteur'.[59]

This group, like for the earlier period, included people who were actively socially upward. Just as in the seventeenth century, the Clerks of Penicuik transformed their success as merchants into significant landownership, the sample for the nineteenth century included people such as Walter Crum, a successful manufacturer, who converted his success into landownership and raised his children in a style commensurate with that of the gentry. The upper ranks continued to combine landownership with politics and occasionally held prestigious military and governmental posts, such as Lord Dalhousie, who was General-Governor of India, and James Stewart Mackenzie, who was Governor of Ceylon and Lord High Commissioner of the Ionian Islands. They were less likely to hold lower-ranking military roles than in the past and many became actively involved in agricultural improvement and land exploitation.

Table 1.1 shows the distribution of men and women across social group. The sample has been divided into heirs and younger children of peerage, and into greater and lesser lairds/middling. People with larger estates and a degree of wider social or political influence have been

Table 1.1 Social grouping of sample[a]

Rank	Pre-1650–99 Male	Female	1700–49 Male	Female	1750–99 Male	Female	1800–50 Male	Female
Eldest son of peer/heiress	16	2	10	0	3	0	6	0
Younger child of peerage	4	12	2	7	1	3	0	6
Greater laird	10	10	11	13	8	6	3	3
Lesser laird/ middling	2	4	6	9	6	9	10	10
Total	32	28	29	29	18	18	19	19

[a] People are grouped by period according to year of marriage. There is discrepancy between the number of women and men in certain categories as the required information was not available.

grouped into the greater laird category. Individuals with small estates and non-lairds, such as those from trade in the nineteenth century, have been classified as lesser lairds. The earlier period contains more individuals from the peerage, as papers for lower ranks were harder to locate. As the period progresses, this pattern changes so that sources from the lesser lairds and wealthy members of the new middle-class predominate in the nineteenth century.

The sample included only English-speaking Scots. It incorporates individuals from the Gaelic-speaking western Highlands of Scotland, but they were from the upper classes and had received a lowland education. The families in this sample were based throughout Scotland from the Scottish Borders to Orkney, from Glasgow to Edinburgh. Younger children of elite families and their kin, if not pursuing opportunities in the military or empire, lived on nearby estates or in the cities, where they were prominent amongst the wealthy merchants and professionals. Scotland's elites often travelled widely, which was reflected in their surviving correspondence. Many aristocratic families had multiple estates throughout Scotland as well as second homes in Edinburgh or Glasgow. Families whose estates were on the west coast and in Lanarkshire tended to have second homes in or near Glasgow, while many Highland families also owned property around Edinburgh.

This reflected the significance of towns to this social group, where visits to the capital, and other metropolises, for business, to attend parliament, to be educated, and to participate in the social whirl of the Scottish 'season' were common. From the eighteenth century, Glasgow boomed and, while it was always an important university town, it became the largest city in Scotland and home to the new industrial middle classes.[60] Edinburgh also expanded, but continued to be home to the professionals that it had housed since the sixteenth century. In Edinburgh, the expansion of the middle class brought with it the formation of the New Town, built in 1767. Here the middle classes isolated themselves from the rest of society with whom their predecessors had worked and lived. In Glasgow, the separation was not so marked, but here too, middle-class neighbourhoods developed. Edinburgh took on many of the functions for the middle class that London did for the upper classes.

There was 'the Edinburgh season', where the wealthier middle classes and elites participated in a social whirl of balls, parties, theatre-going and numerous other amusements. Buildings such as the Assembly Rooms were built in Edinburgh in the latter half of the century to allow the middle and upper classes to meet and mix amongst their own. Many upper-class families from throughout Scotland moved into the cities along with the middle classes, only returning to their estates for the summer vacation. Families that chose to live provincially often had access to similar entertainments in the smaller towns or, like their predecessors, through visiting local friends and family. Only the wealthiest did not participate, preferring to remove to London for its more exclusive 'season', especially after the political union of 1707. Having said this, many of the very richest Scottish families spent considerable time in Scotland and many only visited London for the 'season' when they were looking for a spouse or chaperoning their children.

Despite close ties with England, the sample under study continued to marry into other Scottish families throughout the period. Table 1.2 notes the nationalities of the marriages of the individuals under study. To

Table 1.2 Nationality of spouses

Nationality	1650–1700	1700–50	1750–1800	1800–50
Both Scottish	23	28	14[a]	14
Scottish husband/English wife	2	2	4	2
Scottish wife/English husband	0	0	0	1
Scottish husband/unknown wife[b]	1	3	1	1
Scottish husband/Portuguese wife	0	0	1	0

[a] Includes one case of bigamous cohabitation.

[b] In all these cases, it is most probable that the women were Scottish; they are all individuals where that information is unavailable.

give a fuller picture of Scottish marriage patterns, it includes all the unions of the individuals in the study, even where that particular marriage was not studied. For this reason, it notes Mary Mackenzie's first marriage to the English Sir Samuel Hood, although it is her correspondence with her second husband, James Alexander Stewart of Glasserton, which is used in the study.

Apart from this exception, all the men in the study are Scottish, which is due to the nature of source collection, where family papers are usually held by the husband's family. Of the ten English women in the sample, eight were married to men ranked as Earl or Duke, while two were the wives of Archibald Grant of Monymusk, a greater laird. The choice to marry English women did not appear to be a particular family strategy; six of the men who married English wives also married Scottish women, including Grant who also had two Scottish wives. Before c. 1730, Scottish men had difficulty attracting English wives, who were reluctant to move to a 'foreign' country so far away from family and friends. They also found it difficult to compete in the English marriage market due to their low incomes.[61] There was a premium to certain people on marrying Scottish, as it allowed the furtherance of family networks. Even as late as 1810, when David Robertson wrote from London to announce his marriage, he added, 'her father was from Scotland; her connections are very respectable.'[62] His wife's family originated from his home town.

The Scottish elites held certain values in common that makes it possible to treat them as a homogenous unit. They had a strong sense of their rank and social position (which frequently included a desire for political power); they recognised the importance of family name, legitimacy, blood ties and primogeniture; they valued land-ownership but also frugality; and they shared the same cultural expectations about the duties and responsibilities of marriage. While their experiences were not typical of lower-ranking Scots, they stamped their values on Scottish society through their domination of the law, the economy, culture and society.[63] The extent to which they were successful is a matter of debate.

Rank was central to their sense of self. In the late-seventeenth century, when Susan, Countess of Dundonald married Lord Yester, considerable discussion was given to where she would stand in processions. Would she keep the rank of her first husband as the mother of the new heir, and hence be near the beginning, or would she take her new husband's rank and take her place near the back? Should she ask for the King's exemption to stand with the Countesses as a Duke's daughter?[64] When John Clerk of Penicuik was made baronet, while maintaining trade links and friendships with his merchant roots, he refused to allow his daughters to marry into this social group.[65] Indeed, the level of concern that the Scottish elites gave to maintaining and calculating their relative social position suggests that they had little sense of themselves as a class in a traditional Marxist sense. In many ways, as they drew on cultural norms to outwardly mark their social position, the Scottish elites shared a group identity. But, their allegiances were not with the social group, but with their family, who shared their name, and with their wider kin. Their actions in public, whether in the political sphere, at court, in business or pleasure, were motivated by a desire to advance and protect their family and family name. The importance of name, blood ties and primogeniture was a reflection of this.

An obsession with rank led the elite to share various characteristics, not least of which was a sense of vulnerability, or lack of confidence, in their ability to maintain their social position. Much of this insecurity arose from their vulnerable financial position in relative terms to their English neighbours and from a sense of abandonment from the political process after the Crown moved south in 1603.[66] Even the most politically powerful Scottish families were aware of their relative poverty when compared to their English counterparts as well as their very real geographical distance from the throne. For others further down the social spectrum, this sense of vulnerability was driven by an anxiety over a lack of resources, which many families felt prevented them from adequately performing gentility. Yet, interestingly this was not usually seen as the fault of the family, but of unreasonable expectations driven by English fashions.[67] The result was that frugality was prized at all social levels, emphasised in letters to children and viewed as a necessary quality in a wife.[68]

Over the course of the eighteenth century, these values began to be transformed by changes to the Scottish social structure. The new middle classes had wealth and influence as well as a newly forming sense of class identity, but they were not entirely removed from their elite predecessors. It was not only merchants who were the basis of the middle classes, but landowners, farmers, and those from professions such as law and medicine (the traditional homes of the younger sons of the landed elite).[69] Indeed, the philosopher Adam Smith explicitly envisioned the 'middling ranks', who he argued should hold political authority in Enlightenment Scotland, as landed proprietors.[70] The middle classes had strong ties to the land, as sons of landed gentlemen, landowners and as their friends and associates within new Enlightenment clubs and culture.

Scottish civil society flourished during the eighteenth century, supported by a sympathetic clergy. Intellectual clubs, coffee shops, libraries, lectures and other forms of 'polite society' developed in Edinburgh, and in the later part of the century, Glasgow and the provincial towns. Book sales dramatically increased and those of a middling background had libraries in their homes. For those who could not afford to buy books, circulating libraries, newspaper and periodical press and cheap ephemera provided reading material.[71] Furthermore, in the eighteenth and early nineteenth centuries, the middle classes still sought to transform their business success into landownership, although the opportunity was decreasing.[72] On the one hand, that the middle classes both originated from and shared a desire for landownership and, within the period under study, continued to fulfil their ambitions to transform money into property, meant that the middle and upper classes continued to hold similar values, notably in respect to the importance of family and the marriage contract.

On the other hand, the changing economic landscape and the beginnings of an independent middle-class identity altered some of the core values that had marked the elites of the earlier period. Notably, new-found wealth, which also applied to the landed who found their rents rising due to the demand for land, and the creation of seats in Parliament for Scottish elites, helped raise confidence.[73] Yet, and possibly because this confidence was driven from below as well as the increasing control of print culture by the middle classes, this change in attitude included the filtering of 'middle class' values upwards.[74] This homogeneity was not long-lasting, especially once it became difficult to purchase land and the middle-classes became larger with greater economic wealth, forcing them to reassess the foundation of their social position. Yet, this change was only in its infancy before 1850 in Scotland. Until that point, the wealthy middle and upper classes were linked by shared dreams and shared values that meant that their performance of courtship and marriage, while not unchanging over time, was remarkably similar.

The importance of rank, family and land ownership to this social group influenced courtship practice and behaviour within marriage. As shall be explored in Chapter 3, these core values influenced choice of partner and ensured that family approval and the marital economy remained central to courtship. They also permeated into married life with the performance of gentility, which was intimately tied to rank and land, influencing how people negotiated within marriage. Part of that performance was conforming to patriarchal norms that emphasised male authority and female obedience. These norms were taught and reinforced, in part, through the shared material culture discussed in Chapter 2.

As a relatively cohesive social grouping, there is also evidence that the Scottish elites married across the social group. David Thomas's study of the British peerage shows that fewer than 50% of heirs and 25% of younger sons married within the peerage between 1700 and 1880. The majority of 'out' marriages were to commoners and around 15% married into the gentry. Members of the peerage primarily married landed 'commoners', but there were also significant percentages of marriages into the armed forces, business, Church and law. Those of higher ranks in the peerage were less likely to marry out than the lower ranks.[75] Within the sample under study, a significant number of the peerage married into the lower ranks of laird. Around 30% of the Scottish elites married someone from a different social division, although the sample is too small to be statistically valid.[76] Men more commonly married women of a lower social group than vice versa, which is not surprising as women adopted their husbands' status.

While there was significant inter-marriage, the different social groups that made up the Scottish elites differed in age at first marriage for men, although they followed the British pattern. Martin Ingram has argued that women from English yeomen and gentry families married in their late teens or early twenties, almost ten years younger than women from the lower classes, but that their husbands, while marrying slightly earlier, tended not to marry before the age of twenty-five.[77] Lawrence Stone suggests an average age at first marriage of twenty-two to twenty-three for women and twenty-four to twenty-six for men of the peerage in the seventeenth century.[78] David Thomas' work on the British peerage in the eighteenth century suggests a slightly higher mean age for men of twenty nine to thirty across the period 1700–1849.[79] As detailed in Table 1.3, the women in this study fall closer to Ingram's estimate, marrying in

Table 1.3 Average age at first marriage, with sample size in parenthesis[a]

Pre-1650–99		1700–49		1750–99		1800–50	
Male	Female	Male	Female	Male	Female	Male	Female
24.5	18.8	25.1	19.5	31.9	19.6	30	20.4
(18)	(13)	(14)	(15)	(10)	(8)	(13)	(10)

[a] People are grouped by period according to year of marriage. Due to a lack of data, it was not possible to calculate the age at marriage for all individuals.

their late teens and early twenties, while, with the exception of the period 1650–1700, men married after twenty-five, rising to an average age of thirty after 1750. This significant rise may, at least in part, be caused by sampling difficulties, due to the lack of data for lesser elites in the early category. There is evidence that, even amongst the elites, financial security could impact on age at marriage. Keith Wrightson argues that people married as soon as they were financially independent, allowing the upper and middling classes to marry earlier.[80]

Heirs of the Scottish elites married in their early twenties, several years earlier than younger sons and lesser lairds in the late seventeenth and early eighteenth centuries, who married in their late twenties, but, as shown in Table 1.4, this difference decreased significantly over the period. While the average age of women at first marriage rose slightly over the centuries from eighteen to twenty, there appeared to be little variation across the social group.

While the age at first marriage is important for demonstrating when people chose to marry and for calculating fertility probabilities, Lawrence Stone notes that in England 25% of marriages in the seventeenth century involved at least one party remarrying. This figured dropped to 15% in the eighteenth century.[81] Many of the people in this sample married twice with some marrying three and four times. Men were more likely to remarry than women and this was especially true for people marrying more than twice.[82] It is also notable that many remarrying men married younger, single women rather than widows or divorcees.

Table 1.4 Average age at first marriage by class, with sample size in parenthesis[a]

Rank	Pre-1650–99 Male	Female	1700–49 Male	Female	1750–99 Male	Female	1800–50 Male	Female
Eldest son of peer/heiress	24.3 (11)	20 (2)	24.8 (5)	–	35 (1)	–	28.3 (4)	–
Younger child of peerage	26 (3)	20.2 (6)	28 (1)	20.8 (5)	43 (1)	20.8 (5)	–	21 (4)
Greater Lairds	21.3 (3)	17.7 (6)	23.6 (5)	22.8 (4)	30.8 (4)	22.8 (4)	29.3 (3)	15 (1)
Lesser laird/ middling	30.5 (2)	16 (1)	28.3 (3)	22.5 (2)	34 (2)	22.5 (2)	31.5 (6)	21.6 (5)

[a] People are grouped by period according to year of marriage. Due to a lack of data, it was not possible to calculate the age at marriage for all individuals.

Table 1.5 Remarriage[a]

Number of marriages	Pre-1650–1700 Male	Female	1700–50 Male	Female	1750–1800 Male	Female	1800–50 Male	Female
1	12	18	13	26	11[b]	12	9	12
2	6	3	7	4	2	2[b]	3	2
3	0	0	1	0	0	0	0	0
4	0	0	1	0	0	0	0	0
Unknown	2	2	5	5	3	3	3	3

[a] To calculate this table, each person in the sample was taken as an individual and the number of times they married counted. People who married more than once were dated by their first marriage, hence the smaller sample size for the later period.
[b] Includes one cohabiting couple, which was a bigamous relationship for the wife.

As this suggests, large age gaps were common between men and women when marrying. Men on average married women eight years younger than them; this increased to twelve years over the period 1800–50, due to the rise in age at first marriage of men. A large age gap, it is argued by a number of historians, reflects a more hierarchal, and less equal, relationship between spouses.[83]

While showing significant homogeneity in social values and behaviour, there was some mix of religious belief across the sample. From 1560, Scotland was officially a Protestant nation and papal jurisdiction was repudiated, yet Catholicism remained strong in a small strip from the Northern coast to the Western Isles. The unification of the thrones in 1603 had also brought religious tensions as the Kirk's doctrine differed from the Anglican Church. When Charles I forced uniformity of the Churches in 1629, the Kirk and much of the population were deeply unhappy at the compromise. In 1638, the National Covenant was signed and a significant number of people refused to conform to the Church. This led to significant religious persecution for the next fifty years. In addition, the religious cleavages in Scottish society would come to the fore again in 1689 when the population was split in its support of the Catholic James VII and the Protestant William and Mary. The Catholic population hoped they would regain their social and political rights under James and the non-conforming Covenanters believed that William and Mary would remove the English prayer-book from the Scottish Church, due to the similarities between Dutch Protestantism and Covenanting doctrine.

These tensions, although in slightly different and more politicised forms, would revive in the 1715 and 1745 Jacobite Rebellions, where the population was now divided between a Stuart and Hanoverian monarch. Later in the century, Enlightenment thinkers promoted greater religious tolerance. This was seen in increasing lenience towards non-conformity within the Church of Scotland, marked by multiple splits in the Church over the eighteenth century and the flourishing of protestant sects in the nineteenth century. These divisions, along with increased centralisation of government, reduced the social power of the Church, which previously had significant control over social order and discipline. In 1793, Catholics were emancipated from their social, legal and religious restrictions.[84]

Some Scottish lairds remained Roman Catholic across the period. It is difficult to assess to what extent Catholicism remained in nominally Protestant households. Yet, most Scottish families appear to have adopted Protestantism and actively participated in the faith. Scotland's beliefs diversified in the eighteenth century as the Church of Scotland split into different sects, which affected the elites as much as the rest of the population. By the nineteenth century, much of the landed class were Episcopalian, while the rest of the population was Presbyterian.[85] In the nineteenth century, a number of individuals also began to reject formal religion. Despite being trained for the Church, Thomas Carlyle went through a crisis of faith at University and ranged between agnosticism and atheism for the rest of his life. Robert Chambers, while a practising Episcopalian, rejected the Bible as the basis of knowledge. It is difficult to assess the nature of the beliefs of the people under study as, for much of the period, religion was closely associated with politics. Distinguishing religious belief from political expediency complicates any categorisation.

Within this sample, most families were nominally Protestant, although the degree to which they celebrated their faith and the shape it took varied enormously. The Dukes of Hamilton were strongly Presbyterian, with Ann, Duchess of Hamilton influencing church politics in her local area. Her daughter Katherine, Duchess of Atholl had a similar conviction and it strongly influenced her political beliefs. Various branches of the Home family were persecuted as Covenanters in the seventeenth century. In contrast, John Erskine, 6th Earl of Mar was nominally Episcopalian, yet his nickname 'Bobbing John' reflected his religious beliefs as much as his politics. His involvement in the 1715 Jacobite Rebellion, like his choice to be labelled Episcopalian, may have reflected Catholic sympathies. His brother, the Earl of Panmure, had a similarly complex relationship with religion, yet was married to another daughter of the Presbyterian Ann, Duchess of Hamilton. Most families did not appear to allow the distinctions within the Protestant religion to prevent intermarriage. The exception was the Scottish clergy, who appeared to marry within their own caste and some particularly religious individuals who used religious belief as a primary category when choosing a partner.

The Gordons of Huntley were a Catholic family as were several generations of the Mackenzies of Seaforth. Those individuals who were openly Catholic found it more difficult to marry into Protestant families, yet religious differences would not entirely end the possibility of marriage. The Catholic widow, the Marchioness of Huntley, married the Protestant Earl of Airlie in 1668 when love overcame religious difference. The Earl's mother was particularly against the marriage, noting 'it seimis streng to me that anie thing in eirt [earth] could indous yow to match with on of ane contrie religion trewlie I think no beutie nor honour nor richis nor no qualification unde heavin could do it'.[86] Religious differences made intermarriage difficult, which was complicated by the legal restrictions that meant marriage contracts signed by Catholics were not legally enforceable, yet it was not impossible. Most Catholic families married within their own religious group, like their Protestant counterparts.

While it is often known from other sources that many of the individuals in this study had strong religious convictions or were actively involved in church politics, overt discussions on religious matters were curiously rare in their correspondence with their spouses.[87] There were occasional examples of individuals who quoted from religious texts when quarrelling with their spouse or who discussed the spiritual welfare of their families, but this was far from widespread.[88] In general, abstract, theological or philosophical discussions were absent within couples' letters that tended to focus on the mundane workings of the household, family news and expressions of love. This is not to say that there was no evidence that religious belief was part of their world. Many people, but especially women, used phrases such as 'God forbid', almost superstitiously, when making references to the future or to health. References to religious teaching were found in advice to children from parents on their marriage, notably reminding women to be obedient, and religious platitudes were offered and drawn on for comfort after the death of a spouse or other family member.[89]

Furthermore, the values held by this social group and their understandings of gender were directly informed by religious discourses, which can be seen in references to women as helpmeets or allusions to conduct being related to salvation. This usage of religion suggested that belief was important to this social group, especially during times of change or conflict. Perhaps, it was so much part of the everyday, written into their worldview, that it failed to be newsworthy in correspondence, suggesting that any religious teaching they encountered was not exceptional or remarkable. The religious persecution, and later the memory of persecution, that marked various points in Scottish history may also have discouraged overt discussions of faith in a medium that was at risk of being made public.

There is little sense of the Kirk as a physical or institutional presence within these letters, where the most common reference to church attendance was when men advised their wives not to attend church when they were ill. These references suggest that church attendance was a regular and normal occurrence. Ministers were usually only discussed as family friends or as beneficiaries of patronage. There was almost a sense of ambivalence towards the Church's authority by men and women who exercised patronage, as many of these families considered themselves as superior in rank to the ministers who embodied the Church. It has been suggested that the Kirk's considerable social power was held in check by the Scottish nobility.[90] Yet, even in the writings of ministers and people of similar social rank, the influence of the Church or its place in people's lives was not generally made explicit in their letters. The notable exception to this trend was in the later part of the eighteenth century when people from the middling sorts and lesser lairds, usually in urban areas, used church as a place to meet and to be seen when courting.

Exploring marriage

An investigation of marriage is essentially an exploration of gender and gender relationships. Joan Scott argued in 1986 that gender was a 'primary field within which, or by means of which power is articulated'. She suggests that concepts of gender shape the 'concrete and symbolic organization of all social life'. Gender is a set of references which can be used to determine the distribution of power, and as such 'becomes implicated in the conception and construction of power itself'.[91] Conceptions of gender difference are vital to patriarchy as it is through this difference that lines of power are determined. An analysis of the relationship between gender difference, the distribution of power and the tensions between them, helps to further understandings of the operation of patriarchy. Yet, in the period under study, gender was not the only category that determined distribution of power in the patriarchal system. The importance of class and social position to the operation of patriarchy has been convincingly shown by Susan Amussen.[92] This was further complicated by other aspects of identity, including sexuality and race, which affected the ability, or desire, of a person to conform to patriarchal prescription.[93] Gender can also be a very fluid concept. Scott argues that the tendency to perceive gender difference in terms of binary relationships, and hence to see gender relationships as antagonistic, can obscure historical realities, and with it the production of power.[94]

Concepts of gender, and the patriarchal system that is built upon them, must be understood in their particular historical context. That context is the discourses, ingrained into society, culture and national institutions, that shape how people view the world and which they use to explain their experiences. Penny Summerfield highlights, through her work on oral history, the need for public discourses to allow people to articulate their experience. Where little or no public discourse exists, people found it difficult to construct a narrative, talking in a stilted, fact-giving style.[95] As Drew Gilpin Faust comments, 'we all live within the stories we tell, for these tales fashion a coherent direction and identity out of the discontinuities of our past, present and future.'[96] Discourse offers the language, or cultural scripts, that people use to construct their identities and place limits on how those identities are formed. These scripts are part of a shared language, ensuring that people can relay their personal experience into a public discourse and effectively communicate. Depending on the context, this may be necessary to appreciate a joke or understand the social significance of a statement.[97]

Robert Darnton argues that 'individual expression takes place within a general idiom'. Individuals are shaped by their society, and their expressions or works are a product of that society.[98] In this sense, public discourses can be self-perpetuating. The importance of cultural scripts to communication and the creation of identity ensure that cultural processes are intimately connected with power relationships.[99] Yet, at the same time, discourse is not static but constantly negotiated and recreated in every interaction between people and between people and the physical world. Within the context of the period, the key discourses that gave meaning to people's experience of love, marriage and power were a product of the patriarchal system in which they lived. Through the integration of such discourses with personal experience, the Scottish elites created patriarchal identities. The nature and major features of the Scottish patriarchal system, and how it fits into a wider European context, are described in Chapter 2.

The experience of marriage between the seventeenth and nineteenth centuries happened in a patriarchal context. Yet, while considerable attention has been given to exploring patriarchal society, through studies of popular culture and religious and legal sources, less attention is given to how people negotiated those discourses.[100] This has partly been a problem of sources. Discovering how people negotiated relationships and discourse relies on knowledge of how people communicated in everyday situations that were rarely preserved in writing. One source that has been heavily used for its insights into this picture has been legal records, which have provided a fascinating picture of patriarchal society, especially among the middling and plebeian sorts.[101] Despite the colourful nature of legal records, the picture they provide is of necessity partial. This book draws on correspondence, which is an underused source for the history of the family. While a number of articles have been written using letters to uncover individual marriages, there have been few large scale investigations of marriage using correspondence.[102] This is unfortunate as correspondence can offer a different perspective on marital relationships from other sources, highlighting how couples behaved and talked to each other every day.

The letters used for this project are drawn from the papers of sixty-five elite Scottish families and allow access to thousands of pages of correspondence written by over one hundred couples over a two-hundred-year period. This work, with its focus on love, intimacy and negotiation, is drawn mainly from the correspondence of couples writing to each other. In selecting the sample, except for the period 1650–1700 where there was less available material, correspondences of less than twenty letters were excluded to ensure that a sense of the dynamics of married life could emerge. Between twenty and thirty sets of letters were used for each period of fifty years from 1650 to 1850. Some correspondences were also supplemented with letters to family and friends to give different perspectives on the marriages under study, to gain a sense of whether intimacy between couples differed from wider family intimacy, and to provide missing details and context for family events. The correspondence of family, and particularly parents, was especially important for the discussion on courtship due to the high levels of kin and friend involvement. The purpose of using kin correspondence was to give insight into the conjugal unit. While the wider family is a central part of life and marriage during this period, there was a strong sense of the couple as a discrete and independent unit that allows their relationship to be studied separately from other familial relationships.

The letters were written in a variety of situations, but were in the main between spouses who were absent from each other due to business or family demands. The size of correspondence between individual couples varied depending on the time spent apart, literacy levels, and inclination of the parties, but could range from one letter to several hundred. While the nature of the source and the social group suggests full literacy rates by all parties, varying degrees of literacy were apparent in the writing. In the seventeenth century especially, many wives had quite basic literacy, writing with large characters, erratic spelling, no grammar, and in short bursts. By the mid-eighteenth century, both men and women had high levels of literacy and standardised spelling was increasingly common.[103] Scots language and grammar, common in the earlier period, became increasingly anglicised over the period, until it finally took a shape very similar to that currently used in Scotland. The quality of correspondence also varied enormously from women with poor literacy, who had to be coerced into writing short notes, to women such as Jane Carlyle whose literary talent was evident in witty social commentary and astute observations. Personality impacted on correspondence in multiple ways. Some men, such as the Earl of Marchmont, were almost lyrical in their love notes, while other stumbled over expressions of care, apologising for their lack of poetry. Some women were deferent; others more assertive, but all appeared free to express disagreement and even anger with their spouse.

As a source, letters can offer invaluable insights into the lives of the writer and reader, but should not be used uncritically. Martyn Lyons notes that 'personal letters have traditionally been valued for their spontaneity and their ability to convey personal experience more authentically than official or administrative letters', but adds that this is an overly simplistic approach to these sources.[104] Letter writing is a highly ritualised form of communication that has to be understood in the context of its historical period, or, as Mireille Bossis wittily remarked, the text of the letter 'must never be taken at its word'.[105] Letter writing has rules, or rituals, that govern its performance. These, often unspoken, conventions determine the structure and content of the conversation that takes place between writer and reader. They operate differently depending on the relationship between the writer and reader and are historically specific. Such rules determine forms of address and farewell, the length of the letter, frequency of writing and content. They are influenced by social conventions but also physical realities such as the frequency of the post, the cost of paper, ink and postage, and the geographical distance between the reader and writer. Letters are not a faithful reflection of the past but a cultural practice.[106]

In a Scottish context, couples who were apart in the seventeenth and early eighteenth centuries would write to each other once a week, although this gap could be longer if one party were abroad. By the end of the eighteenth century, spouses frequently wrote to each other daily when apart. This change appears to be partially due to the greater frequency and speed of the post in the later period, allowing shorter times between returns. Many couples had agreements to write with particular frequencies, even if there was little to report. Letters also tend to date to particular times in a person's life. Correspondence is rare during the 'honeymoon' period and for many couples tends to cluster over periods that may last years, but do not reflect the entire length of the marriage.

Each letter is a performance where a person creates an identity that is personal to her or him, but which also conforms to the rules of presentation that are demanded by letter writing convention. These conventions ensure that similar forms of correspondence look alike and have comparable content. Lyons' work on nineteenth century love letters shows that they not only shared similar forms of address, but that commonly authors contrived spontaneity of emotional expression through a suggestion of disordered thoughts.[107] This form of writing was a socially acceptable form of expressing emotional sentiment. This is not to suggest that the feelings described were not real, but that the form of expression was socially controlled.

The performative nature of correspondence is complicated in the period under study due to the potential for a wider audience for individual letters.[108] Letters were often read aloud in family groups, passed on to friends, and for much of the period, if they were posted, could be read and censored by the Crown. There was also ample opportunity for letters to be waylaid and read by interested parties and servants. The sense of the public nature of writing, in part, helps to explain the existence of letter writing etiquette books. Etiquette books gave guidelines on the formal rules of letter writing including the correct forms of address and farewell, the structure of letters, and even appropriate content. They existed because the letter is a public form of communication, and not usually a window to the private, free expression of the soul.[109]

Having said this, letters between husbands and wives often indicated an expectation of privacy. That letters or portions of letters were only meant for the eyes of the recipient was occasionally stated, but many others revealed an expectation of privacy through indicating parts to be read aloud; asking to send on particular messages to family members; describing other members of the household in less than complimentary ways; through the disclosure of intimacy or politically sensitive information; and through the insistence that wives write in person, rather than using scribes. Many couples wrote with the expectation that their letters would only be read by each other. Yet, there was often awareness that privacy was not possible in practice. The Duke and Duchess of Hamilton appeared to have an expectation that their letters were private, often sharing sensitive political or family gossip, but they occasionally resorted to a cipher to disguise names or events. The Duke also refused, on occasion, to pass on details by post, asking his wife to trust his judgement. The potential for publicity may also have influenced self-presentation on a more personal level.

It is unhelpful to think of letters as having no relationship with the personal. People require a narrative, a social discourse, to compose their experiences. Every form of communication involves a form of performativity as every conversation has rules that guide it. As Judith Butler argues, 'language is not an *exterior medium* or *instrument* into which I pour a self and from which I glean a reflection of that self'.[110] Letters allow time for composition and thoughtful presentation of the self, but this self is always a performance. This process is similar to how people construct their identities in most social situations. Linda Pollock, in her discussion of emotional expression in correspondence, notes that 'the prevailing assumption is that these paradigms get in the way of access to true feelings, that they are, in fact, a hindrance to historical understanding. But cultural scripts are an essential part of the communication of emotion in personal relationships.' She continues that these cultural scripts allow for both parties to be able to communicate, to make sense of what is otherwise a very personal experience.[111]

Understanding cultural scripts can be especially important when dealing with abstract concepts such as emotions. Leslie Baxter argues that people have difficulty expressing abstract thoughts so they use a set of common cognitive metaphors to explain their experiences. Through a study of how American undergraduates described their relationships with their partners, Baxter shows that certain metaphors, such as the relationship as a journey, as a container, as a fire, were used to express abstract ideas. These metaphors reoccurred frequently throughout her sample. The interviewee assumed that Baxter would understand her or his metaphor and, through understanding the metaphor, understand her or his personal experience.[112] Heli Tissari has performed a similar study on early modern texts and the use of the word love and found that the word was commonly used alongside metaphors that expressed love as a duty.[113] Cultural scripts are a basic part of communication and necessary for ensuring that both parties can understand each other. They change over time, requiring the historian to tread cautiously when studying past cultures.

This shared language or collective conventions for communication are not used unsophisticatedly by letter writers. Pollock notes that 'letter writers knew how to manipulate and exploit the regulations governing the correct phrasing of sentiments. They enable us to see how cultural scripts were enabled or amended in everyday life.'[114] Disrespect or anger could be shown through incorrect use of address forms, while a play on words was a useful form of negotiating power. From a Foucauldian perspective, the social conventions of language are what ensure power in this society, while the rejection or reinterpretation of these conventions allowed resistance.[115] The multiple interpretations available in social expression and convention help contribute to the instability of the system of power as well as ensuring that authority never lies entirely in one place. It is also important to recognise that there is never only one cultural script, but a multitude that have to be negotiated and prioritised depending on the social situation.[116]

Letter writing by its very nature involves negotiation. The letter is not an isolated text, but part of a conversation. Many letters form part of chain of a much larger correspondence and, while some instigate a new topic, others can only be understood as a response to a former question. It is important to understand the content of letters in the context of this conversation if the meaning is to be understood. Every letter relies on the fact that the writer and reader talk the same language, yet this cannot be taken for granted. Misunderstandings and misinterpretations were common and not always accidental. Bossis argues that every letter is a collaboration between the writer and the reader, and so has to be understood as portraying more than the identity of one individual.[117] This informed how individuals expressed themselves. Couples were usually careful in expressing criticism of the other, so when provoked to anger tone noticeably changed. To protect their spouse's feelings, individuals underplayed illness or the seriousness of a political crisis. In times of marital conflict, they chose to misread or even ignore letters, to deflect disapproval, and to represent themselves in the best possible light. Spouses played off each other, offering multiple interpretations of the same behaviour, in a negotiation for power.

The letter is usually written in absence and/or at a distance. It is an attempt by the writer to extend her or his everyday life across time and space to the reader. This distance can allow the writer to say things or express emotions that he or she would not have done in person, while the opposite is also true. When using letters to study people's marriages, this is an important consideration. Many couples resented the distance between them, while for others it allowed them vital space. How a marriage functioned when performed through correspondence and over distance may have very little in common with how a couple behaved when together. It should not be forgotten that the space gained in a letter was not only physical. In the 1730s, Archibald Grant of Monymusk found it easier to write to his wife about his feelings of anger from his bedroom than confront her face to face in the next room. At a practical level, distance also affected content. Long absences required discussion of the household economy, estates and family businesses, while shorter visits only required the passing of family news or no news, but expressions of care and remembering.

A number of other sources were used to interpret the cultural scripts found within letters. Legal texts, religious writings, and prescriptive and popular literature were used to explore the culture of marriage and the operation of patriarchy in Scotland. They are used to provide the historical context discussed in Chapter 2, but also give insight into the meaning of cultural scripts found within letters. Due to the low incidence of discussions of marital violence within letters, evidence from separation for cruelty cases conducted at the Commissary Court in Edinburgh across the period 1714–1830 are used in Chapter 7, alongside correspondence, to create a larger sample for discussion.[118] The sample was restricted to cases that involved couples from the Scottish elites, many of whom were relatives of the couples whose correspondence was studied. John Home of Kimmerghame, whose wife sued for separation, was the cousin and nephew of two of the couples. Grisell Baillie, who sought a separation from her husband Alexander Murray, was the niece of one of the couples under study, as well as the second cousin of John Home above. One of Alexander Murray's letters to his wife is also extant. Elenora Cathcart, who received a separation from her husband, John Houston, was the aunt of Mary Graham, whose correspondence with her husband provided evidence for the late eighteenth century. Court records are used alongside correspondence to give a broader picture of the nature of marital violence amongst the Scottish elites.

This book uses the correspondence of the Scottish elites to explore how they negotiated their marriages within a patriarchal context. Chapter 2 provides the institutional and cultural framework for marriage in Scotland. It explores how the Church, judiciary and popular writers created the context which people used to interpret married life, highlighting the concern with a husband's obligation to love, protect and provide for his wife, and a wife's duty to obey her husband. Yet, it also shows that within that broad framework, meanings of husbandly authority, wifely obedience, and the duties of married life were flexible, open to negotiation and change over time. This created a structure for Scottish marriage that reinforced patriarchal values, but allowed adaptation to personal circumstances and experience. Chapter 3 expands on this theme through a discussion of the role of wider kin and the place of economic security and love within courtship. It demonstrates that courtship, as well as being part of the life-cycle, was a time where couples negotiated the terms and framework of their future marriages. It highlights that courtship behaviour adapted as the purpose of marriage shifted from consolidating family networks to reinforcing the new conjugal unit in the eighteenth century, but that throughout the period the bargaining over the marriage settlement was also a debate about power in later life.

Following on from this, the remainder of the book explores in more depth how people negotiated marriage in the everyday through correspondence. Chapter 4 looks at how couples used the language of love. It demonstrates that seventeenth-century models for loving behaviour were closely associated with fulfilment of duty, so that love was demonstrated through a husband's benevolent provision and protection, and a wife's obedience. It then explores how understandings of love changed with the culture of sensibility to reflect the new emphasis on the conjugal unit. Yet, this new way of thinking about loving did not reduce a wife's obligation to obey, and indeed, built into its structures was the need for wives to sublimate their self beneath that of their husband in the process of shoring up the new male individual. Despite these patriarchal constructions of loving, women continued to find spaces to negotiate the meaning of love, creating a space for the female self within marriage.

Chapter 5 discusses the place of intimacy within the patriarchal marriage. It explores the way that a close relationship, particularly an interdependent relationship such as marriage, complicates social hierarchies through the need for cooperation and compromise. The nature of such cooperation and compromise, and thus the nature of intimacy itself, is historically specific and reflects how people understood the relationship between intimate partners. As a result, this chapter looks at how Scottish culture and the elites understood and practised the concepts of obedience, duty, friendship and finally domesticity, as it was through the negotiation and practice of these key concepts that they practised intimacy. It concludes that hierarchy, and thus patriarchal power, was not dissolved due to the intimate relationships of spouses, but that intimacy added democratic potential to marriage.

The ambiguities of patriarchal power in practice are continued in Chapter 7, which explores the marital economy. The high level of cooperation between spouses required to manage a household and estate, and particularly the access to economic resources that managing a home gave to women, threatened male authority and potentially gave power to women. In particular households, this gave individual women significant authority, yet they had difficulty transforming this into power beyond the home. In the seventeenth century, society shunned 'domineering' women, while in the later eighteenth century, the cult of domesticity, which separated the home from the public sphere where power was exercised, structurally severed the link between women's authority over household resources and public power. As a result, the potential threat that access to economic resources posed to patriarchal society was limited to disputes over power within private houses.

The threat that women's agency offered to the patriarchal system is at the heart of Chapter 7. It explores how the Scottish elites conceived and reacted to marital violence within their own households, before discussing the central motivations for violence. It highlights that marital violence was closely connected to disputes over economic resources and to female sexuality, both areas where women's agency potentially undermined the hierarchies of the patriarchal system. It concludes that marital violence reflected the failure of negotiation within the marital relationship, but was still implicated in its processes as its purpose was to restore order in the patriarchal home. Throughout, this book demonstrates that the practice of patriarchy was more complicated than male dominance and female subordination as couples cooperated, fought and negotiated the terms of their relationship, but at the same time, this very process of negotiation ensured that the Scottish elites never stepped outside the patriarchal framework that they used to define their relationships, ensuring the continuance of the patriarchal system.

Notes

1   National Archives of Scotland [hereafter NAS] GD18/5215 Christian Kilpatrick to John Clerk, 17 September 1698.
2   E. Ewan and J. Nugent (eds), *Finding the Family in Medieval and Early Modern Scotland* (Aldershot: Ashgate, 2008).
3   Leneman's main works are: L. Leneman, *Alienated Affections: The Scottish Experience of Divorce and Separation, 1684–1830* (Edinburgh: Edinburgh University Press, 1998); L. Leneman and R. Mitchison, *Sexuality and Social Control: Scotland 1660–1780* (Oxford: Basil Blackwell, 1989). Other historians have discussed marriage in the wider context of the family or women's experiences, yet the list is not extensive,

see: R. Marshall, *Virgins and Viragos: A History of Women in Scotland from 1080 to 1980* (London: Collins, 1983); K. Brown, *Noble Society in Scotland: Wealth, Family and Culture from Reformation to Revolution* (Edinburgh: Edinburgh University Press, 2000); E. Ewan and M. Meikle, *Women in Scotland, c. 1100–c. 1750* (East Linton: Tuckwell Press, 1999); E. Gordon and G. Nair, *Public Lives: Women, Family and Society in Victorian Britain* (London: Yale University Press, 2003); L. Abrams, *Myth and Materiality in a Woman's World: Shetland 1800-2000* (Manchester: Manchester University Press, 2005); L. Abrams et al., *Gender in Scottish History since 1700* (Edinburgh: Edinburgh University Press, 2006); A. Clark, *The Struggle for the Breeches* (Berkeley: University of California, 1995).

4 A. Erickson, 'The marital economy in comparative perspective', in M. Ågren and A. Erickson (eds), *The Marital Economy in Scandanavia and Britain 1400-1900* (Aldershot: Ashgate, 2005), pp. 3–22.

5 L. Stone, *The Family, Sex and Marriage in England 1500-1800* (London: Weidenfeld and Nicolson, 1977); E. Shorter, *The Making of the Modern Family* (London: Collins, 1976); R. Trumbach, *The Rise of the Egalitarian Family* (Oxford: Academic Press, 1978).

6 Stone, *The Family*, pp. 270–391.

7 Shorter, *Modern Family*; W. Goode, 'Marriage among the English nobility in the 16th and 17th centuries: comment', *Comparative Studies in Society and History*, 3 (1961), 207–14; W. Goode, 'The theoretical importance of love', *American Sociological Review*, 24 (1959), 38–47.

8 J. Amato, 'A world without intimacy: a portrait of a time before we were intimate individuals and loves', *International Social Science Review*, 61 (1986), 155–68. Norbert Elias makes a similar argument suggesting that people became increasingly controlled in their emotional expressions: see N. Elias, 'On human beings and their emotions: a process-sociological essay', *Theory, Culture and Society*, 4 (1987), 339–61.

9 Stone, *The Family*; Shorter, *Modern Family*.

10 K. Wrightson, *English Society 1580-1680* (London: Hutchison, 1982), p. 92.

11 E. Foyster, *Marital Violence: an English Family History, 1660-1857* (Cambridge: Cambridge University Press, 2005), p. 11; Gordon and Nair, *Public Lives*, pp. 71–3; A. Vickery, *The Gentleman's Daughter: Women's Lives in Georgian England* (London: Yale University Press, 1998), p. 40; B. Capp, *When Gossips Meet: Women, Family, and Neighbourhood in Early Modern England* (Oxford: Oxford University Press, 2003), p. 11.

12 B. Taylor, 'Feminists versus gallants: manners and morals in Enlightenment Britain', in S. Knott and B. Taylor (eds), *Women, Gender and Enlightenment* (Houndmills: Palgrave, 2005), p. 38. See also J. Popiel, 'Making mothers: the advice genre and the domestic ideal, 1760-1830', *Journal of Family History*, 29 (2004), 339–50; I. Tague, 'Love, honour and obedience: fashionable women and the discourse of marriage in the early eighteenth century', *Journal of British Studies*, 40 (2001), 85.

13 J. Hardwick, *The Practice of Patriarchy: Gender and the Politics of Household Authority in Early Modern France* (University Park: Pennsylvania State University Press, 1998); J. Bailey, *Unquiet Lives: Marriage and Marriage Breakdown in England, 1660-1800* (Cambridge: Cambridge University Press, 2003); and D. O'Hara,

Courtship and Constraint: Rethinking the Making of Marriage in Tudor England (Manchester: Manchester University Press, 2000).

14 D. Sabean, *Property, Production, and Family in Neckarhausen, 1700–1870* (Cambridge: Cambridge University Press, 1990), p. 24.

15 Stone, *The Family*; Shorter, *Modern Family*; Trumbach, *Egalitarian Family*.

16 J. Kelly, 'Did women have a Renaissance?', in J. Kelly, *Women, History and Theory: the Essays of Joan Kelly* (Chicago: Chicago University Press, 1984), pp. 20–50; J. Bennett, 'Confronting continuity', *Journal of Women's History*, 9 (1997), 73–95, continues this discussion by pointing out that we need to explore both continuities and change.

17 A good discussion of the need to study the 'long eighteenth century' can be found in Foyster, *Marital Violence*, pp. 7–9.

18 M. Weber, *The Theory of Social and Economic Organisation* (New York: Oxford University Press, 1947), p. 152. For a discussion see L. Lamphere, 'Strategies, cooperation, and conflict among women in domestic groups', in M. Zimbalist Rosaldo and L. Lamphere (eds), *Women, Culture and Society* (Stanford: Stanford University Press, 1974), pp. 97–113.

19 M. G. Smith, *Government in Zazzau* (London: Oxford University Press, 1960), pp. 18–20.

20 b. hooks, *Feminist Theory: From Margin to Centre* (Boston, MA: South End Press, 1984), p. 89.

21 S. Walby, *Theorising Patriarchy* (Oxford: Blackwell, 1990), pp. 20–1.

22 J. Bennett, 'Feminism and history', *Gender and History*, 3 (1989), 260; Bennett, 'Confronting continuity', footnote 9.

23 Bennett, 'Confronting continuity'. See also C. Smart, *The Ties that Bind: Law, Marriage and the Reproduction of Patriarchal Relations* (London: Routledge, 1984), pp. 6–13.

24 M. Ezell, *The Patriarch's Wife: Literary Evidence and the History of the Family* (London: North Carolina University Press, 1987), pp. 1–8; see also M. Hunt, 'Wife beating, domesticity and women's independence in eighteenth century London', *Gender and History*, 4 (1992), 10–33.

25 A. Fletcher, 'Manhood, the male body, courtship and the household in early modern England', *History*, 84 (1999), 419–36; A. Fletcher, *Gender, Sex and Subordination in England 1500–1800* (London: Yale University Press, 1995); L. Pollock, 'Rethinking patriarchy and the family in the seventeenth-century England', *Journal of Family History*, 23 (1998), 3–27; A. Shepherd, 'Manhood, credit and patriarchy in early modern England c. 1580–1640', *Past and Present*, 167 (2000), 75–106; S. Amussen, *An Ordered Society: Gender and Class in Early Modern England* (Oxford: Basil Blackwell, 1988); J. Scott, 'Gender: a useful category of historical analysis', *American Historical Review*, 91 (1986), 1053–75; E. Foyster, *Manhood in Early Modern England: Honour, Sex and Marriage* (Harlow: Longman, 1999), p. 65.

26 M. Foucault, *Discipline and Punish* (London: Penguin, 1979), p. 194.

27 Capp, *When Gossips Meet*, p. 1. I argue that this is the definition of a system.

28 P. Bourdieu, *Outline of a Theory of Practice* (Cambridge: Cambridge University Press, 1972), p. 183; M. Foucault, *The Will to Knowledge: the History of Sexuality*, vol. 1 (London: Penguin Books, 1998), pp. 135–59.

29 Capp, *When Gossips Meet*, p. 25.

30 D. Kandiyoti, 'Bargaining with patriarchy', *Gender and Society*, 2 (1988), 285.

31 Foucault, *Will to Knowledge*, p. 92.

32 J. Bennett, *History Matters: Patriarchy and the Challenge of Feminism* (Manchester: Manchester University Press, 2006), pp. 72–9.

33 D. Hall, *Fixing Patriarchy: Feminism and Mid-Victorian Male Novelists* (New York: New York University Press, 1997).

34 Bourdieu, *Outline of a Theory*, p. 170.

35 Foucault, *Will to Knowledge*, p. 97.

36 Other than in a Marxist sense that groups with differing interests are in conflict by virtue of those interests.

37 This investment also applies to never married women who until recently rarely headed households, spending their lives as members of extended families, based around a nuclear unit. They also had strong ties with kin; see A. Froide, *Never Married: Singlewomen in Early Modern England* (Oxford: Oxford University Press, 2005).

38 Even if we argue that in Western culture today women have a sense of gender identity outside of the family, some feminists have pointed out that the present focus on difference within gender stops any sense of 'commonality derived from subordination under patriarchy'. An interesting discussion of this is: J. Hoff, 'A postmodern category of paralysis', *Women's History Review*, 3 (1994), 149–68.

39 Bennett, 'Feminism and history', p. 261.

40 A. MacFarlane, *Marriage and Love in England: Modes of Reproduction 1300–1840* (Oxford: Basil Blackwood, 1986), pp. 119–210.

41 The best summary of Scottish history throughout this period is T. C. Smout, *A History of the Scottish People, 1560–1830* (London: Fontana Press, 1985).

42 Erickson, 'The marital economy', p. 6.

43 Brown, *Noble Society*, pp. 8–14.

44 Leneman and Mitchison, *Sexuality and Social Control*, p. 55.

45 M. Meikle, *A British Frontier? Lairds and Gentlemen in the Scottish Borders, 1540–1603* (East Linton: Tuckwell, 2004), pp. 11–20.

46 For a fuller discussion see: Leneman and Mitchison, *Sexuality and Social Control*, p. 56.

47 R. A. Houston, 'British society in the eighteenth century', *Journal of British Studies*, 25 (1986), 458–59.

48 Brown, *Noble Society*, p. 11 and Meikle, *British Frontier*, p. 19.

49 S. Nenadic, *Laird and Luxury: the Highland Gentry in Eighteenth Century Scotland* (Edinburgh: John Donald, 2007).

50 Nenadic, *Lairds and Luxury*; A. Cathcart, *Kinship and Clientage: Highland Clanship, 1451–1609* (Leiden: Brill, 2006).

51 Nenadic, *Lairds and Luxury*, p. 21.

52 Leneman and Mitchison, *Sexuality and Social Control*, pp. 54–5.

53 I. G. C. Hutchison, 'The nobility and politics in Scotland, c. 1880–1939', in T. M. Devine (ed.), *Scottish Elites* (East Linton: John Donald, 1994), p. 135.

54 Leneman and Mitchison, *Sexuality and Social Control*, p. 56.

55 The significance of military careers to the Scottish elites is noted by S. Nenadic, 'The impact of the military profession on Highland gentry families, c. 1730–1830', *Scottish Historical Review*, 85 (2006), 75–99.

56 Smout, *Scottish People*, pp. 205–13.

57 K. Bowie, *Scottish Public Opinion and the Anglo-Scottish Union, 1699–1707* (Woodbridge: Royal Historical Society, 2007).

58 Smout, *Scottish People*, pp. 240–7; Nenadic, *Laird and Luxury*.

59 Fred Kaplan, 'Carlyle, Thomas (1795–1881)', *Oxford Dictionary of National Biography*, (Oxford: Oxford University Press, 2004).

60 For a wider discussion see Smout, *Scottish People*. For a discussion of the implications of change see S. Nenadic, 'Experience and expectations in the transformation of the Highland gentlewoman, 1680 to 1820', *Scottish Historical Review*, 80 (2001), 201–20.

61 This is also noted by Marshall, *Virgins and Viragos*, p. 64.

62 NAS GD1/616/264 David Robertson to his sister Miss Robertson, 26 December 1810.

63 Leneman and Mitchison, *Sexuality and Social Control*, p. 56.

64 NAS GD406/1/6358 Earl of Rutherglen to Earl of Arran, 9 January 1697/8.

65 NAS GD18 Papers of the Clerks of Penicuick.

66 M. Lee, 'Scotland and the "General Crisis" of the seventeenth century', *Scottish Historical Review*, 63 (1984), pp. 144–5. The extent of this 'vulnerability' is questioned by Brown, *Noble Society*.

67 This is commented on in A. Campbell, Marques of Argyll, *Instructions to a Son* (London: Richard Blackwell, 1689), pp. 79–80.

68 NAS GD18/5186/7 John Clerk to Elizabeth Clerk, [c. 1690]; GD155/851 Robertson of Strowan to Margaret Robertson, 23 May 1755; GD345/799/1 Francis Grant of Monymusk to Archibald Grant, [c. early 18th century]; M. Pittock, *Scottish and Irish Romanticism* (Oxford: Oxford University Press, 2008), p. 19.

69 Smout, *Scottish People*, p. 232.

70 John Dwyer, 'Ethics and economics: bridging Adam Smith's Theory of Moral Sentiments and Wealth of Nations', *Journal of British Studies*, 44 (2005), 670.

71 D. Allan, 'Provincial readers and the book culture in the Scottish Enlightenment: the Perth library 1784–c1800', *Library*, 3 (2002), 367–89.

72 Houston, 'British society', 458–9. Smout, *Scottish People*, p. 263.

73 Smout, *Scottish People*, pp. 263–5.

74 N. T. Phillipson, 'Culture and society in the eighteenth century province: the case of Edinburgh and the Scottish Enlightenment', in L. Stone (ed.), *The University in Society*, vol. 2 (London: Oxford University Press, 1974), pp. 411–48.

75 D. Thomas, 'The social origins of marriage partners of the British peerage in the eighteenth and nineteenth centuries', *Population Studies*, 26 (1972), 99–111.

76 When the categories of peerage, greater and lesser laird are used. For more, see K. Barclay, '"I rest your loving obedient wife": marital relationships in Scotland, 1650–1850' (PhD dissertation, University of Glasgow, 2007).

77 M. Ingram, *Church Courts, Sex and Marriage in England, 1570–1640* (Cambridge: Cambridge University Press, 1987), p. 129.

78 Stone, *The Family*, pp. 37–51.

79 Thomas, 'Marriage partners', 100.

80 Wrightson, *English Society*, pp. 68–70; For an alternative perspective see: J. Gillis, '"A triumph of hope over experience": chance and choice in the history of marriage', *International Review of Social History*, 44 (1999), 47–54 and D. Levine, '"For their

own reasons": individual marriage decisions and family life', *Journal of Family History*, 7 (1982), 255–64.

81 Stone, *The Family*, pp. 37–51.

82 R. Grassby notes of the business classes in England that the number of men marrying widows declined across the period 1580–1740 from 12.1% to 7.9%, see *Kinship and Capitalism: Marriage, Family, and Business in the English- Speaking World, 1580–1740* (Cambridge: Cambridge University Press, 2001), p. 51.

83 M. Segalen, *Love and Power in the Peasant Family* (Oxford: Blackwell, 1983), p. 13; M. Hartman, *The Household and the Making of History: a Subversive View of the Western Past* (Cambridge: Cambridge University Press, 2004), p. 32.

84 C. Brown, *Religion and Society in Scotland since 1707* (Edinburgh: Edinburgh University Press, 1997).

85 Hutchison, 'The nobility', p.132.

86 NAS GD16/34/200 Isobel Hamilton to the Earl of Airlie, 1668.

87 H. Kelsall, *Scottish Life 300 Years Ago: New Light on Edinburgh and Border Families* (Edinburgh: John Donald, 1986).

88 For example, NAS GD345/1148/5/27 Archibald Grant to Anna Potts, 6 April 1739.

89 For example, NAS GD18/5186/7 John Clerk to Elizabeth Clerk, [c. 1690]; GD155/851 Robertson of Strowan to Margaret Robertson, 23 May 1755; GD345/799/1 Francis Grant of Monymusk to Archibald Grant, [c. early 18th century].

90 K. Boyd, *Scottish Church Attitudes to Sex, Marriage and the Family 1850–1914* (Edinburgh: John Donald, 1980), p. 1; M. Graham, *The Uses of Reform: "Godly Discipline" and Popular Behaviour in Scotland and France, 1560–1610* (Leiden: Brill, 1996), pp. 259–79.

91 Scott, 'Gender: a useful category', 1069.

92 Amussen, *Ordered Society*.

93 For example, A. Fletcher, 'Men's dilemma: the future of patriarchy in England 1560–1660', *Transactions of the Royal Historical Society*, 6:4 (1994), 61–81; L. Boose, 'Scolding brides and bridling scolds: taming the woman's unruly member', *Shakespeare Quarterly*, 42 (1991), 179–213; F. Easton, 'Gender's two bodies: women warriors, female husbands and plebeian life', *Past and Present*, 180 (2003), 131–74; D. Dugaw, *Warrior Women and Popular Balladry, 1650–1850* (Cambridge: Cambridge University Press, 1989).

94 Scott, 'Gender: a useful category', 1064.

95 P. Summerfield, 'Culture and composure: creating narratives of the gendered self in oral history interviews', *Cultural and Social History*, 1 (2004), 65–93.

96 Quoted in K. Halttunen, 'Cultural history and the challenge of narrativity', in V. Bonnell and L. Hunt (eds), *Beyond the Cultural Turn: New Directions in the Study of Society and Culture* (Berkeley: California University Press, 1999), p. 171.

97 An interesting discussion of this concept in operation is P. Bailey, 'Conspiracies of meaning: music-hall and the knowingness of popular culture', *Past and Present*, 144 (1994), 138–71.

98 R. Darnton, *The Great Cat Massacre and Other Episodes in French Cultural History* (London: Vintage Books, 1985), p. 6.

99 R. Johnson, 'What is cultural studies anyway?', *Social Text*, 16 (1986/7), 38.

100 A few examples include: J. Wiltenburg, *Disorderly Women and Female Power in the Street Literature of Early Modern England and Germany* (London: Virginia University Press, 1992); A. Friedman, 'Love, sex and marriage in traditional French society: the documentary evidence of folksongs', *Annual Meeting of the Western Society for French History*, 5 (1978), 146–154; A noticeable exception is A. Kugler, 'Constructing wifely identity: prescription and practice in the life of Lady Sarah Cowper', *Journal of British Studies*, 40 (2001), 291–323.

101 A good example of use of legal records for the plebeian and middling sorts, includes: Bailey, *Unquiet Lives;* Capp, *When Gossips Meet* and O'Hara, *Courtship and Constraint.* Leah Leneman used legal records for Scotland, looking at all social groups, see footnote 3 for her main publications.

102 Some examples include: B. Harris, 'Power, profit and passion: Mary Tudor, Charles Brandon, and arranged marriage in early Tudor England', *Feminist Studies*, 15 (1989), 59–88; B. Hill, 'The course of the marriage of Elizabeth Montagu: an ambitious and talented woman without means', *Journal of Family History*, 26 (2001), 3–17; M. Slater, 'The weightiest business: marriage in an upper-gentry family in seventeenth century England', *Past and Present*, 72 (1976), 25–54. A notable exception is S. Whyman, *Sociability and Power in Late-Stuart England* (Oxford: Oxford University Press, 1999).

103 For a discussion of Scottish literacy see: L. Stone, 'Literacy and education in England, 1640–1900', *Past and Present*, 42 (1969), 120; R. A. Houston, 'The literacy myth?: Illiteracy in Scotland, 1640–1760', *Past and Present*, 96 (1982), 90–2; T. C. Smout, 'Born again at Cambuslang: new evidence on popular religion and literacy in eighteenth century Scotland', *Past and Present*, 97 (1982), 121–7.

104 M. Lyons, 'French soldiers and their correspondence: towards a history of writing practices in the First World War', *French History*, 17 (2003), 81.

105 M. Bossis and K. McPherson, 'Methodological journeys through correspondences', *Yale French Studies*, 71 (1986), 75.

106 M. Lyons, 'Love letters and writing practices: on ecritures intimes in the nineteenth century', *Journal of Family History*, 24 (1999), 237.

107 Lyons, 'Love letters', 232–9.

108 For a discussion of the balance between publicity and privacy in letters, see: J. Brewer, 'This, that and the other: public, social and private in the seventeenth and eighteenth centuries', in D. Castiglione and L. Sharpe (eds), *Shifting the Boundaries: Transformation of the Languages of Public and Private in the Eighteenth Century* (Exeter: Exeter University Press, 1995), pp. 10–12.

109 L. Pollock, 'Living on the stage of the world: the concept of privacy among the elite of early modern England', in A. Wilson (ed.), *Rethinking Social History: English Society 1570–1920 and its Interpretation* (Manchester: Manchester University Press, 1993), pp. 78–96.

110 J. Butler, *Gender Trouble: Feminism and the Subversion of Identity* (London: Routlege, 1999), pp. 182–3.

111 L. Pollock, 'Anger and the negotiation of relationships in early modern England', *Historical Journal*, 47 (2004), 573.

112 L. Baxter, 'Root metaphors in accounts of developing romantic relationships', *Journal of Social and Personal Relationships*, 9 (1992), 253–75.

113 H. Tissari, *Lovescapes: Changes in Prototypical Senses and Cognitive Metaphors since 1500* (Helsinki: Societe Neophilologique, 2003).

114   Pollock, 'Anger and negotiation', 573.
115   Foucault, *Will to Knowledge,* pp. 83–6.
116   Pollock, 'Anger and negotiation', 573.
117   Bossis and McPherson, 'Methodological journeys', 63–75.
118   For more information on these cases, see: Leneman, *Alienated Affections.*

2

Marriage within Scottish culture

Like in most of Europe, patriarchal social relations underpinned all forms of human interaction in Scotland through the seventeenth and into the late nineteenth century. A male head of household presiding over his subordinates, which included his wife, resident adult offspring, young children and servants, was the ideal form of household and the very basis of the social order. Symbolically, the conjugal relationship was the epitome of patriarchy, which all other social relationships, including that of king and subjects, should emulate. The ideal marriage featured a benevolent husband who offered wise and kind rule to his obedient wife. As both husband and wife benefited from the good order of the home, their shared interest ensured that they followed patriarchal prescriptions. Husbands had the authority to discipline their wives, yet, if their relationship worked according to the ideal, this should be unnecessary. Language, law, religion and popular culture reinforced belief in the patriarchal model, yet even its strongest advocates acknowledged that in practice this social system had flaws.[1] This chapter will provide the institutional and cultural context for marital relationships in Scotland, highlighting how the Church, State and popular culture created a patriarchal context for marriage that helped frame the nature of the marital relationship in Scotland. This framework informed how people negotiated the marital relationships explored in the remainder of the book.

Church, State, law

The Scottish State, through legislation and the operation of law, and a socially and politically influential Church, underpinned the patriarchal model for marriage, 'construct[ing] and maintain[ing] the gendered hierarchies that … provided an explicit basis for social and political organization on the notion of household patriarchy.[2] The law, in part, defined the form and character of the marital relationship. Marital law, during this period, took its shape, like much of Scottish law, from Canon and Roman (civil) law, some gifted judicial writers, the Kirk and popular demand. The body of the law was written before 1650 and there was almost no statute change before 1830. The Commissary Court, which dealt with all forms of family law, the Court of Session and institutional writers compensated for this with increasingly sophisticated case law.[3] Marital law was publicised through the teachings of the Church, through the publishing of scandalous legal suits in ballads and pamphlets, and through participation in legal processes by the Scottish public.[4] The Scottish elites were often intimately involved in the making of the law itself as politicians, lawyers, judges, jury members, and their wives.

MAKING MARRIAGE

Marriage in Scotland was peculiarly easy to contract, 'requiring no particular solemnity, nor even written evidence but deliberate and unconditional consent alone'.[5] This had been the case in most of Catholic Europe until the strictures on the Council of Trent came into force in 1564, using the decree *Tametsi* to nullify all marriages not performed by the Church. Some of the reformed central European states adopted similar legislation restricting clandestine marriage, but in northern Europe and Britain the formation of marriage remained remarkably unregulated into the eighteenth century and beyond.[6] 'Unconditional' consent required that marriage was understood and intended by both parties. Marriage through intimidation or force, intoxication or where the parties were underage or insane was not legally binding.[7] Until 1929, the legal age for marriage was twelve for women and fourteen for men.

Unlike in most of Catholic Europe and parts of Protestant Germany, parental consent was not needed, although the issue was debated in Parliament in 1698.[8] No act was ratified as a result of this discussion. This was possibly due to Lord Stair's contention that while the government could make a marriage without parental consent unlawful, and so open to sanction, it would not annul the marriage.[9] But, it also reflected Scotland's Presbyterian values, which viewed arbitrary authority – within the family as elsewhere – as problematic. The question again arose 1755, but never made it past the drafting stage; partly because the Scots were very sensitive about the British parliament interfering in Scots law, but again because they saw it as a form of 'Church Tyranny' infringing on the religious freedom of Presbyterians.[10] As a result of this decision,

when Hardwicke's Marriage Act (1753) in England and similar legislation in Ireland required people under 21 to have parental consent at
marriage, Scotland developed a flourishing trade in irregular marriage,
most notably launching Gretna Green into the limelight.

The Church, in conjunction with the State, defined marriage as
either regular or irregular. Following the Catholic formula, regular
marriage required the proclamation of banns, notice of intention to
marry in the local parish church on three successive Sundays and the
issue of a certificate verifying their reading, followed by a ceremony
performed by a Church of Scotland clergyman in front of two credible
witnesses. The right to perform a marriage was extended to clergymen of
the Episcopal faith in 1711 and to Quaker leaders and Jewish Rabbis in
1834. Irregular marriage was any that did not conform to Church regulations, but was usually divided into irregular marriage or cohabitation
with habit and repute. Irregular marriages were valid and so could not be
annulled, but were punishable by the Church and State as contravening
church discipline and social order. The State recognised two forms of
irregular or private marriage, which centred on the wording of the promise to marry. *Verba de praesenti* was where two people consented to
marry at that time. Alternately, *verba de futuro* plus *copula* was a promise to marry in the future followed by sexual intercourse. The validity of
the latter form was highly controversial amongst legal commentators.
Most people who chose to marry this way were rebuked by the Church as
fornicators and made to marry regularly.[11]

A no less controversial form of marriage was cohabitation plus habit
and repute, although this was ratified by an Act of Parliament in 1503.
Where a couple lived together, treated each other as man and wife, and
were commonly acknowledged as husband and wife by the local
community, the law upheld their marriage and the legal benefits that it
entailed. The controversy arose over the issue of how to prove 'habit and
repute', as concubinage, where an unmarried couple cohabitated, was not
a valid form of marriage.[12]

Irregular marriage became increasingly popular over the eighteenth
century. Leneman and Mitchison demonstrate that in regions, such as
Troqueer in southwest Scotland between 1751 and 1780, irregular
marriage made up a third of all marriages, while in Dysart in Fife and
Muiravonside in the Central Lowlands, they comprised around 10%
from the beginning of the eighteenth century. Julia Sperling shows a
similar pattern in pre-Tridentine Spain and Portugal, arguing it reflected
more equitable inheritance practice amongst siblings and less parental
control over marriage.[13] Most irregular marriages were structured events

in front of family and friends, and were conducted by a celebrant. They were often marked with a meal or drinks.[14]

Regular marriage was established by church law, but was enforced by the State through fines and imprisonment for those who married irregularly, and banishment for celebrants. By the nineteenth century, couples were rarely penalised and even in the seventeenth century gaol terms were unusual.[15] While there was no obligation to have a ceremony for a marriage to be valid, the Kirk reluctantly regularised marriages of couples who appeared without a certificate. There usually had to be substantial evidence of habit and repute before the Church accepted the marriage and did not punish the couple for fornication.[16] Over the course of the seventeenth and early eighteenth centuries, the Kirk actively sought to bring order to the celebration of marriages, effectively ignoring civil law to encourage the perception that a ceremony, irregular or otherwise, was essential to a valid marriage. This made it easier to monitor and protect sexual unions, ensuring that denial of marriage, desertion of spouses and popular divorce were more difficult. It also meant that, despite little legislative change, Scotland followed a similar pattern of increased regulation of marriage as the rest of Europe, although in a form that emphasised free choice over parental control.[17]

This evolving framework for establishing a marriage was as relevant to the social elites as other social groups. Despite the prevalence of irregular marriage in Scotland across the period, the need for demonstrably legitimate heirs heightened the importance of marrying regularly for this social group. However, regular marriage was difficult for those outside the Church of Scotland who desired to marry in their own church – perhaps more important for Catholics for whom marriage was a sacrament than for Protestants. For such people, the legal validity of irregular marriage enabled them to combine a religious ceremony with a binding contract, which was reinforced by greater regulation of irregular marriage practices.

The increased regulation of the formation of marriage coincided with broader social changes in the policing of Scottish society. As the governance of the local community and clan was withdrawn from the social elites in favour of centralised state control, more formal mechanisms were needed for monitoring marriage-making.[18] At the same time, as shall be explored in the next chapter, these changes were not just about public order, but the nature of the family. Previously large areas of Scotland were policed through the family network of the clan, using marriage, fosterage and adoption to consolidate family ties, reinforce friendships and ensure social order.[19] With the increased centralisation of local governance, the social significance of the elite family altered in Scottish society. Yet, as will be explored throughout this book, this was not a straightforward story of the decline of the family in favour of the individual.

MARRIED LIFE

Once a couple married, they found themselves obliged to conform to legislation that determined their rights and responsibilities within marriage. The marriage contract was peculiar in Scottish law. Lord Stair noted in his *Institutions of the Laws of Scotland* of 1693 that the marriage contract 'is not human, but a divine contract'. It is created by the consent of individuals, but its nature, as Bell noted, is 'established and regulated by public law'. Unlike human contracts, which can be negotiated and defined by the contracting parties, the marriage contract could not be altered in 'substantials', although any clause could be inserted that was not inconsistent with that form of life. The substantials noted by Stair included, 'to make the marriage for a time, or to take power over the wife from the husband, and place it in any other, or the right of provision or protection of the wife from the husband', while Lord Bankton's *Institutes* of 1713 limited his to 'no proviso in a contract of marriage can divert the husband of the administration as head of the family, or deprive him of his marital power over the wife'. As late as 1839, Bell notes, 'the husband's administration as head of the household is absolute; and his jus mariti comprehends every subject that is part of the common stock'.[20] By definition a marriage under Scottish law was patriarchal.

With the marriage contract came rights and duties for both husband and wife. The nature of these rights and duties was an area of debate by the State, Church and legal writers, but in the main they remained rather vague. The regular marriage ceremony performed by the Church detailed the duties of the wife as 'to study to please and obey her husband, serving him in all things that be godly and honest, for she is in subjection, and under the governance of her husband as long as they continue both alive'. The duty to obey was not removed from the marriage ceremony until 1912. The husband's duties were not mentioned until his vows, when he promised 'to keep her, to love and intreat her in all things, according to the duty of a faithful husband'.[21]

The Kirk embedded the patriarchal model for marriage from childhood, within Church-run schools, and reinforced it with weekly sermons, a strict moral code and effective discipline for offenders that also applied to the social elites. Sermons published in Scotland had a similar understanding of marital duties as the law, emphasising that marriage entailed mutual responsibility and complementarity. Ralph Erskine preached in 1722 that the duty of the husband was 'to make over himself to her; all he is, all he hath, all he hath purchased, all he hath promis'd'. He continued that a husband was 'to provide for her, protect her, direct her, pity her, clothe her, to encourage and comfort her; and to do all for her she needs'.[22] William Secker, in 1715, described the husband's duty as a helpmeet to his wife, to protect her from injury, provide for her needs and to cover her infirmities, while he notes the wife's duties as to be a help to her husband, being obedient and faithful, not wandering abroad, and shunning idleness.[23] George Whitfield warned women not to rule over their husbands.[24]

The civil courts also recognised that marriage came with obligations. Institutional writings gave the legal definitions of the rights and duties of husband and wife. Bankton notes under the heading of duties:

> among the first are the conjugal love and affection between the married persons; the protection due from the husband to the wife from all injuries; the obligation of aliment and provide her suitably with all necessaries; and obedience from the wife to the husband.[25]

Lord Stair's work noted that with marriage comes a 'natural obligation of affection, but an outwardly obligation of cohabitation or adherence … and the obligation of the husband to aliment and provide for the wife all the necessaries for her life, health, and ornament according to their means and quality'. He adds that with marriage came rights:

> Rights arising from marriage is the jus mariti, or conjugal power of the husband over the wife, her person and goods, and therewith by consequence the obligement of her debts. 2. his power, and the wife's security, whereby during the marriage she cannot oblige herself. 3. the husband's obligement to entertain the wife and provide for her after his death. 4. her interest in his goods and moveable estate at the dissolution of the marriage.[26]

Patriarchy was not unchecked male authority. It was rare for a wife's duty to obey not to be mentioned alongside a husband's duty to love, protect and provide. Patriarchy was not seen as an abusive system of power, but as good order. The requirement upon a husband to love and protect ensured that marriage was not tyranny, a concern of many authors of prescriptive literature. The minister William Secker announced in his sermon of 1715 that 'to force fear from this relation [marriage], is that which neither benefits the husband's authority to enjoyn, nor the wife's duty to perform'.[27]

This framework for marriage, where male power was balanced with obligations and responsibility, was meaningful to the Scots of the period, as it reflected their understanding of the nature of married life. It was also flexible enough to allow women and men a space to negotiate the terms of their marriage. As shall be explored in later chapters, women who believed that their husbands had not fulfilled their responsibilities could argue that they were not required to be obedient. Husbands could use their wives' disobedience as an excuse not to support them. Yet, the nature of obedience or provision was not legally defined, leaving it open to interpretation. Similarly, the requirement upon men to love and protect allowed wives to complain about mistreatment and violence. It allowed women to seek external intervention, from family and friends or from the law/church courts, when a husband failed in his legally required duties.

BREAKING MARRIAGE

Women who were in abusive marriages could seek redress in the courts. Under Scots law, separation was voluntary or judicial. Men could voluntarily separate from their wives for any reason, as long as they provided for them. Women had to seek a judicial separation for either adultery or cruelty as their husbands had a legal right to their person. They could not leave their husbands unless their lives were in immediate danger. Separation for cruelty was designed to protect a wife from future harm, not punish her husband for past misdeeds. A woman had to prove she was in danger if she remained with her husband.

Early Scottish legal experts did not define cruelty and Lord Stair's *Institutions* did not even explore the possibility of separation for cruelty within Scottish law, although it was available in practice. Lord Brougham in the Evans case of 1790 defined cruelty as: 'personal violence as assault upon the woman, threats of violence which induce the fear of immediate danger to her person, maltreatment of her person so as to injure her health … furthermore, any conduct towards the wife that leads to any injury, either creating danger to her life or danger to her health'.[28]

Bell argued in the early nineteenth century that maltreatment included 'continued annoyance, wearing out and exhausting the party'.[29] Over the course of the nineteenth century, the definition of cruelty expanded to include deliberate communication of a sexually transmitted disease, not providing sufficient necessities of life, cruelty to children to inflict pain on the mother, and unreasonably confining wives to the house.[30] Parallel to similar developments in England, there is some evidence that the court was increasingly hostile to domestic violence against elite women as the period progressed. By the nineteenth century, only a few physical altercations or even threats were needed for a separation to be granted and judges were more likely to express their disgust at such behaviour.[31]

Having said this, throughout the period the right of husbands to use violence against their wives remained an area of tension in the judicial system. A husband's legal right to his wife's body included his right to discipline it. The legal writer Patrick Fraser noted in 1846 that 'our ancient law gave the husband a right moderately to chastise his wife by corporeal punishment, and the doctrine has been so laid down even as the law at the present day'.[32] Wives had to show that they had in no way failed in their duties or given cause for their husbands to punish them to win a separation suit. The law protected wives from husbands who failed in their duties to love and care, but the courts' reluctance to interfere, except in extreme circumstances, underlined the unwillingness of the court to diminish a husband's patriarchal authority. If a separation was granted, a husband had to provide his wife with alimony and neither party could remarry.

Like in other protestant states, remarriage was available after divorce, which was available equally to men and women in Scotland from 1560 on the grounds of adultery or desertion.[33] Neither of these events in themselves dissolved marriage, but were justifications that the injured party could use to end one. On divorce, the guilty party was declared as dead to the pursuer who became entitled to the property they would have received on the death of their partner, unless a private settlement had been reached. As a result of the inequitable property laws discussed below, women were usually disadvantaged by divorce even when they were the innocent party. Divorce rates remained low in Scotland until the passing of the Scottish Married Woman's Property Act of 1881.[34] Yet, that divorce was an option may have ensured that some forms of unreasonable behaviour within marriage were held in check. In this way, the law provided the boundaries for acceptable behaviour in marriage that were played out in the everyday.

MARITAL PROPERTY

The patriarchal nature of the marital contract was reinforced by the restrictions placed upon a woman's body and property after marriage. According to church doctrine, upon marriage man and woman became the property of the other. As the exhortation at the wedding ceremony stated 'the husband hath no more right or power over his own body, but the wife; and likewise the wife hath no more right or power over her body, than the husband'.[35] While this suggests that all property brought to the marriage was owned jointly, in practice, the law placed restrictions upon what property was shared and what remained separate. Furthermore, like in the Scandinavian states, joint ownership did not imply equal right to administration. As Stair notes, the husband has the privilege of distributing and governing marital property.[36] The details of property ownership in marriage were subject to a considerable amount of case law during the period, but as Eric Clive comments, 'it is not much of an oversimplification to say that the governing principle throughout was the supremacy of the husband'.[37]

Matrimonial property law in 1650 had its origins in some of the earliest statutes on record. Upon marriage, the moveable, or personal, estate of both parties formed part of the common stock. Heritable property, such as land, houses, and buildings attached to land, and paraphernalia remained separate, although a woman's property and any income received from it were administered by her husband. Under Scottish law, paraphernalia was defined as any dress or ornaments, not included in the dowry, that were proper to her rank, as well as any furniture in which those items were stored. This included any necklace, earrings, breast or arm jewels given to her husband before or on her marriage, and the 'lady's gown', which was any gift, usually money, given to a wife by the purchaser of land on her renunciation of her liferent right in said land. In addition to her paraphernalia, women were entitled to their terce, or a liferent in a third of their husband's property, as well as half of his moveables if they had no children and a third where they did on his death. Husbands were entitled to a liferent in all their wives' property on her death, providing that a living child was born of the marriage.

Paraphernalia offered a degree of financial protection to wives. Even modest apparel was relatively valuable in this period. Amy Erickson's work indicates that land values were relatively low in comparison to the value of moveables. She suggests that for inheritance purposes receiving items of clothing and furniture could be of similar value to receiving a piece of land.[38] Garthine Walker's work on theft shows that clothing often had considerable financial value and there was a flourishing resale market.[39] Allowing women control over their wardrobes allowed them access to potential income in times of need.[40] Wives' separate estate also advantaged families as it could not be claimed by creditors in repayment for debts. Until 1832, when the law changed, men could also transfer their property to their wives by deed to protect it from creditors.

Although men had the final say over administration of property, the law allowed women a degree of authority within the home. As the wife was 'formed by nature for the management within doors', she was *præposita negotiis domesticis*, having the power to purchase whatever is proper for the family. This power could be removed, but only when the wife abandoned the family, if the husband was granted an order from the Court of Session, or in the nineteenth century, expressly informed traders that he had removed his consent (a general notice in newspapers was not sufficient). This power was extended tacitly or expressly where a wife was concerned in the management of her husband's business.[41] This law was intended partly as a security for creditors, but wives' rights to the management of the home and property were staunchly defended by women.

Over the course of the eighteenth and nineteenth centuries, case law developed that altered and clarified the definition of marital property. The most significant debate was over the legitimacy of marriage contracts. Marriage contracts were known in Scotland since at least the fourteenth century and were increasingly common at all social levels. The purpose of the contract was to define any monies or property brought by the families to the marriage and to provide for the wife if the husband predeceased her. It covered issues such as the marriage settlements for any children, especially daughters of the marriage, pin money, and the renunciation of the *jus mariti*. Under Scottish law, it was not in the power of the husband to renounce his *jus mariti*, his right to administer his wife's property, as it was 'a right so inseparable from the character of the husband, that all reservation of it by the wife, or renunciation of it by the husband, even in an antenuptial contract, was ineffectual'.[42] This fact was confirmed by all institutional lawmakers of the seventeenth century, with the exception of Dirleton, and by the case law of the period.

The first challenge to a husband's right to his wife's property, Lord Collingtoun versus Lady Collingtoun (1667), found that although the husband had renounced his *jus mariti* in an antenuptial contract, 'yet he was found to have the power to manage it to the use of the family'. During the eighteenth century, attitudes began to change and the Walker case of 1730 established that a husband had the right to renounce his *jus mariti*. The only exception was established in the Gordon case of 1832 whereby a marital contract made after marriage fell by the way on bankruptcy. While the development of this law increased women's control over their property, it was primarily seen, like pin money, as a protective measure against the power of a wastrel husband. Furthermore, Scottish thinkers continued to view women's separate property suspiciously. As late as 1779, the Scottish historian William Alexander complained that 'such a bargain overturns the natural order of things and destroys that authority which the gospel and the laws of this country give a man over his wife and that obedience and subjection which the rules of Christianity prescribe in the deportment of a wife toward her husband'.[43] The renunciation of the *jus mariti* did not commonly appear in marriage contracts in Scotland before the nineteenth century.

While a husband could renounce his right to a wife's property, it was possible for him to retain his curatorial power. This ensured that his wife could not enter any contract or dispose of her own property without his permission. It was possible for a husband to renounce his curatorial right and it could be excluded, like the *jus mariti*, by a third party when giving property to a married woman.[44] The distinction between the right to administer and ownership of property differentiated Scottish from English property law and was to have interesting repercussions in the later nineteenth century. The Scottish Married Woman's Property Act of 1881, unlike its English counterpart, retained the curatorial right of the husband over his wife's property. This anachronism was not resolved until 1920.[45]

Unlike their counterparts in England, France and parts of North America, Scottish wives were not subject to coverture, but were legally in the power of their husbands. They retained their rights as legal persons in certain contexts. Scottish married women could be prosecuted in criminal procedures and while a husband's 'coercion' could be used to argue for a reduced sentence it did not remove their culpability. If they had a separate estate, married women could contract debt, so far as it extends, with their husband's permission. Similarly, they could act as independent traders (with their husband's consent) and contract debt in the normal line of business. Scottish women could also bequeath their heritable property and paraphernalia, although they needed their husband's consent to will property that was part of the common estate. This resulted in considerably more women in Scotland leaving wills than in England.[46] Scottish women sued for their own seduction, unlike in England and Ireland where a woman's parents or employer sued for loss of services. Married women could also sue for seduction if they could prove their virtue was overcome by seductive wiles, rather than willing consent.[47] Their right to utilise household resources gave unusual legal backing to a common and recognised custom across the continent. Yet, they were not in a privileged position in Europe. Scandinavian wives had greater rights over heritable property after their husband's death, while in parts of France and Portugal, wives often managed marital property jointly with spouses in life, although legislative and social change increasingly restricted this practice.[48]

Scottish marital law focused on the marital economy and much of its concern was with ensuring its harmonious operation. The rights and duties entailed by the marriage contract emphasised the husband's right to manage his wife and her property, while a wife's right resided in her interest in her husband's property and the expectation that she be provided for. The law's interest in the marital union was in its role as an economic unit, not as may be expected as a procreative unit.[49] There was no requirement for a marriage to be consummated in Scotland for it to be legally binding. While a marriage where one party was impotent could be annulled, this was due to procreation being one of the purposes of marriage, not its primary function.[50] This reflected the significance of the marital economy to Scottish society and the good order of the community. This legal and religious context for marriage impacted on the amount of social power women could exercise within marriage as well as the resources that they could draw on, which in turn effected their negotiations with their spouse.

Popular culture

Patriarchal ideals were not just to be found in the formal proscriptions of law and Church, but within Scottish popular culture. A large number of cultural products were available to the public, including prescriptive literature, novels, newspapers, plays, songs and gossip, although not all forms were always available throughout the period.[51] Scottish popular culture was situated within a broader British material culture, drawing heavily on ideas from the rest of Britain and Protestant Europe, and incorporating them in full, or adapting them to the Scottish context. By the late eighteenth century, Scottish authors, particularly the Enlightenment literati (themselves members of the Scottish elites), were also creating works that were distinctly Scottish, but well received and influential throughout Britain and Europe. The Scottish public were not passive, but actively engaged in creating a distinct national culture. Different discourses were weighted discretely in this process of identity creation, depending on whether it was more important to the individual to be Scottish or British, an obedient wife or a benevolent husband. While the elite classes are usually associated with high culture and prescriptive texts, the libraries of the Scottish elites reflected their engagement with a broad range of cultural products from conduct literature to broadside ballads. The Kirk was particularly influential as it not only provided cultural products, such as sermons and religious discourse which were found in large quantities in elite households, but the ideals it promoted were endowed with authority. Having said this, as Joy Wiltenburg notes, people combine social models in unique and idiosyncratic ways when creating their identities, values and culture.[52]

Scotland was a patriarchal society and its popular culture reflected its values. The conduct or prescriptive literature found in the libraries of the Scottish elites offered guidelines and advice on the construction and maintenance of social and gender roles based on a patriarchal model. George Savile, Marquis of Halifax, commented in 1688:

> You must lay it down for a foundation in general, that there is inequality in the sexes, and that for the better œconomy of the world, the men who are to be the law-givers, had the larger share of reason bestowed upon them; by which means your sex is the better prepared for the compliance that is necessary for the better performance of those duties which seem'd to be the most properly assigned to it.[53]

This understanding of the marriage relationship was still prescribed in the nineteenth century. William Giles informed his female reader in 1813 that:

> By marrying you have committed yourself to the care of one whose province is government and direction: the duty on your part therefore is subjection and obedience … With this truth coincides experience; for the wife, as the weaker vessel, naturally cleaves to her husband, and expects from him both assistance and advice. And here, it is presumed, you will have no reason to complain.[54]

Authors founded female subordination in scripture and in nature. It was not only commanded by God, but evidenced by female behaviour and characteristics. Similarly, man was created to hold authority and protect his family.[55]

Even within broader culture where patriarchal ideals faced greater critique, there was no alternative system of life. Ballads and plays available in Scotland portrayed marriage as a battle between the sexes. David Garrick's *Miss in Her Teens* (1753) saw the comic husband and wife team, Puff and Tag, compete for authority within marriage, taking turns to have the upper hand. Ballads, like *Be Valiant Still &c*, (1700–20) or *A Fully True, and Particular Account of that Awful Bloody Battle for the Breeks!* (1825), used the metaphor of war to explore power within marriage. But women were never victorious for long and those that found themselves in positions of power were never happy, unable to cope with the responsibility. Whether an author was critiquing the present system of marriage or expounding on ideal behaviour, the loving husband and the obedient wife were the norm that all other behaviours were contrasted with. They were present in every marriage, real or fictional, because marriage could not be understood without them. The patriarchal system was naturalised to the extent that it was no longer necessary to justify it. Yet, while this model was long-lasting, the nuances of its operation changed over time.

Across the eighteenth century, definitions of what made a loving husband or an obedient wife were shaped by shifting models of appropriate gendered behaviour. As has been highlighted in a broader European context, the eighteenth century saw a move from representations of womanhood as disorderly and sexually insatiable to that of women as innately chaste and virtuous.[56] A similar picture emerged within Scotland during the period. The disobedient wife quickly disappeared as a model for femininity for elite women, although, as shall be explored below, there was a distinct class dimension to this phenomenon. Previously, although always a figure of disdain, she appeared regularly within the writings of seventeenth century authors. William Ramesay noted in 1672 that 'to have a scold, a fool, a whore, a fury, is the worst of plagues, and an hell upon earth'.[57] The ideal wife was regularly compared to her antithesis. Allestree compared the frugal wife with the spendthrift, the obedient wife with her domineering sister.[58] The disobedient wife, for the seventeenth century commentator, caused considerable damage to the family economy and, through this, society. In the eighteenth century, references to the insubordinate wife declined. While in the seventeenth century, the wayward wife was considered dangerous; in the eighteenth, she was merely inconvenient. Where authors referred to her, it was simply to comment on the ineffectual nature of such behaviour. Lord Kames in 1781 noted that 'sullenness or peevishness may alienate the husband; but tend not to sooth his roughness, nor to moderate his impetuosity'.[59] Any wider social implications were not noted.

Similarly Scottish popular culture saw a decline in the sexual power of women. The motif of the sexually frustrated wife forced to cuckold her impotent, and thus powerless, husband was popular in seventeenth and early eighteenth-century ballads and chapbooks. Sex was an act where power was negotiated and the bedroom a place where a virile husband brought his wife under his control. By the nineteenth century, the sexually voracious woman was no more. Ballads, such as *The Bloody Battle* or *Watty and Meg*, where couples fought for power, no longer used sex as a means to control women.[60] Instead, the bedroom was a symbol of reconciliation after a husband subdued his wife, usually through violence or an assertion of his economic power. The act of sex was still implicated in the system of power negotiation, representing good order and the submission of wife to husband, but it was no longer a form of control or discipline in itself.

The ease with which the disobedient, sexually insatiable wife disappeared from Scottish elite culture, in part reflected the significance of elite Scottish authors in the creation of the modern woman. Enlightenment intellectuals working within Scottish universities, such as William Alexander, Adam Smith and John Millar, actively promoted a 'stadial' model of history that placed the newly commercialised British empire as the pinnacle of human development. At this stage of history, the 'civilised' treatment of women allowed them to flourish and demonstrate their innate feminine qualities of chastity, morality and 'natural attachment' to men. This was coupled with the rise of the culture of sensibility, which created an emotional framework to express these new gendered identities.[61] These ideas were given a wider audience through the best-selling prescriptive literature of Scottish writers, John Gregory and James Fordyce, the sermons of James' brother, David Fordyce, as well as appearing in the periodical press.[62] Yet, unlike earlier models of femininity that were theoretically applicable to all women, if complicated by rank, the modern woman was an ideal only achievable by the elites.

The stadial model for history argued that humanity progressed through stages of development from the savage to the modern. Commercial and industrial progress had allowed the elite classes in Britain to leave behind their unenlightened past, but this was not true of everyone. The non-European world was understood to be several steps behind, justifying imperialism, colonialism and slavery.[63] Similarly, the lower classes of society, who were unable to engage in commercial culture, had not achieved modernity. This belief was to reinforce the strict class divisions that were to develop in the nineteenth century, but also distinctions between elite and lower-class women in the eighteenth century. Elite women, married to men engaged in the culture of sensibility and part of commercial society, were protected from harsh treatment due to their refined and delicate natures, leading to greater scrutiny of domestic violence and maltreatment. In contrast, lower-class women needed no protection as their innate feminine qualities had not been allowed to develop; they were hardened by their engagement in a more savage society.

The legacy of the violent, disobedient early modern woman lingered in representations of lower-class women, although there were alternatives, such as the chaste shepherdess of Romantic pastoral poetry. Domestic violence in lower-class homes was expected by elite society and poor women were not believed to be in need of protection by the

State, except in the most severe cases of barbarity. In practice, the Kirk got involved in domestic disputes, but usually when they threatened the good order of the wider community, rather than to protect women. This changed in the mid-nineteenth century as the memory of the disobedient wife faded and was replaced with the violent, socially disruptive working-class man. Working-class woman, in the elite imagination, moved from viragos to victims, allowing the protective legislation of the period.[64]

The development of distinctive social classes had implications for material culture. Whilst seventeenth- and early-eighteenth-century balladry involved actors of different ranks and presented social models that were applicable across rank, possibly due to the continued control of the press by the elites; in the late eighteenth century, they become a medium of, and for, the lower classes. The models of masculinity and femininity presented within them had less resonance for the elite classes. Similarly, the prescriptive literature of the late eighteenth-century presented a model of behaviour that had little relevance to the lower classes, as it was unachievable without an engagement with commercial society. The removal of the disobedient wife from social discourse destroyed a possible exemplar of resistance for elite women, but the new model of femininity that replaced her was not entirely powerless, especially in the hands of female writers.

Drawing on older models of behaviour, many authors recognised that women held influence over their husbands. In the seventeenth century, Savile commented to his female reader that: 'you have it within your power not only to free yourselves but to subdue your masters and without violence throw both their natural and legal authority at your feet … You have more strength in your looks, than we have in our laws; and more power by your tears, than we have by our arguments'.[65] The ability of women to 'persuade' was considered by many to be a natural female characteristic and a limit to male power. The wife who persuaded her husband to work toward her interest was not disobedient, but ensured balance and the well-being of the household. Eighteenth-century authors similarly believed in a woman's ability to influence her husband, with it becoming the only medium for women to exercise power. Lord Kames noted in 1782 that 'he governs by law, she by persuasion. Nor can her influence ever fail, if supported by sweetness of temper and zeal to make him happy.'[66]

Not everyone was happy with this understanding of women's role. Hannah More argued that it was only through education and the ability to hold a rational argument that women would truly recognise their social subordination. She argued that tears and artifices were the cause of 'the most absolute female tyranny'.[67] Similarly Hestor Chapone's work suggested that a good education taught women how to serve those they loved. A rational education and the ability to converse politely ensured mutual happiness in marriage.[68] There was a tension within conduct literature between wifely obedience and a woman's ability to influence her husband, particularly for the female authors of the late eighteenth century who campaigned for a more rational education for women. They could not reconcile persuasion and tears with the effective management of the household. If a woman's advice was to be followed, it should be because it was reasonable, not because she manipulated her husband. To behave otherwise was folly.

The reliance of these authors on mutual respect and rational conversation led to a rethinking of women's place within marriage by female authors. Hester Chapone emphasised friendship, mutuality and shared interest within marriage and never overtly discussed the expectation that women obey their husbands. While she thought it was a woman's place to serve those she loved, she emphasised shared interest. When discussing household accounts, she expressed concern that some men did not disclose such information to their wives, noting, 'I think it a very ill-sign, for one or both of the parties, where there is such want of openness'.[69]

Hannah More's *Strictures* promoted a similar relationship between husband and wife, although she explicitly acknowledged that women were to be subordinate to their husbands. This belief occasionally came into conflict with other ideas within her writings. More simultaneously argued that a good education would ensure that women knew their social place, unlike the woman who ruled with tears, and allow them to manage a weak husband within their marriage. She maintained that women were the private property of their husbands, yet critiqued a marriage system that treated women like paintings to be purchased.[70] These issues were not reconciled within her work. In many respects, the values and ideals promoted by More and Chapone were not significantly different from their male counterparts. Where they differed was in their refusal to reduce female agency to persuasion. They were not challenging what was considered to be a fundamental truth, women's subordination, but an ideology that ensured that female power was only exercised through their husbands.

Even Lady Pennington, whose work drew heavily on the older writings of Savile and Allestree, was reluctant to reduce women's agency, calling on women to exercise prudence in their obedience.[71] These women called on their male readers to recognise their wives as partners with whom they negotiated a relationship, rather than imagining women as an extension of themselves over whom they exercised control. The new model of femininity was not as disruptive as its predecessor, but it could be interpreted by women to allow them to retain some agency within their marriages.

Shifting conceptions of femininity were mirrored by changing ideas of manliness. Unlike women, whose identities were inseparable from their role as wives for most authors, men held multiple social roles. The duties and responsibilities of husbands are often given little consideration in comparison to wider discussions of masculinity. Scottish conduct literature from the seventeenth and early eighteenth centuries aimed at men, such as George Mackenzie's *Moral Gallantry*, or James Forrester's *The Polite Philosopher*, had little to say to husbands, focusing on men's public role and emphasising reason, calmness, good nature, respect for religion and patriotism.[72] Those writings that gave some consideration to a husband's role emphasised the duties of provision and protection promoted by the Kirk and the State.[73]

Before the eighteenth century, elite Scottish men drew heavily on a model of martial manhood, where men defended both family and country through battle, and where honour was central to identity.[74] While these ideas were not always explicitly associated with marriage, as Elizabeth Foyster and Robert Shoemaker demonstrate for England, they informed men's role within the home. Men were without honour if they could not rule their families, using reason and physical strength, ideals that women were not believed to possess.[75]

As was the case in other parts of Europe, whether it was the behaviour of the husband or wife that was at fault, both reflected badly on the husband.[76] An unruly wife undermined her husband's masculinity and social reputation, which shifted the burden of a wife's actions to her husband. The ballads *My Wife Shall Have Her Will* (c. 1720), where a demanding wife is allowed her every desire, and *My Husband has no Courage in Him* (1701), where a woman asks for someone to cuckold the husband who cannot satisfy her sexual needs, highlighted the insecure nature of male authority and offered no reassuring victory for men. Early modern conceptions of manhood were always vulnerable, in no small part to the unruly women who, at all times, threatened to undermine it.

The replacement of this model of femininity within elite culture in Enlightenment Scotland put men on a more secure footing. As Rosi Carr demonstrates, the eighteenth century saw the replacement of the noble warrior with the refined gentleman, marked by 'courteous behaviour, benevolent actions and a sympathy for others'.[77] Like his female counter-part, the refined gentleman was a product of commercial culture; his civility enabled through an engagement with polite society in the form of enlightenment print culture, coffee houses, urban clubs and mixed-sex gatherings.[78] Elite women encouraged this form of masculinity through their natural sympathy and aversion to conflict, but enlightenment manhood was driven by engagement in commercial society and homosocial relationships. As William Alexander argued, while women 'give an elegance to our manners ... If perpetually confined to their company, they infallibly stamp upon us effeminacy'.[79] As a result, women were less central to male honour, making it more difficult for them to emasculate their husbands. Having said this, an ability to control the household (and particularly its finances) remained the key marker of male authority into the nineteenth century – a point the Scottish legal professor John Millar made clear in *The Origin of the Distinction of Ranks* in 1779.[80]

The nature and extent of a husband's authority within marriage was the central concern of writers exploring the duties of men within marriage throughout the period. Unlike in early modern England, the dialogue of male authority in Scotland tended to be part of a wider discussion of gender roles and responsibilities, rather than an attempt to emphasise and enforce patriarchy as a concept.[81] Authors offered advice on how to live under patriarchy, how to wield authority and the limita-tions upon that authority. Richard Allestree reduced the austerity of the command to obey by limiting compliance to those commands that were scripturally lawful.[82] He assured women it was not disobedient to ques-tion their husband's instructions if they were unreasonable, as long as they did so calmly, quietly and accepted his final decision.[83] Similarly, Lady Pennington noted in 1761 that wives should obey their husbands as long as their commands were scriptural and did not leave their wives open to censure by the world. She argued that it was not wrong for wives to question their husbands' decisions as long as they did so in a 'strong, plain good-natured manner'.[84]

A key concern was ensuring that marriage was not tyrannical. References to tyranny were popular across the period. A tyrant was someone who ruled without regard to law, but it was closely tied to discussions of marriage. It referred not only to abusive men, but those who were not fulfilling their contracted duties and responsibilities as husbands.[85] This rejection of absolute authority was a central tenet of Scottish Protestantism, reflected in the Presbyterian structure of the Kirk. Absolute rule, whether by king over State or husband over wife, placed a human in the position of God, and thus was believed to be a form of idolatry.[86] The rejection of absolute authority continued into the eighteenth century, although it was converted into a secular form by Enlightenment thinkers. Literati, such as Adam Smith, saw 'liberty', the ability to employ reason in the making of decisions and a rejection of arbitrary power, as central to both 'civilised' society and independent, refined manhood.[87] This rejection of absolute authority spilled over into marriage, restricting husbandly power. The philosopher John Millar linked a wife's 'implicit obedience to [a husband's] will' with 'savage' societies, while in 'civilised' society 'women become neither the slaves nor the idols of the other sex but the friends and companions'.[88]

The most common check on male abuse of power was the husband's duty to love. Throughout the period, love was expected within marriage to temper authority and was particularly, though not exclusively, required of men. Richard Allestree argued in the 1670s that love was a husband's primary duty and that this:

> utterly forbids all harshness and roughness to them [wives]; men are to use them as their own bodies, and therefore to do nothing that may be hurtful and grievous to them, no more than they would cut and gash their own flesh. Let those husbands that tyrannize over their wives, that scarce use them like humane [sic] creatures, consider whether that be to love them as their own bodies.[89]

He believed that a marriage without love was 'only a bargain and compact, a tyranny perhaps on the man's part, and a slavery on the woman's. 'Tis love only that cements the hearts, and where that union is wanting, 'tis but a shadow, a carcase of marriage'.[90] Love ensured that both men and women fulfilled their duties.[91] William Ramesay similarly required men to love their wives, but added that a husband should not allow his love to 'enervate thy rule over her, nor that lessen thy love'.[92] In a different genre, Thomas Otway's *The Orphan* (1726) demonstrated that authority within marriage could be given and taken away as signs of love and hate. When the heroine Monimia weds Castalio, she offered obedience as a sign of her love, commenting, 'you shall not fear't: indeed my nature's easy, I'll ever live your obedient wife, nor ever any privilege pretend beyond your will, for that shall be my law'. Castalio perceived himself wronged by Monimia, 'Nay you shall not, madam, by you bright heaven, you shall not; all they day I'll play the tyrant and at night forsake thee; till by afflictions and continued cares, I've worn thee to a homely houshold [sic] drudge'. Castalio abused his authority over his wife as a sign of hate.[93]

The use of love to temper male authority was still evident over a century later. Samuel Stennett, when discussing the duties of the conjugal relationship, summarised them as 'love on the one part, and reverence on the other'. He maintained that a loving husband would work for his wife's comfort, make his home happy for her and their children and alleviate his wife's domestic burdens.[94] William Giles similarly noted, when discussing the wife's duties of 'subjection and obedience', that the ideal husband is 'a man blessed with too much good sense to request what is unreasonable; and his love too great to solicit attention to any thing but what conscience demonstrates to be right and urges as a duty'.[95] Happy marriage required male authority to be curbed, yet authors were cautious about defining limits. Love provided a solution to this tension. Male writers did not have to define strict boundaries to male authority, but could advise men to use their judgement on what was appropriate behaviour from a loving husband.

While love was always required within marriage, eighteenth-century literature increasingly promoted love as requirement for marriage. In the seventeenth century, love did not feature when discussing the properties necessary for a happy match. Men and women were advised to look to the external qualities and circumstances of a partner, selecting a spouse of similar social background and values and with a secure financial standing.[96] Authors of conduct literature, ballads and even proverbs emphasised that love flourished within the correct material conditions. That the basis of love was considered to be tangible, external qualities made it no less real.

During the eighteenth century, love was increasingly conceived as a motivation for marriage as well as duty within it. William Giles observed in 1813 that: 'every man is induced by some motive to marry this woman in preference to that. Some men are influenced by the love of gain; some by other motives equally detestable; and some it is hoped, though comparatively few, by the dictates of affection.'[97] Similarly, John Moir noted in 1784, 'without an exchange of hearts, what in the eyes of God or man can sanctify their choice?'.[98] This was influenced by the rise of the culture of sensibility that emphasised emotional display and the expression of the internal workings of the mind.[99] Late eighteenth-century society, reacting to the Earl of Chesterfield's *Letters to His Son* (1774), were concerned with proving that politeness was not just display, but motivated by a genuine sense of morality.[100] This was portrayed in displays of sympathy. Men wept, fainted and expressed their feelings in an overt fashion.

Yet, eighteenth-century authors were not blinded by love. They argued that love was correctly placed when it corresponded with the qualities that were conducive to a successful marriage. Most authors expected people to choose their mates wisely, selecting them for their virtues and marrying with parental approval.[101] They were slightly more suspicious of marrying for wealth than their seventeenth century predecessors, emphasising shared social background and mindset over money. William Giles noted that those who married unequally in age, rank or religious belief were 'excluded from a league that requires not only unity of design, but a choice of the same means; in which the parties ought to feel equal interest and ardour; and where joint efforts are indispensably requisite to permanent success'.[102] Marriage was a union where equality at least in respect of circumstances was essential.

One tension that arose from the eighteenth century's emphasis on love before marriage was the role that women played as lovers. Wifely love within marriage had received little discussion within seventeenth century texts, beyond its ability to ensure obedience. In the eighteenth century, female love was no longer constrained to marriage but granted to women to help them make their choice of marriage partner. This was problematic as it granted to women the power that men had traditionally held through their act of loving. Love had always been crucial to the operation of power within the patriarchal marriage. It was an act that men performed on women as a symbol of their authority and of their benevolence in restraining that authority. Writers were concerned about granting this authority to women and many put a concerted effort into restraining and denying female expressions of love. John Gregory, the best-selling advice author, advised women in 1784 that: 'if you love him, let me advise you never to discover to him the full extent of your love, no not although you marry him. That sufficiently shews your preference, which is all he is intitled to know'.[103]

While authors expected both spouses to perform their duties, when the system failed, or rather when men did not fulfil their role, the responsibility was placed upon women to try to ensure its operation. While in plays and ballads, failings by men or women and the resultant breakdown of the marital relationship were often left unresolved, conduct literature placed the burden of failure on wives. Women were berated for and expected to correct both their own mistakes and those of their husband. Savile argued in his book, *The Ladies New-Years Gift*, of 1672, that if women moulded themselves around their husband's faults, they could compensate for them and, perhaps, reform their partners. He argued that a wife should be grateful for a drunk as 'his wine will veil your mistakes', while gentleness would reform an ill-humoured husband.

Finally, Savile stated that a wife should be glad of a weak, incompetent husband as she would have dominion over the household.[104] Richard Allestree argued in 1673 that it was a wife's responsibility to 'preserve this flame' of love, ensuring that her marriage was not a tyranny, while she could reclaim her husband from sin with 'patient submission', not 'storms and loud outcries'.[105] Both Savile and Allestree acknowledged that men were at fault if they failed to conform to prescribed roles, yet they did not spend time berating male behaviour.

The expectation that women mould themselves around their husbands continued into the late eighteenth and nineteenth centuries. Henry Home, Lord Kames, noted in 1782 that 'women, destined by nature to be obedient, ought to be disciplined early to bear wrongs, without murmurings'.[106] Lady Pennington similarly argued that while a wife may discreetly mention her husband's faults in a friendly manner, if they were habitual she should 'let them pass as unobserved'. If a woman married a man with a 'morose tyrannical temper', there was little she could do but bear it with 'patient submission'.[107] Samuel Stennett in the nineteenth century suggested a more equitable understanding of marriage, noting that 'the woman who is married to a man, has as much right to his love, confidence and support, as he has to hers', yet even he noted that a wife's love for her husband lessened his flaws in her eyes and ensured her obedience.[108] It could be argued that these authors offered practical advice, reflecting the reality that women were most likely to suffer from the patriarchal marriage, yet it put an inordinate amount of pressure on women to moderate and control their behaviour. While the patriarchal system placed responsibilities on both spouses, the burden of its successful operation continually fell to women.

Marriage law in Scotland was established before 1650 and underwent little statute change across the period; yet, the Kirk and judiciary adapted its flexible framework to meet the needs of society. As social order became increasingly state-controlled in the seventeenth and early eighteenth centuries, the Church attempted to regulate marriage more strictly to meet the needs of a changing society, before its disciplinary authority eventually dissolved towards the end of the eighteenth century. Yet, throughout the period, its Presbyterian values shaped how it interpreted familial authority, limiting, but not removing, the power of husbands and fathers. The courts similarly used case law to restrict male violence, recognise marriage contracts and reinforce women's property rights within a system where male authority and female obedience was at the heart of the marriage contract.

While the obedient wife and the benevolent husband were the mainstays of Scottish popular culture across the period, what it meant to be obedient or benevolent adapted over time. The rise of Enlightenment thought and the culture of sensibility from around the 1730s disrupted traditional constructions of femininity built around good order, where the disobedient wife remained a constant threat, and replaced it with the innate virtues of chastity and humanity enabled by commercial society. At the same time, martial manhood, where husbands relied on physical prowess and honour to defend their households, was replaced by the polite gentleman, who was engaged in commercial society, homosocial networks and who replaced violence with self-control. New models of gender shaped how people envisioned the marital relationship, allowing some female writers to envision a more equal relationship. For others, it simply reinforced women's subordinate role and need for love and protection. The patriarchal framework for marriage established the boundaries of how people negotiated marriage, but it gave them ample space to reconcile their experiences with these patriarchal discourses and negotiate the terms of their relationship. Yet, in doing so, as shall be highlighted in the remainder of this book, they continued the operation of the patriarchal system.

Notes

1   Fuller discussions of the basis of patriarchy during this period have been given elsewhere, see: A. Fletcher, *Gender, Sex and Subordination in England 1500–1800* (London: Yale University Press, 1995), pp. 44–82; S. Amussen, *An Ordered Society: Gender and Class in Early Modern England* (Oxford: Basil Blackwell, 1988), pp. 34–66; B. Capp, *When Gossips Meet: Women, Family, and Neighbourhood in Early Modern England* (Oxford: Oxford University Press, 2003), pp. 3–14.

2   J. Hardwick, 'Women "working" the law: gender, authority, and legal process in early modern France', *Journal of Women's History*, 9 (1997), 29.

3   E. M. Clive, *The Law of Husband and Wife in Scotland* (Edinburgh: W. Green, 3rd edn, 1992), pp. 1–16. For more information, see N. Busby et al., *Scots Law: a Student Guide* (Edinburgh: T. & T. Clark, 2000); R. Rait, 'The Scottish parliament before the union of the crowns continued', *English Historical Review*, 15 (1900), 417–44; J. Wormald, 'Bloodfeud, kindred and government in Early Modern Scotland', *Past and Present*, 87 (1980), 92.

4   Examples include: *An Account of the Most Remarkable Trials and Executions which took place in Scotland for above 300 years* (1826); *Answers and Duplies for Mrs Anna Muir, to the Replies given to the Lord's Commissars of Edinburgh, by Walter Nisbet of Craigintinnie* (1726); and *The Trial of Divorce at the instance of Peter Williamson printer in Edinburgh, against Jean Wilson, daughter of John Wilson, bookseller in Edinburgh, his Spouse* (The booksellers of Edinburgh: 1789). This last pamphlet, which included the lawyer's and witness' statements, sold for 1 shilling.

5   G. Bell, *Principles of the Law of Scotland* (Edinburgh: Thomas Clark, 4th edn, 1839), p. 555; J. Dalrymple, Viscount of Stair, *The Institutions of the Law of Scotland* (Edinburgh: Edinburgh University Press, [1693] 1981), p. 108 and A. D. M. Forte, 'Some aspects of the law of marriage in Scotland: 1500–1700', in E. M. Craik (ed.), *Marriage and Property* (Aberdeen: Aberdeen University Press, 1984), pp. 104–18.

6   J. Watt, *The Making of Modern Marriage: Matrimonial Control and the Rise of Sentiment in Neuchâtel, 1550–1800* (London: Cornell University Press, 1992), pp. 40–7; A. Erickson, 'The marital economy in comparative perspective', in M. Ågren and A. Erickson (eds), *The Marital Economy in Scandanavia and Britain 1400–1900* (Aldershot: Ashgate, 2005), pp. 3–22.

7   Dalrymple, *Institutions*, p. 108.

8   J. Sperling, 'Marriage at the time of the council of Trent (1560–70): clandestine marriages, kinship prohibitions, and dowry exchange in European comparison', *Journal of Early Modern History*, 8:1/2 (2004), 67–108; Watt, *Making of Modern Marriage*, p. 42.

9   Dalrymple, *Institutions*, p. 108.

10 B. Dempsey, 'The Marriage (Scotland) Bill 1755; Lord Hardwicke's attempt to abolish clandestine and irregular marriage in Scotland', *Stair Society Miscellany* (forthcoming).

11 L. Leneman and R. Mitchison, *Sexuality and Social Control: Scotland 1660–1780* (Oxford: Basil Blackwell, 1989), pp. 99–100. For the debate among legal commentators, see: Dalrymple, *Institutions*, p. 106; H. Home, Lord Kames, *Elucidations respecting the Common and Statute Law of Scotland* (London: Routledge, [1777] 1993), pp. 31–9, and Bell, *Principles of the Law*, p. 559.

12 Bell, *Principles of the Law*, p. 559.

13 J. Sperling, 'Dowry or inheritance? Kinship, property, and women's agency in Lisbon, Venice, and Florence (1572)', *Journal of Early Modern History*, 11:3 (2007), 197–238.

14 Leneman and Mitchison, *Sexuality and Social Control*, pp. 79–103.

15 Bell, *Principles of the Law*, p. 558.

16 Leneman and Mitchison, *Sexuality and Social Control*, p. 100.

17 Watt, *Making of Modern Marriage*, pp. 40–56; Sperling, 'Dowry or Inheritance?'.

18 T. C. Smout, *A History of the Scottish People, 1560–1830* (London: Fontana Press, 1985), pp. 205–13.

19 A. Cathcart, '"Inressyng of kyndnes, and renewing off thair blud": the family, kinship and clan policy in sixteenth-century Scottish gaeldom', in E. Ewan and J. Nugent (eds), *Finding the Family in Medieval and Early Modern Scotland* (Aldershot: Ashgate, 2008), pp. 127–38.

20 Dalrymple, *Institutions*, pp. 105–7; A. McDouall, *An Institute of the Laws of Scotland in Civil Rights* (Edinburgh: A. Kincaid and A. Donaldson, 1713), p. 107; Bell, *Principles of the Law*, p. 572.

21 *The Book of Common Order for the Church of Scotland* (Edinburgh: William Blackwood and Sons, 1901), pp. 128–33. This form of marriage ceremony was taken by the Church of Scotland from the 'Book of Geneva', which lifted it almost verbatim from Neuchâtel's Liturgy of 1533. It was still in use in this form up until 1912, when the word 'obey' was removed from the woman's troth.

22 R. Erskine, *The Best Match; or the Incomparable Marriage between the Creator and the Creature* (Glasgow: William Smith, 1771), p. 7.

23 W. Secker, *A Wedding Ring Fit for the Finger or the Salve of Divinity on the Sore of Humanity* (Edinburgh: James Watson, c. 1715), pp. 15–16 and 22.

24 G. Whitefield, *The Marriage of Cana; a Sermon Preached at Black-heath* (Edinburgh: James Beugo, 1739), pp. 10–11.

25 McDouall, *An Institute*, p. 124.

26 Dalrymple, *Institutions*, p. 111.

27 Secker, *Wedding Ring*, p. 15.

28 F. P. Walton, *A Handbook of Husband and Wife according to the Law of Scotland* (Edinburgh: W. Green, 1893), p. 58.

29 Bell, *Principles of the Law*, p. 559.

30 Walton, *A Handbook*, pp. 58–71.

31 L. Leneman, *Alienated Affections: the Scottish Experience of Divorce and Separation, 1684–1830* (Edinburgh: Edinburgh University Press, 1998), p. 26; A. J. Hammerton, 'Victorian marriage and the law of matrimonial cruelty', *Victorian Studies*, 33 (1990), 269–92.

32 P. Fraser, *Treatise of the Laws of Scotland as Applicable to the Personal and Domestic Relations* (Edinburgh: 1846), pp. 460–1.

33 Watt, *Making of Modern Marriage*, p. 47. Erickson, 'Marital economy', p. 15.

34 See Leneman, *Alienated Affections*, p. 16 and Report of the General Register's Office of Scotland, 2002, Appendix 1 Table 1, 'Population and vital events Scotland 1855–2001'.

35 *The Book of Common Order*, pp. 128–33.

36 Dalrymple, *Institutions*, p. 111.

37 Clive, *Law of Husband and Wife*, p. 5.

38 A. Erickson, *Women and Property in Early Modern England* (London: Routledge, 1993), pp. 64–8.

39 G. Walker, 'Women, theft and the world of stolen goods', in J. Kermode and G. Walker (eds), *Women, Crime and the Courts in Early Modern England* (London: University College London Press, 1994), pp. 81–105.

40 For discussion, see S. Staves, 'Pin money', *Studies in Eighteenth-Century Culture*, 14 (1985), 47–77; S. Staves, *Married Women's Separate Property in England, 1660–1833* (London, Harvard University Press, 1990), pp. 131–61.

41 J. Erskine, *An Institute of the Law of Scotland* (Edinburgh: The Law Society of Scotland, 8th edn, [1871] 1989), pp. 152–8; Bell, *Principles of the Law*, p. 574.

42 Dalrymple, *Institutions*, p. 111.

43 W. Alexander, *The History of Women, from the Earliest Antiquity to the Present Time* (London: C. Dilly, 1782), p. 431.

44 Erskine, *An Institute*, pp. 148–55.

45 A discussion for the motivations in passing the Women's Property Acts can be found in: B. Griffin, 'Class, gender and liberalism in parliament, 1868–1882: the case of the married women's property acts', *Historical Journal*, 46 (2003), 59–87.

46 Erickson, 'Marital economy', p. 17.

47 Walton, *A Handbook*, pp. 296–8. Men also sued their wives' paramours for 'seduction', although it appears to be rare before the end of the eighteenth century; 'criminal conversation' does not exist in Scottish law. Scottish parents could not sue for 'loss of services'.

48 Erickson, 'Marital economy', p. 12; Sperling, 'Dowry or inheritance?', 201–3.

49 E. Leites, 'The duty of desire: love, friendship, and sexuality in some Puritan theories of marriage', *Journal of Social History*, 15 (1982), 383–408; L. Stone, *The Family, Sex and Marriage in England 1500–1800* (London: Weidenfield and Nicolson, 1977), p. 263.

50 Erskine, *An Institute*, p. 142.

51 K. Barclay, 'Scottish Marriage Texts 1650–1750', (MPhil Dissertation, University of Glasgow, 2004).

52 J. Wiltenburg, *Disorderly Women and Female Power in the Street Literature of Early Modern England and Germany* (London: Virginia University Press, 1992), p. 4.

53 G. Savile, Marquis of Halifax, *The Ladies New-Years Gift* (Edinburgh: Matt. Gillyflower and James Partridge, 1688), p. 23.

54 W. Giles, *The Guide to Domestic Happiness* (London: Whittingham and Rowland for William Button, 10th edn, 1813), p. 144.

55 Fletcher, *Gender, Sex and Subordination*.

56 M. Legates, 'The cult of womanhood in eighteenth-century thought', *Eighteenth-Century Studies*, 1 (1976), 21–39; D. Dugaw, *Warrior Women and Popular Balladry, 1650–1850* (Cambridge: Cambridge University Press, 1989); I. Tague, *Women of Quality: Accepting and Contesting Ideals of Femininity in England, 1690–1760* (Woodbridge: Boydell Press, 2002), pp. 30–1; Wiltenburg, *Disorderly Women*, pp. 156–7; P. M. Spacks, '"Ev'ry Woman is at Heart a Rake"', *Eighteenth Century Studies*, 8 (1974), 27–46.

57 W. Ramesay, *The Gentleman's Companion* (London: E. Okes for Rowland Reynolds, 1672), pp. 91–2.

58 R. Allestree, *The Ladies Calling* (Oxford: Theatre in Oxford, 1700), p. 204.

59 H. Home, Lord Kames, *Loose Hints on Education* (Edinburgh: John Bell, Geo. Robertson and John Murray, 1782), p. 256.

60 *A Fully True, and Particular Account of that Awful Bloody Battle for the Breeks!* (Edinburgh: A. Turnbull, [c.1825]); [Alexander Wilson], *Watty and Meg, or the Wife Reformed* [1790–1810].

61 G. J. Barker-Benfield, *The Culture of Sensibility: Sex and Society in Eighteenth Century Britain* (London: Chicago University Press, 1992), pp. 35–6.

62 R. Carr, 'Gender, national identity and political agency in eighteenth century Scotland', (PhD Dissertation, University of Glasgow, 2008), 145–9.

63 Carr, 'Gender, national identity', 192.

64 M. Wiener, 'Alice Arden to Bill Sikes: changing nightmares of intimate violence in England, 1558–1869', *Journal of British Studies*, 40 (2001), 184–212; F. Dolan, *Dangerous Familiars: Representations of Domestic Crime in England 1550–1700* (Ithaca: Cornell University Press, 1994).

65 Savile, *New-Years Gift*, pp. 27–8.

66 Home. *Loose Hints*, pp. 257–8.

67 H. More, *Strictures on the Modern System of Female Education* (London: T.Cadell Jun. and W. Davies, 1799), pp. 130–2.

68 H. Chapone, *Letters on the Improvement of the Mind* (London: J.F. Dove, 1827).

69 Chapone, *Letters*, p. 125.

70 More, *Strictures*, pp. 130–75.

71 S. Pennington, 'Unfortunate mother's advice to her absent daughters', *The Young Lady's Parental Monitor* (Hartford: 1792), pp. 87–100.

72 J. Forrester, *The Polite Philosopher* (Edinburgh: Robert Freebairn, 1734), pp. 40–8; G. MacKenzie, *Moral Gallantry* (London: 1821), pp. 19–36.

73 Barclay, 'Scottish Marriage Texts'.

74 Carr, 'Gender, national identity', 134–5.

75 E. Foyster, 'Male honour, social control and wife-beating in late Stuart England', *Transactions of Royal History Society*, 6:6 (1996), 215–25; R. Shoemaker, 'Male honour and the decline of public violence in eighteenth-century London', *Social History*, 26 (2001), 190–208.

76 M. Segalen, *Love and Power in the Peasant Family* (Oxford: Blackwell, 1983), pp. 156–7; Fletcher, *Gender, Sex*, pp. 3–29; Wiltenburg, *Disorderly Women*, p. 102; M. Ingram, 'Ridings, rough music and mocking rhymes in early modern England', in B. Reay (ed.), *Popular Culture in Seventeenth Century England* (London; Croom Helm, 1985), pp. 176–7.

77 Carr, 'Gender, national identity', 136.

78 Carr, 'Gender, national identity', 193.

79 W. Alexander, *The History of Women, From the Earliest Antiquity to the Present Time* (London: C. Dilly and R. Christopher, 3rd edn, 1782), p. 495.

80 L. Carter, 'British masculinities on trial in the Queen Caroline Affair of 1820', *Gender and History*, 20 (2008), 248–69; J. Millar, *The Origin of the Distinction of Ranks* (Edinburgh: William Blackwood, [1779] 1806), p. 234.

81 K. Davies, 'Continuity and change in literary advice on marriage', in R. B. Outhwaite (ed.), *Marriage and Society: Studies in the Social History of Marriage* (London: Europa, 1981), pp. 58–80; A. Fletcher, 'The protestant idea of marriage in early modern England', in A. Fletcher and P. Roberts (eds), *Religion, Culture and Society in Early Modern Britain* (Cambridge: Cambridge University Press, 1994), pp. 161–81.

82 Allestree, *Ladies Calling*, p. 201.

83 R. Allestree, *The Whole Duty of Man* (London: R. Norton for Robert Pawlet, 1675), pp. 323–4.

84 Pennington, 'Unfortunate mother', pp. 94–7.

85 J. Rudolph, 'Rape and resistance: women and consent in seventeenth century English legal and political thought', *Journal of British Studies*, 39 (2000), 157–84. The use of the word tyranny within conduct literature may also reflect the desire of some writers to speak to the relationship between king and State as well as man and wife, see: A. McLaren, 'Monogamy, polygamy and the true state: James I's rhetoric of Empire', *History of Political Thought*, 25 (2004), 446–80.

86 D. G. Mullen, *Women's Life Writing in Early Modern Scotland* (Aldershot: Ashgate, 2003), pp. 2–3.

87 Carr, 'Gender, national identity', 150; J. Dwyer, *Virtuous Discourse: Sensibility and Community in Late Eighteenth-Century Scotland* (Edinburgh: John Donald, 1987), pp. 38–51.

88 Millar, *Distinction of Ranks,* pp. 41–2 and p. 86.

89 Allestree, *Whole Duty of Man*, p. 327.

90 Allestree, *Ladies Calling*, pp. 180–1.

91 Allestree, *Whole Duty of Man*, p. 326. I. Tague, 'Love, honour and obedience: fashionable women and the discourse of marriage in the early eighteenth century', *Journal of British Studies*, 40 (2001), 76–106.

92 Ramesay, *Gentleman's Companion*, p. 94.

93   T. Otway, *The Orphan or the Unhappy Marriage: A Tragedy* (London: J. Darby, 1726), p. 56.

94   S. Stennett, *Discourses on Domestic Duties* (Edinburgh: J. Ritchie for J. Ogle, 1800), p. 136.

95   Giles, *Domestic Happiness*, pp. 144–5.

96   For descriptions of the qualities desired within marriage see, Ramesay, *Gentleman's Companion*, p. 94 and A. Campbell, Marques of Argyll, *Instructions to a Son* (London: Richard Blackwell, 1689), pp. 41–3.

97   Giles, *Domestic Happiness*, p. 19.

98   J. Moir, *Female Tuition; or an Address to Mothers on the Education of Daughters* (London: J. Murray, 1784), p. 260.

99   Barker-Benfield, *Culture of Sensibility*, p. xix; P. Carter, *Men and Emergence of Polite Society, Britain 1660–1800* (Harlow: Pearson Education, 2001), conclusion.

100 For a discussion of this see: A. Bryson, *From Courtesy to Civility: Changing Codes of Conduct in Early Modern England* (Oxford: Oxford University Press, 1998).

101 For an example of the combination of love and prudence, see Chapone, *Letters*, p. 112.

102 Giles, *Domestic Happiness*, p. ix.

103 J. Gregory, *A Father's Legacy to his Daughters* (Edinburgh: 1774), p. 87; K. Barclay and R. Carr, 'Love, Enlightenment (and equality?)', Early Modern Research Seminar Series, Department of History, University of Glasgow, 26 January 2009.

104 Savile, *New-Year's Gift*, pp. 32–46.

105 Allestree, *Ladies Calling*, pp. 180–93.

106 Home, *Loose Hints*, p. 256.

107 Pennington, 'Unfortunate mother', pp. 94–7.

108 Stennett, *Discourses*, pp. 115 and 136–8.

3

The first step to marriage: courtship

While this book primarily explores marriage and the relationship between spouses, understanding the motivations for marriage and how people selected their partner can give insights into power later in their relationship. A number of factors intersected when selecting a spouse, of which it is argued the most significant in Western Europe were parental approval, economic security and the potential for love.[1] At different times, individual factors had greater precedence than others, but choosing a partner always involved multiple considerations. Within a Scottish context, family held a significant role within courtship throughout the seventeenth to nineteenth centuries, as elite marriage could not be separated from issues of lineage, land and political power. Yet, the changing economic environment of the eighteenth century, as well as cultural changes around ideas of self and individualism, shifted the focus of the purpose of marriage from bilateral kinship to the conjugal unit. These same changes had practical implications for the form of marriage settlements, while they were coupled with the increased use of romantic language, which, for some historians, has disguised the economic and social contracts that were being negotiated through it.

As the first step to marriage, the negotiations that took place within courtship set the stage for later life. As Julie Hardwick argues for France, property arrangements agreed in courtship 'were key elements in shaping who exercised power and how that power was exercised in everyday life'.[2] Yet, this held true in Scotland beyond the economic. The changing relationship between men, women and their natal families shifted positions with the family network that were related to the power held within that network. Similarly, while the rise of 'romantic love' has been seen to reduce male authority, in practice, it reshaped the terms of the negotiation in a manner that left women at a structural disadvantage that would continue into married life.[3] This chapter explores how Scottish couples selected their spouses over the period 1650 to 1850 and the implications for the distribution of power within their future relationships.

Parental control and child interest

The relationship between family and personal interest in courtship has been a topic of debate amongst a number of historians.[4] For some this has been a story of the decline of the family and community, with its interest in economic and social stability and dynastic power, in favour of the needs of the individual – sometimes seen as being a case of love conquers all. Yet, for others, as marriage continues to be fundamentally about the formation of new households, which form the basis of community life, the economic and social ramifications of courtship continued long after the rise of 'romantic love', ensuring that the individual was never entirely free of the family.[5] Family or 'friends', as they were referred to throughout the period, played a vital part in Scottish courtship, although the role they played altered over time.[6] Parental consent was not necessary for marriage in Scotland to be valid, yet it was a topic of enough importance for it to be debated within parliament in 1698.[7] The tension between parental and child interest was recognised within Scottish cultural discourses and manifested within people's lives. As shall be demonstrated, during the seventeenth century, a cohesive network of friends was vital during courtship to represent the interests of the individual and family, provide patronage/clientage and to offer economic, social and emotional support. Over the course of the eighteenth century, a changing emphasis on the purpose of marriage altered the role that the family and the individual played in negotiating marriages, but this was not a straightforward victory for the individual over community.[8]

During the late seventeenth century, marriage was more than the union of two people. It was the joining of two families with an emphasis on bilateral kinship. Marriage was expected to expand and solidify kinship networks, bringing political, economic and social advantages to all parties. Archibald Campbell, Marquess of Argyle, described a successful marriage in his *Instructions to a Son* as one where both families were strengthened by the union. He continued that where families were unequally matched the weaker family 'suck up moisture from the root, while the branches are withered … never like to reflourish again'.[9] Many marriages were arranged within a tight network, but even as early as 1650 forced marriages were disapproved of. In Scotland, as in England, most families worked to ensure their children made marriages that brought benefits and increased their reputation, and were wary of marrying their children to families who were unknown to them, even if the suitor had independent means.[10]

Like in France and the Nordic countries, women in Scotland kept their own surnames on marriage, reflecting the need for both the bride and groom to retain their independent familial identities.[11] This reinforced the sense that marriage connected two networks, rather than subsuming women into new families as happened in England.[12] Diane Purkiss suggests that the retention of surnames indicated that Scottish women were often marginal to their husband's family.[13] There are examples that suggest women's usefulness lay in their links to their natal family, particularly amongst certain highland clans, where they were often sidelined or returned to their parents after they were widowed.[14] Yet, the social observer Thomas Morer argued in the seventeenth century that the retention of their surname indicated that Scottish women were more independent of their husbands than their English counterparts.[15] It allowed women identities that were separate from their husbands' and gave them authority as the gatekeepers to their families and any related benefits. Within marriage, this conception of women's role was more usually a position of power.

While this marriage strategy has been considered to prioritise the needs of the family over the individual, it is important to recognise that modern conceptions of the self as an individual with his or her own rights and needs were only beginning to emerge during this period in Scotland. The 'individual' understood themselves in reference to their place in a particular family and not only their interest, but their sense of self lay within it.[16] In this context, the history of courtship during this period was less about tension between individuals, with their own interests, and families, than about negotiation over what role a person held within the family network, what resources they were entitled to, and what power they held.

Proficient use of family networks was vital to the success of new households. It was in children's interests to marry within the network and, as they understood themselves in terms of their place in the family, the extent to which people recognised the need for family goodwill to their future success should not be underestimated.[17] Parental control over the process became most evident in times of conflict – where children disputed their place within the network (perhaps demanding too large a portion), or, as ideas of individualism began to emerge, where they failed to recognise their self-interest lay within the family. Ensuring that children made the right choice was understood as an act of love and protection.[18] Richard Allestree's conduct literature argued that girls often foolishly wished to marry for love, but, for the sake of their happiness, should follow the advice of their parents, while George Savile similarly noted that parental consent ensured that women did not conspire 'against herself' by loving an unsuitable 'conqueror'.[19]

Letters from courting couples and their families reveal this system in operation. Alexander Mackenzie, when selecting a spouse, noted to John Clerk in 1729, 'my first and chief rule was to match in a good family by which I would have honour & esteem as well as a person of virtue & good qualitys'.[20] As Alexander suggests, rather than being judged on their own merits, individuals were understood to gain their personal characteristics from their family, allowing family reputation to be a determining characteristic in spouse selection. At the same time, as the Marquess of Argyle suggested above, the joining of two families should be symbiotic, allowing both sides to flourish. The courtship of James, Earl of Arran and the daughter of Lord Crewe in 1693 ended when Lord Crewe discovered James' parents disapproved. Lord Crewe realised that his family would get no benefit from this marriage without parental consent.[21]

As James himself recognised in later years, marriage brought with it responsibilities from the wider family. He encouraged his sister's suitor, noting, 'no body wishes you more happiness then I doe, nor shal be readier then I am to enter into all the friendships & concern for your self and family, that so near ane alliance ought to produce'.[22] Similarly, the Marquis of Atholl commented to the Duke of Hamilton in 1682, during the marriage negotiations of their children, 'noe match in Britain would have made me goe the lengths I have don in this, my desire is soe great to have the honour of an alliance with your noble family which has bin always my ambition'.[23]

The relationships formed through marriage were not just formalities but had tangible benefits. Helen Gray asked her brother-in-law in 1673 to vet her future husband's finances before she married him.[24] The Duke of Atholl, although now a widower, asked his former mother-in-law's advice on prospective partners for his son in 1710.[25] Both of their requests were answered. Wives were often used by husbands to utilise their family network effectively, which offered women considerable power. Archibald Grant tried to persuade his wife to ask her parents for money, but she consistently refused. He noted in 1740: 'Oh my dear nancy, you should speak no more of love, when you can so easily withhold, what is so much in you power, and what you know to be so materiall to my comfort; especially when at the same time you know I have so much occasion for comfort'.[26] The responsibilities that marriage brought to wider kin required individuals to consider the needs of the broader family when making a selection. Yet, as people thought of both themselves and their future partners in terms of their position within their natal family, the aim of the individual in picking a compatible spouse and that of the family in picking a suitable alliance were often combined.

While families played a considerable part in negotiating marriages, the individual was not superseded. In the 1690s, Margaret, Countess of Wemyss, was approached by Lord Southesk to seek permission to marry her young daughter. Margaret noted:

> I am very unwilling to dispose of her she is so young, so I positively told my ld [Lord] Southesk it was needless for him to speak anie more of that matter since I thought it my daughters & my interest not to marry her in haste & I knew all his relations thought it his interest to marry now so I shuld wish happy in another choice but hee is so earnest to have her, that he offers to take noe portion with her & to give her what jointure I please & which I think most of all to waitt the time I shall think fitt to bestow her upon him; I would say nothing to all this till I speak with her selfe curiouslie about it, & after I had done soe, I found she thinks herselfe obliged to belive hee has a great kindness for her & more then she can possibly expect from anie other, so she desired mee to ask my friends advice in it.[27]

Her friends informed her that Southesk was 'not only a very witty man, but one that has been all his life free of all manner of debaucherie' and that his estate was acceptable.[28] In this instance the marriage does not appear to have gone ahead.[29]

Men and women often had their own agendas when choosing partners, and could be no less mercenary than their parents. In the late seventeenth century, James, Earl of Arran's primary criteria in a wife was that she brought £20,000 to the marriage to pay his extensive debts. In turn, James was frequently rejected by his choices as his mother (the head of the family) would not offer a suitable settlement. His mother, the Duchess of Hamilton, desired James' bride to bring £10,000 (to pay his sisters' portions, not James' debts) and was only prepared to offer a jointure proportionate to this amount, leaving James at a disadvantage in negotiations.[30] Lady Cavers Douglas in 1700, while negotiating her own terms that were later ratified by her father, demanded a settlement of 20,000 merks from her suitor and asked that if she survived her husband and had no children that the fee be provided to her (giving her control over who inherited the family property).[31]

Family control over marriage choice depended upon the individual's place in the family, age and marital status. As Susan Whyman notes for

England, 'birth order and gender clearly affected choice.'[32] Heirs, reliant on their inheritance, were obliged to conform to their parents' wishes. As Charles Hay noted on the slow process of his marriage negotiation in 1697, 'I am afraid that I must run the common fate of all heirs of familys which is (if I may say so) to be keeped under by their parents.'[33] Parents often had less control of younger children's options – even wealthy Scottish families could not provide substantial settlements for all of their children.[34] Younger sons were increasingly expected to have independent finances and used this, sometimes along with a settlement from their parents, to marry.[35]

Age and marital status also limited family control over marriage choice. Women were customarily and men legally independent at twenty-one and many families felt that at this age children should have greater freedom of choice. In 1701, when James Pringle asked George Home for his permission to marry Katherine Hepburn, he 'told him she was now of age and would choose for herself'.[36] Twenty-one was also the usual age that children came into any trusts or settlements that had been previously held by parents. Children's, especially daughters', marriage portions were often stipulated in their parents' marriage contracts and were normally paid on marriage or at twenty-one. This restricted parental power over children, as was recognised by some contemporaries. During the marriage negotiation of Julian Home, there was concern over specifying the children's settlements in the marriage contract. George Home noted that 'My Lo: Harcasse alledged that that provision would take off the dependency of the children on their parents', but the rest of the party disagreed, noting 'that this was ordinary in all such as this.'[37] While in reality it was difficult to enforce payment of money held by parents, these stipulations gave children a degree of financial independence. Once daughters married, they usually became independent of their parents, even if widowed at a young age. The young widow Susan, Countess Dundonald, although seeking her family's advice, made her own choice of partner in 1697, selecting a poorer but loving suitor over a rich match. On criticising her selection, her brother was curtly informed by their mother, 'she is only judge her selfe of whom to choise'.[38]

Parental consent in the late-seventeenth and early-eighteenth centuries could even be an area of tension. There were children, risking the wrath of their parents, who married without consent. Elopement appeared reasonably common in the seventeenth century, especially among younger children of elite families. Almost every family under study had at least one instance of elopement in every generation. The 3rd Duke of Hamilton's brother eloped as did his son George and grandson

Basil. John Clerk's daughter, son and nephew eloped. Elizabeth Baillie of Jerviswood secretly married the poor Weems of Grange Muir despite the risk of losing her 16,000 merk portion.[39] Most children returned or wrote home after the event to tell their parents their news. Family reaction to elopements was varied, although it was expected that such behaviour resulted in being disowned.

Isobel Hay noted of her son's marriage in 1682: 'If his choice be hapy, it will be the beter for him however, madam, I am not resolved to understand that by any particular acquaintance with the gentlewoman or further intimate correspondence with him, who to my sade grief hath behaved in such a foolish and undutiful manner towards me'.[40] Other people found it difficult to entirely reject their families. The Duke of Hamilton responded to his brother's elopement in 1687 by telling his son, 'I desire you may tell him from me that he say nothing of it to me & I will not ask questions at him or say any thing of it to him but converse with him as a formerly but intends never to visit his choice which I make no doubt he will leave [live] to repent'.[41] The Duke's wife similarly showed conflicting emotion over their son, George's, choice, saying she intended never to write to him again, or at least that was her intent for now.[42]

The number of people who eloped with members of their own social class made exclusion harder. Elizabeth Baillie was wealthier than Weems, but he was also a member of the Scottish elite. George Hamilton married the wealthy Elizabeth Villiers, who would have been an acceptable match had she not been at one time mistress to William III. Basil Hamilton secretly married Isabella Mackenzie as she was already contracted to marry another, not because she was a poor match. His aunt noted, 'tho on some respects its well he is married tho I wish he had done it more advisedly'.[43] At a lower social level, the daughter of an advocate eloped with her cousin, while being courted by another.[44]

While elopement suggests a rush of love or a complete disregard for parental interest, it is worth noting, as Steven King has for the lower-classes in England, that many eloping individuals were involved in previous failed courtships that involved their families and typical courting behaviour.[45] Familial control had its limits and ultimately the decision of whom to marry fell to the person. This was not to say that eloping couples in the seventeenth century were all early adopters of modern individualism. For some it was a breakdown in family negotiation or a sense of displacement within the network that forced them to action; for others, it was the impulses of youth that momentarily blinded them to consequences. It may even have been a calculated risk to force wider family into a particular alliance – made easier in Scotland by the legality of post-nuptial marriage settlements. That most individuals returned home and expected some form of reconciliation into the family network highlighted that eloping was not viewed as exiting the family by seventeenth century Scots.

Yet, at the same time, Scotland was undergoing changes that raised questions about the relationship between the family and the individual, especially younger sons. Whereas in the sixteenth and early seventeenth century, younger children continued to be found roles and positions within the family economy, notably being placed on cadet lands in a number of wealthier families, this became increasingly uncommon.[46] Younger sons were instead educated for the professions, went into the military or forced to become entrepreneurial to make a living. The family could not offer the same benefits as in past generations.

The many failed courtships of William Clerk – a younger son – provide a useful example of both sides of this equation. While a young man, still being educated at university, William selected a number of unsuitable brides that all required a larger portion than his father was willing to give. He became increasingly frustrated with his father's stance as he (in his mind) tried to make a good match and failed. After leaving university and working in his profession for a number of years, he eloped with his bride.[47] Given his repeated attempts to select a suitable bride, William showed that he believed his interest lay within the family, and his elopement can be seen to reflect a sense of displacement and despair at pleasing an exacting father, rather than an act of individualistic self-interest. Yet, that he was increasingly financially independent of his father, no doubt gave him the confidence to take this risk as well as shaping how he viewed the relationship between himself and his family network.

Following patterns in the rest of Europe, parental permission was to remain an important part of marriage into the nineteenth century, but the involvement of family in courtship was to take on different significance in the eighteenth century. The concept of forced marriage, always disapproved of, became increasingly repulsive and the occasional cases of kidnapped heiresses that occurred in the seventeenth century disappeared.[48] Overt parental interference was more likely to promote conflict than obedience in the eighteenth century. As one woman was said to have told her suitor, 'tho she will obey her father in what he commands her, yet if the thing be left to her own choice, & that death were laid in one balance & he in the other, she had rather choose death'.[49] Marriage choice, reflecting Enlightenment ideas, was increasingly understood to be about meeting the needs of the individual rather than the family. As Ruth Perry has shown within English novels of the period, there was a move from consanguinity to conjugality, where the interest of the individual was no longer placed with the natal family, but the newly formed conjugal unit.[50] Resembling a similar phenomenon in eighteenth-century France where individuals increasingly represented their marriages as personal unions rather than 'dutiful submissions to family', parents and children in Scotland were less likely to discuss marriage in terms of benefits to kin in the eighteenth century.[51]

In 1738, Lady Down, with no mention of family interest, advised her son: 'when you resolve to marry and settle as you value your own interest and happiness make a prudent choice of some young discreet wellborn virtuous woman, with whom who may reasonably expected to live comfortably: study to make her happy and in return she will do the same by you.'[52] With increased emphasis on individual happiness, parents became more tolerant of eloping children and allowed children greater choice over partner. Despite its popularity in English literature, by the end of the eighteenth century elopement had become a social anomaly among the elites as children felt less constrained in their choice and so found themselves in less conflict with their parents.[53] Lord Elibank, when seeking forgiveness from the Earl of Airlie on behalf of the Earl's son who had secretly married in 1743, noted, 'we know that when we ourselves were young we were liable to do imprudent things from the violence of our passions'.[54] Dorothy Hobart wrote to her family in 1752 asking for forgiveness after she eloped, noting that she realised it may be some time before they forgave her, but she hoped it was not forever. She appeared genuinely distressed when she learned her grand-parents did not offer her the quick forgiveness that she expected.[55]

That people now talked of marriage in terms of individuals did not mean there was no role for the family. Colin Mackenzie noted in 1731 the complex mixture of parent and child roles in the process of finding a spouse:

> My daughter is upon the point of being marry'd to a neighbour gentle-man Mackenzie of Aplecross, whose person & conversation is agree-able to Anne, and whose estate can afford a suteable living both living & dead; the first I have left, intirely to the G.[entle] woman she being to marry not I; the 2d I have deliberately considered and find that tho in burden yet such as good conduct & management may soon overcome and Anne being willing to take her hazard I freely gave my consent.[56]

Parents still wished for their children to make good matches and helped guide their children in their choice as well as negotiated suitable settlements. Access to credit, business connections and political power still came through social networks created by marriage. The key change was that these benefits were now sought for the new marital unit rather than the wider family. Children were still conscious of these benefits as can be seen by the fact that most people continued to marry those of similar social background.[57]

The new economic and social climate of the late eighteenth century helped ease this transition. Whereas previously marriages had been negotiated through family networks, new arenas, such as ballrooms, racecourses, gardens and theatres, now existed and allowed children to choose their partners from a suitable and restricted social group. People had access to a larger number of possible partners than in the past. They believed they were making a choice, while their parents were secure knowing that choice was limited to the right sort of people. Having said this, these new arenas could be exploited. The advent of consumerism and shopping significantly helped those who wished to meet in private. Thomas Macknight, in the 1790s, met his sweetheart in a music shop on a weekly basis, as neither party was sure he would receive permission to court her.[58] Similarly in 1819, Anne Kirkwood clandestinely visited her beau in his business, a bookshop, in the early days of their relationship.[59]

While these new arenas widened the marriage market, the role of parents and wider family was still important when selecting mates. Parents chaperoned their children to social events, making and monitoring introductions, while the relationships made were consolidated at home. In 1824, Dugald G— was invited to the home of Jane Welsh after meeting her and her mother at a racecourse. He visited shortly afterwards with his sister and while there proposed marriage to Jane, but was rejected.[60] Many children continued to marry friends of the family. Jane Welsh on another occasion refused the proposal of a childhood friend,[61] while Loudon Robertson in 1781 married a friend whose family vacationed with hers.[62]

The role the family played in courtship impacted on the power relationship between husband and wife. As gatekeepers to their family networks, wives were provided with a negotiating tool in their relationship with their husband. A decline of the importance of these networks in society may have had a corresponding impact on the power of wives, but change was slow in coming. While they were used differently, family connections were still important to the political, economic and social success of the elites throughout the eighteenth and nineteenth centuries.[63] Family support offered protection to wives as some husbands could not afford to alienate their spouses' families.

Economic resources and spouse selection

The role of the family in the process of selecting a partner was closely related to that of economic resources. As has been noted above, families were often involved in providing resources, helping negotiate contracts, and ensuring the secure economic foundations of the new marital unit. John Gillis and Helen Berry emphasise the importance of fiscal security in marriage throughout the seventeenth to nineteenth centuries, noting that marriage was associated with economic independence.[64] Whether financial security came in the form of a dowry, jointure, inheritance, savings or a secure profession, many historians have accounted for the late age at marriage in Western Europe as motivated by the desire to maintain a separate household.[65] That the upper ranks married at a younger age is thought to reflect that much of their wealth was inherited rather than earned. Yet, as the high number of people willing to elope suggests, economic security was not always essential.[66] In Scotland throughout the period, like in much of Europe, it was expected that both men and women would bring economic resources to the marriage, and with it they brought tools to negotiate for power.[67] The form those resources took and their significance within courtship negotiations altered over the period.

As is highlighted in the words of Archibald Campbell above, in the seventeenth century elite families expected that couples marry to the economic, social and/or political benefit of both families. As a result economic resources were central to discussions of marriage in seventeenth century conduct books. William Ramesay in 1672 advised his male readers to 'look well to the main chance of her estate; especially if thine be impaired, and in the wane. For, a comfortable estate is, next to virtue, the only means to extenuate the innumerable inconveniences, and miseries of a married life'.[68] Similarly Campbell noted that 'Money is the sinew of love as well as war, you can do nothing happily in wedlock without it'.[69] Both of these authors were concerned that economic resources impacted on power relationships within marriage. They attempted to resolve this by advocating class endogamy. Ramesay noted that 'if they [the couple] be unequally matcht, live at variance, no greater torment or misery', while Campbell emphasised to his sons that to marry below their rank was dishonourable and 'will soon breed distaste and dislike in yourself, which will cause malice and revenge in her'.[70] Other forms of popular culture exposed the threat that women with economic resources posed to their husbands, while from the opposite perspective *Montrose, He Had a Poor Shepherd* described a beautiful shepherd's daughter who initially refused a wealthy marriage proposal due to fear that her beau would treat her with disdain.[71]

Despite the concern with exogamy within popular culture, a significant number of people in this study married outside their social rank, if not by significant degree. As is noted for other parts of Europe, this was resolved in the late seventeenth and early eighteenth centuries by allowing economic resources to function as a symbol of social worth that compensated for differences in rank.[72] This resulted in the marriage contract and its negotiations holding importance within the courtship process. Both men and women investigated and knew the financial standing of their potential spouse, and their letters and those of their families are full of discussions on this issue.[73] Men who were willing to settle large sums on their wives demonstrated how much they valued them, while those who quibbled over minor amounts showed disrespect. In 1701, James Pringle's marriage negotiation faltered when his fiancée, Katherine Hepburn, learned he quibbled over the jointure. She declared she would 'never come in communing with him, though he should offer the 300 merks more'.[74] When Susan Dundonald married the impoverished Lord Yester in 1697, her family agreed to the match as he provided the best terms his condition allowed. When the negotiations were going badly, Susan told her brother that he should remain civil to Yester as he had done everything in his power to meet the terms of the contract.[75]

By offering a suitable settlement, men showed that they valued their wives. While this did not remove their husband's authority over them, it suggested to women that they would be treated with respect during marriage. From the opposite perspective, suitors who could not suitably match their beloved in rank and fortune risked their authority within marriage. When William Clerk asked his father in 1713 to increase his portion so he could marry a woman of higher rank with a sizable estate, his father responded that a little more money would not make his proposed wife respect him.[76] Similarly, during the marriage negotiation of Julian Home and Dr Trotter, the question of husbandly and also future parental authority underpinned concerns about this mismatched pair with the financial terms being explicitly weighted to counterbalance this problem. After they had successfully negotiated financial terms, her uncle George Home noted, 'we had some difficulties about the meanesse of his birth, yet thought that might be past if she had ane inclination to the man'.[77] Economic resources were used as tools in negotiations of power. Men had to show they had equal fiscal standing to their wives, if they wished to have authority after marriage, while women understood that the money that was settled upon them symbolised the authority and respect they would hold within the home.

As the eighteenth century progressed, the fore-grounding of finances within courtship negotiations became increasingly distasteful to conduct authors and elite letter writers alike. Suitors continued to extract the best terms from marriage contracts, but in letters emphasised their social background, education and potential earning capacity, rather than fiscal worth.[78] Hestor Chapone advised her readers in the late eighteenth century, a happy match relied on 'suitableness of character, degree and fortune – on mutual esteem, and the prospect of a real and permanent friendship ... a mercenary marriage is a detestable prostitution'.[79] Lady Pennington urged her female readers to concern themselves with the personal character of their future spouses, leaving 'fortune and family' as the province of their fathers.[80]

Eighteenth- and nineteenth-century courting couples avoided discussing financial terms too explicitly. In the 1820s, Jane Welsh was reluctant to explicitly address her suitor's poor financial situation. She delicately advised Thomas Carlyle to take up a regularly paid tutor's post, arguing that his friends had worked hard to find him the opportunity, not that it made him a more desirable match. Her letters are littered with hints for him to save and look to his future financial well-being. Thomas never realised her meaning and continuously opted for the poor but satisfying life of a writer. After five years of correspondence, Jane admitted outright that she would marry him if he offered her financial security. Thomas immediately found the money to marry her as well as the means to maintain them in the future.[81]

Many suitors wished to disassociate themselves from mercenary motives. David, Earl of Airlie noted to his fiancée Clementina in 1812 that he had not visited as his father's agent was meeting her guardians to discuss their marriage contract. He continued that: 'I think it would appear rather indelicate for me to [be] present while these matters are settling. My motives God knows are not mercenary. If matters are arranged speedily and to meet the approbation of you and your friends it is all that I care or wish for – it is you who have taken possession of my heart and can make me happy – Lawyers writers and guardians I want to have nothing to do with.'[82] Yet, despite many eighteenth- and nineteenth-century suitors' protests, the marriage contract remained a vital prerequisite to marriage for the elites. The importance of economic resources in marriage negotiations did not diminish in the eighteenth century, but their use as a marker of love and value declined. Eighteenth- and nineteenth-century suitors used the language of romantic love to highlight their respect for their future spouse, where their predecessors in the seventeenth century used economic resources.

The nature of marriage contracts and how they changed over the period reflected the increasing importance laid on the couple, rather than the family. Marriage contracts were often of significant legal impor- tance due to their association with inheritance, being used to bestow estates on heirs.[83] For most people, marriage contracts laid out the provi- sions for support of the marital unit, the amount brought to the marriage by both parties, the nature of the wife's economic support after her husband's death (the dower or increasingly jointure) and usually the children's marriage portion. As Robert Rutherford observed in 1731, not having a marriage contract was a disadvantage to both men and women. He noted after his son eloped, 'he hess gott a tender wife to try his steill but a tender tocherless wife is a bad bargaine and she runs a risk if she live long to be in a bad situation not being to be expectit that he make a settlement'.[84]

In the seventeenth century, women usually brought a dowry, referred to as the tocher, or a portion, which was used to provide her with a jointure and usually pay the portions of future children. While references to the tocher were not unknown, it was common by the seven- teenth century for women to receive their portion, or share of the family inheritance, when marrying. The advantage of the tocher or portion was that it usually brought lump sums of money into families who were land- rich but cash-poor. In return, families settled pieces of land on brides, the income of which supported them as widows. Occasionally parties brought land or goods if their families did not have cash, such as the family who provided several 'boolls' of meal annually as a jointure.[85] As the period progressed and land became increasingly scarce, cash was used by all parties. Money set aside for jointures was placed in bank accounts or in stocks to earn interest. It was also common in Scotland for men to add to their wives' tochers during settlement negotiations, so that children's portions were viewed as an inheritance from both parents.[86] Julian Home's portion was the same as that allocated in her marriage settlement to her first daughter, and it was noted during negotiations that 'it was hard that in case of one daughter she should have nothing of her father'.[87] This expectation, like that of bilateral kinship, emphasised that this was a joining of two families, and later two individuals, rather than the subsuming of women into their husband's person.

Like in other parts of Europe, the settlement of large pieces of land or money on wives for their future use could be problematic.[88] Land that was allocated for jointures could not be sold or allocated for any other use, which was difficult for families with financial problems. The families of widows often resented the burden they put upon the estate, especially when land was needed for the jointures of the wives of heirs. Yet, that women had control over a substantial piece of property could be used as a negotiating tool with their families. In 1686, the Countess of Findlater found herself inundated with requests to renounce her right to the lands settled on her so they could be used for her son's wife's settlement.[89] Whether she agreed is unknown. Margaret Ogilvy, in similar circumstances in 1660, refused to consent, to the annoyance of her husband and son. She noted to her father, 'I sie no way layed down for privyding of my children which displeased me more nor any thing concerning my self and I really think if I wale remmince, that ther wale be small cair had of their provisions'.[90]

In another instance in 1730, Jean Wilsone gained significantly through negotiating with her husband over land, although in this case it was her own heritable property. In return for selling half of her lands for 3000 merks and giving up her liferent in the money, Jean received after his death 400 merks, a 'house in Langside called the forehouse', the 'yeard', and one dozen good hens, as long as there was no children. If they have children, she was to receive 100 merks with one chalder of victual half beer oatmeal as well as the said house, yard and hens. If she remarried, she lost her right to the property and received a yearly payment of 200 merks. She was to have all household furnishings and a large section of land. She also received 100 merks on her death.[91] At the same time, as Stana Nenadic points out, some widows relinquished their property under family pressure, leaving themselves in penury in old age.[92]

Over the course of the eighteenth century, the nature of contracts changed, reflecting a greater concern with the individual as well as the changing nature of the economy. Personal property was not so rigidly allocated, was often bequeathed to the longest liver and women were given rights to bequeath marital property. Settlements were increasingly made in cash or investment, allowing the couple to live off the interest, and reducing the financial benefit to the wider family. By the nineteenth century, settlements upon the couple were made in both their names and were usually of the same amount. This money was expected to support the wife and children after her husband's death. The nineteenth century also saw husbands beginning to renounce their *jus mariti*, their legal right to their wife's property, in marriage contracts, although before 1850 this was far from universal. In 1801, Laurence Oliphant renounced his *jus mariti* over the £500 Hannah Johnston brought to the marriage.[93]

While certain financial requirements had to be met for a contract negotiation to be successful, individuals could offer generous terms and add to the contract over time. John, Earl of Hopetoun's original settlement with his wife, Elizabeth, in 1767 granted her a jointure of £500 per annum, a bond of annuity worth £1,000 annually, and the household furniture and parks of Ormiston during her life. In 1768, he gave her an additional bond worth £1,000 and in 1778 one for £1,200. In 1775, he added a clause creating Elizabeth tutrix and curatrix to all her children. In 1771, he added to his children's provisions, giving £8,000 to his eldest son over and above the estates, and a bond of £8,000 to his younger son. He also gave his four daughters a bond of £5,000 each to be paid at twenty-one or at marriage.[94] As family wealth increased or husbands' trust in their wives grew, they could give more advantageous terms to their partners.

Despite these changes, this is not a straightforward narrative of progress. Just as jointures linked to income from land could be withheld from widows (illegally) by resentful heirs, marriage jointures in the eighteenth and nineteenth centuries were often held in trust, potentially leaving women in the hands of paternalistic and controlling trustees. Susan Staves suggests for eighteenth-century England that woman's increasing rights to own separate property was coupled with an unwillingness of the courts to recognise that ownership except under very particular conditions.[95] While a similar study has not been written for the Scottish court system, the continued suspicion of married women's property ownership, discussed in Chapter 2, and their changing role in marriage settlement negotiations, may suggest that this was not unique south of the border.

While contract negotiations have been seen as male arenas, mothers were often present alongside, as well as representing or replacing absent and deceased husbands. Andrew Home's mother was present with her spouse at the settlement of his marriage contract, criticising her husband for the poor condition of his estate, while Loudon Robertson's mother organised and negotiated the terms of her contract as her father was fighting in the American War of Independence.[96] Furthermore, Scottish women were generally aware of their future husbands' and fathers' financial situations and the state of the negotiations. There was evidence that many women had already decided the terms they would agree to in advance and their fathers were merely their advocates, although this may have been regional and declined over the eighteenth century.[97]

Women from the Scottish borders appeared to be particularly active in their marital negotiations. George Home of Kimmerghame was employed by Katherine Hepburn in 1701 to represent her in her contract negotiations, at which both her suitor and father were present. Her suitor would not meet her demands so, although her father was willing to agree to his terms, Katherine rejected his proposal. Her father and advocate had to continually relay the state of the negotiations to Katherine and heed her opinion.[98] When Julian Home met her future husband in 1698, she was concerned that her parents may not agree as he was not wealthy. She used her knowledge of his financial situation and her portion to create terms for a suitable contract and then approached her parents to ask permission to marry.[99]

On the other hand, as Stana Nenadic highlights, women from families in the north-west of Scotland appeared to have a lot less control over their futures.[100] This appeared to have mirrored wider inheritance strategies. Families where women could not inherit the main estate due to their gender allowed women less freedom to negotiate their marital contracts; whereas, in families where women could inherit (usually on the failure of a male heir), they had more freedom to interfere. There was also some relationship with religious belief, with the northern clans expressing more Episcopalian sympathies, while families from the Scottish Borders often had close ties to the Covenanting movements. This may suggest that the hierarchal structures of the Episcopalian church and the spiritual equality of the Covenanters were reflected in family practice. Having said this, the estates of the staunchly Presbyterian Dukes of Argyll had a male entail, excluding women from inheriting, so the relationship between belief and behaviour is far from perfect.

As the eighteenth century progressed, the need to distance oneself from 'mercenary' motivations for marriage reduced the ability of women to participate in negotiating their marriage contracts. While women still appeared to be aware of what was being discussed, the need to appear above such concerns meant that women were less active in negotiations, or had to intervene in a less overt manner. A similar restriction should have applied to men, who were also meant to rise above the distasteful financial considerations of marriage, but in practice they had a number of opportunities to get involved. Men who were already heads of families had little choice but to participate in contract negotiations, while lawyers generally drew up their own marriage contracts. Furthermore, as the model of the nuclear family with a male 'breadwinner' became more culturally important among the elites in the nineteenth century, men could use the model of the fiscally responsible husband as a justification for actively ensuring a settlement that benefited the new nuclear unit. Although, as Amanda Vickery and Nicole Eustace suggest, women were able to manipulate their expected passivity to influence men in their favour, their inability to speak explicitly in this area subtly shifted the balance of power that had been traditionally negotiated during the marriage settlement in favour of the husband.[101] Marriage contracts were not just negotiations between men but between couples.

Love and courtship

While the concept of romantic love has been explored in the context of changing values across time, such as proffered by Lawrence Stone and Edward Shorter, and by those who wish to rebuff their theory that at the end of the eighteenth century 'love conquered all', the role of love in courtship has received relatively little attention.[102] Love was expected to temper male authority and acted as a tool in negotiations of power. The importance placed upon love in courtship and its role in courtship rituals provides important insights into the relationship between love and power throughout the period.

Although seventeenth century conduct writers believed that love was an indispensable aspect of the marital relationship, they were relatively silent on the issue of love within courtship beyond a few warnings to women that passionate love 'hath friends in the garrison'.[103] Passionate love was problematic as it threatened the parent's right to consent and thus the patriarchal social order. Similarly, lavish expressions of love were given a low priority in seventeenth-century Scottish letters, but this did not imply an absence of affection between writers. For most people, love was necessary within marriage and the potential for love had to exist before marriage went ahead. The courtship of Nelly Poulett and James, Earl of Arran faltered in 1679 when she heard he had a long-term mistress. She expressed concern about marrying him as, 'your heart is already fixt, without the power of allowing the least sheave to her you marrie'.[104] Nelly, although not requiring fidelity, expected love within marriage and was unwilling to marry where it would be absent. James Ogilvie noted in 1686 of his brother's suit, 'he hes gained the primates daughter her affection and lykwayes hes goten the bishops ladys consent, and that nothing does hender my brothers marriage bot that the primat is not yet returned from London'.[105] The gaining of the lady's affection was considered necessary for the marriage to go ahead.

Correspondence indicates that affection was part of courtship, with couples showing concern for each other's welfare. Asking after a recipient's health or offering to work in his or her interest were marks of affection within courtship correspondence. The Marchioness of Huntley, writing to her suitor the Earl of Airlie in 1668, asked after his health and noted 'if I could advance your lordship saetisfaction in anie business wharin my self war not concernt I wad exteim myself oblidged to doe it for your own diservid faveors'. The Earl's response was humorous and more openly affectionate. He noted, in response to her jest that she had a separate interest from him, that he had gone blind for fifteen minutes, stressing that his affection for her was so great that a rebuffal affected his health. Couples also showed affection through offering tokens such as jewellery and hair. The Earl noted to the Marchioness that there was a rumour that he had a ring and a bracelet of hair, but told her, 'those stories should not vex you seeing ye knowe to well [I] was not so hapie as to have had so great a trust allowed me'.[106] Numerous other couple's letters contained lockets of hair that they had carefully preserved along with their correspondence.

As the eighteenth century opened, the idea of love and affection within courtship, as well as marriage, became increasingly important. In 1700, John Clerk noted of his marriage negotiation that: 'as for me I shall be verie blyth & content with any condition you may make with them for although I'm no ways in love, yet I shall dispaire of over having the offer of such another … I say this not that I am indifferent of the woman bot verie much to the contrary'.[107] While John did not believe that love was a requisite for marriage, his letter indicated that the idea of 'love' before marriage was not unfamiliar. By the 1720s, people referred to their feelings before marriage as 'love', even though the usage of the term suggests they were referring to the emotion that an earlier generation referred to as 'affection'. James, Earl of Wemyss' first comment to his friend David, Earl of Leven on his proposed marriage in 1720 was: 'I am in love with Miss Charters [Charteris]. I have been often in her company. I have informed myself of her humour from others whom I can tryst that know her better than it is possible for me to do. I flatter myself with the hopes that you lordship will approve of my choice'.[108] While, as James recognised, his knowledge of his future wife was based on reputation rather than intimacy, he understood his admiration for her as love.

By the mid-eighteenth century, letters between courting couples commonly used emotive language. This reflected the expectation within popular culture that love was a motivation for marriage, highlighting that the Scottish elites experienced the 'glamourisation' of romantic love during the period similarly to the rest of Britain.[109] Couples emphasised the necessity of love before marriage progressed and their letters became increasingly informal with the use of pet names. Hugh, Earl of Marchmont's correspondence with Elizabeth Crompton in 1747 reveals the language of love letters. He noted to her on one occasion, 'My dearest my Betty, that I should say when I lost you I lost everything, would surely not surprise you, since it is what any common lover would say'.[110]

He constantly reiterated that he only wished her to marry him if she loved him: 'Lay your reason out of the question, don't say, I ought to do so & so to Lord Marchmont, but ask your heart, if there will be pleasure felt in giving up all its objects to Lord Marchmont, in preferring him to every one of 'em, be they what they will. If your heart hesitates, then your reason will tell you, you owe it to my love & esteem for you to say no.' To marry without love was abhorrent to Hugh, yet, like conduct writers, he was not above practical considerations. He discussed the importance of receiving the blessing of his children from his first marriage and asked others for information on her reputation, noting to her, 'I saw the attorney general at court, who has given me his opinion, that you will make a very good wife'.[111]

Love as a form of power became increasingly visible in the emotive language of Hugh Marchmont and his contemporaries. Hugh's letters expected his future wife's love for him to encompass her whole being. He noted, 'If I should not have my wish in the absolute possession of all your heart, I have but one wish to make, & that is you may not undertake to make his happiness, who cannot be happy unless you have constant pleasure in making yourself absolutely subservient to this end', while in another he states, 'I shall make endless demands of love, friendship, unreserved confidence, & entire trust in me; I shall expect you not only to think of yourself as my property, but to be delighted with being so. Will this be tyranny? If not I have all my wish.' On the one hand, this was the language of love, of affection and mutual interest, yet, on the other, love was clearly understood to remove women's power.

In the eighteenth century, female love was no longer constrained to marriage but granted to women to help them make their choice of marriage partner. As was shown in the previous chapter, eighteenth-century authors wished to ensure that female usage of the language of love, and thus the power inherent within the act of love, was restricted. Like their counterparts in colonial North America, they wished for female passion to be controlled by a male suitor or spouse.[112] The number of surviving letters written by women during courtship is limited, but there is some evidence that women absorbed such prescriptions. Jessie Graham's letters to her future husband Walter Crum in 1825/6 described their relationship in terms of his love for her, while she expressed her feelings in terms of friendship. She noted on one occasion: 'I would not leave town without telling you how very sorry I felt that you should for a moment have supposed me annoyed by your calling as a friend. I should always be most happy to see you and surely you would not wish me to deceive you by saying that at present I felt more than grateful for the very kind interest you seem to take in me, yours with esteem, Jessie Graham.'[113] In another letter Jessie remarked that she was 'very happy on the prospect of having your love again. I am my dear Walter your most affectionate friend.'[114] Jessie's letters implied that she understood love as male action towards her, while she only offered friendship.

When Margaret Bruce accepted the Earl of Airlie's marriage proposal in c. 1838, she demonstrated her understanding that with marriage she gave herself and her affection into the hands of her husband. She wrote:

> I take my time in assuring you that heart and hand are alike free and that I will bestow both upon you in the full confidence that my happiness will be in safe keeping and as I do or do not my duty to you, yr little girls & Ogilvy as a wife and mother … I trust I need hardly add that even if I did not consider the so doing sinful nothing could tempt me to give my hand unaccompanied by my affections. I am now my dear lord Airlie yours with sincere affection Margt. Bruce.[115]

Margaret did not speak of love, but of affection, yet even this emotion was offered to her husband as a symbol of his full possession of her person. Love was something that men offered women and which women passively accepted.

From the late eighteenth century onwards, the conflict between the inexpressive woman and the emotive male suitor developed into an elaborate game. A suitor bombarded his beloved with gifts and declarations of love, while the woman expressed reserve and behaved in a noncommittal fashion. When she finally relented, usually just before they married, he was seen as the victor who had wooed and won his sweetheart. While Vickery and Eustace have viewed this as giving women power during the courtship, in fact his victory was almost always inevitable and she had a very restricted and prescribed role. The only real area she could exploit was if she has more than one lover to play off against each other and even then she eventually must make a choice.

The courtship of Anne Kirkwood and Robert Chambers utilised this ritual in 1829. Robert's letters were always affectionate and expressed longing for Anne, whereas she was always reserved. In the first few months of the relationship, she told Robert of another suitor and sent him his letters so he could give her advice. In contrast, Robert was devoted to Anne. He commented that while in a 'fever of sentiment … I took out all your letters from their bosom place in my clothes, and there lay for an hour, reading them kissing them, and bedewing them with my tears. They have lain beneath my head all night and my first action after waking was to seize them and press them to my lips.' Robert noted that Anne did not respond in kind, saying, 'My mother used always to prophesy that if ever I was married I would write no more books; but if I find the same result almost effected by a mere acquaintance with a young lady, which the said young lady calls friendship. Ah this friendship!' The game advanced with Anne becoming increasingly friendly and finally relenting. Their courtship began in January 1829 and they married in December.[116]

James Balfour's courtship with Anne Macintosh in 1806 followed a similar pattern. He attempted to awaken love within Anne and through doing so take possession of her and her feelings. He wrote:

> You confess an anxiety to know how I am, and you cannot help feeling an interest in my health and welfare. These are not the expressions of ordinary friendship or of common politeness and far less of cold indifference. They must proceed from some other source more nearly connected with the warmer influence of the heart. Shall I trace them to a return of sentiments similar to those which it is my pleasure to avow I have towards you?[117]

He was not successful on this occasion and she did not relent for over a year. Letter writing rituals of this form placed men as the aggressors, while women remained passive and inactive. They were not allowed to express emotion, until they finally accepted a proposal of marriage. This ensured that female love was immediately placed under the control of her spouse, and that the power that love offered remained in male control. At the same time, as Nicole Eustace suggests for North America, when courtship negotiations failed it allowed men to blame a lack of affection from a beloved, rather than acknowledge that they lacked the appropriate economic, or familial, resources needed to close the deal – important to men in a world where social position was increasingly related to commercial success.[118]

This ritual also related to the increasing idealisation of female chastity. It allowed a woman to correspond with several men and even develop intimate relationships, but as it was always framed in the terms of friendship, she could withdraw honourably at any time. A woman's silence represented her chastity, perhaps drawing on traditional early modern associations of the tongue with genitals. As the Scottish proverb noted, 'Ane glib'd tongued women seldom chast ar found'.[119] Men, less concerned with sexual reputation, were freer to express themselves. As love gained force as a form of power, so the patriarchal system adapted to limit its usage by women.

While the active man/passive woman dichotomy was the dominant discourse for male and female behaviour within courtship, there is evidence of alternative behaviours. Enlightenment discourses of rationality influenced some writers to emphasise their choice of partner was rational and their expression of love contained.[120] Anne Mylne, when trying to free herself from a courtship in the late 1760s, explained:

> I have a great opinion of my own head, it has extricated my heart out of so many scraps, that its found quite insolent both to it and other people and treats its feeble emotions, as the weakness of an idiot that's perpetually going wrong, take this my dear for an answer about hearts, I tell you again and again, that it would be just as well if we had none, to be sure it would be somewhat like wanting a nose, and therefore that we may not appear to maime it, but right to talk of having one, But while we are compelled to act ten times out of a dozen, in direct opposition to its feelings its just as well that this member born only to suffer or lead us astray were quietly out of the way, by suffocation strangling or any way, but poisoning.[121]

Anne strongly believed in love within marriage, noting to her niece: 'I hope some time to see you disposed of to one whom your heart and reason can approve', but wished to observe a balance between affection and pragmatism.

Reason was meant to control the violent excesses of love and rational suitors were meant to consider more than love when selecting a partner.[122] Additionally, at least in this instance, Anne's assertion of rationality in matters of the heart allowed her to have active emotions. While she acknowledged that her heart was contained, it was through her own exercise of reason rather than an inability to conceive of love as a female behaviour. In practice, this meant that her behaviour in courtship was similar to her contemporaries, but this discourse acted to allow women ownership of their emotions and some sense of power in their emotional relationships. This conception of love tied into a broader discussion amongst groups of elite British and American women in the mid-eighteenth century who attempted to use ideas of rationality to promote equality amongst the sexes and friendship as a basis for marriage.[123]

In the 1820s, Jane Carlyle felt social pressure to conform to cultural norms of submissive and polite feminine behaviour, but privately critiqued the irrationality of the system. In a letter to her cousin, she described a visit from a suitor, who she had previously rejected:

> Mother and I received him more politely 'than was to have been expected, all the circumstances of the case considered'; and we proceeded to walk, and play at battledoor, and talk inanities, about new novels, and new belles, and what had gone on at a splendid party the night before, where he had been (he told us) for half an hour with *his arm under his hat*; and then he corrected himself, and said, *with his head under his arm!* It was of very little consequence where his head was; it is not much worth.

He followed up his visit with letters and gifts, including several pieces of music, and later a further marriage proposal, which she rejected firmly, and then passed the matter to her mother to end. In private, however, she railed against his behaviour, commenting, 'Hitherto there had been nothing of *hope*, nothing more of love or marrying; but now my gentleman presumed to flatter himself, in the expansion of the folly of his heart, that *I might possibly change my mind*. Ass! I change my mind, indeed! and for him!'[124]

Jane was intolerant of men who showed too much sensibility, noting of her suitor Dugald G— that 'the more he is kicked about, the more he fawns and cringes. I told him, among other things, in tolerably plain English, that he was given to lying! (and good reason I had for saying so.) In reply, he kissed my hand!' Yet, she also engaged with this model of courtship playfully, responding to a piece of Goethe, translated by her future husband, by noting, 'All the sentiment in me was screwed up to the highest pitch; I could hardly help crying like a child or Dugald G— and I kissed the seal with a fervour which would have graced the most passionate lover.'[125] Her courtship with the man she married was very conventional. Jane played the passive, disinterested woman, and he pursued her with a mixture of romantic hope and paternalistic advice. In her interactions with men, Jane conformed to socially acceptable models of behaviour, but in her letters to her close female friends, she critiqued this restricted role, even adopting male behaviours to expose the absurdity of her position. Despite her problematic relationship with courtship rituals, Jane still operated within them, unable to imagine an acceptable alternative.

There is also some evidence that some women transgressed from their expected role within courtship more overtly. Within John Clerk's papers survives 'observations' relating to the illicit affair of 'Miss Cathcart' and her brother in law, Sir John Houston. Miss Cathcart was probably Marie Anne Cathcart, daughter of Charles, 8th Lord Cathcart and only sister of Elenora Cathcart.[126] The 'observations' criticised Miss Cathcart for her disregard for her sister in maintaining this illicit relationship, but also noted 'she has been so madly in love with him as to write & speeke directly as he inclined she would' and that 'her real intentions was to ingross [sic] all from johns affection to her self'. Miss Cathcart's active behaviour in their relationship was as significant and derisory as her illicit affair. The note continued that 'Miss Cathcart had employed most of her time wil & memory in reading romances in all languages & she seemes very weel acquainted with all the theory of love matters'.

Unfortunately Miss Cathcart's letters have not survived, but her unfeminine behaviour was explained by the writer of the 'observations' as her too detailed knowledge of love. As is noted by Ruth Yeazell, women who understood desire were seen to be in danger of using its power for their own purposes.[127] Miss Cathcart's expertise in love was thought by the writer to originate from the romances of the period, which held an ambiguous social role. Novels were condemned within sermons and prescriptive literature for their corrupting role.[128] Hannah More argued that novels promoted unconstrained passion and endangered women's chastity.[129] Yet, many novels advanced the values and displayed the courtship rituals practised in society. Samuel Richardson, author of the best-selling novel *Pamela*, summarised the moral of his work as 'that a young lady should be in love, and the love of the young gentleman undeclared, is a heterodoxy which prudence, and even policy, must not allow'.[130] The criticism of Miss Cathcart indicated that moral women were not supposed to show action within courtship, but her behaviour suggests that not all women conformed to this expectation. Furthermore, as the writer acknowledged, there were social discourses available for women who chose a different path.

The increased use of the word love and emotive expressions of affection found within eighteenth-century courtship letters led historians such as Lawrence Stone to argue that how marriage was negotiated underwent serious change and one that favoured the individual, emotion and equality between spouses, over family and finances.[131] Yet, as has been demonstrated, in Scotland this shift and its implications for power were not so straightforward. There was no simple decline of the family in favour of the individual across the eighteenth century, rather that elite estates could no longer support large extended kin networks led to an emphasis on the conjugal unit as the basis of the household and community. The family were still involved in the practical negotiation of courtship and marriage settlements, but their goal was the future well-being of the new married unit. The emphasis on the conjugal unit brought with it a greater concern with individual happiness and so choice, demonstrated through the language of love, became of increased importance. But, this did not remove the fact that marriage continued to be primarily an economic relationship and that practical considerations remained central to a successful match.

Just as courtship was a time to negotiate the economic terms of marriage, it was also the time to negotiate power in married life. The emphasis on bilateral kinship in the seventeenth century where husband and wife represented the resources provided by their family networks and reinforced by marriage settlements based around equally matched unions (if one where rank could be balanced by wealth) which provided a joint inheritance from both spouses for their future children, subtly indicated the degree to which marriage was expected to be a partnership, if one where authority was vested in the man. Women, who were often involved in negotiating their marriage settlements, also had an active say in determining the nature of the contract that was the basis of their future relationship. This gave them space to negotiate the terms of their married life.

Over the course of the eighteenth century, the shift towards individual choice subtly shifted the balance of power. The rise of romantic love, which silenced women and emphasised that women's emotions were to be held by men, and its concomitant distaste of 'mercenary' marriage, that removed women from active involvement in negotiating marriage settlements, reduced the opportunities for women to have a say on the shape of their future married life. They were increasingly asked to trust their parents and then their lover in protecting their interests. In this sense, the move from consanguinity to conjugality was not a shift that empowered men and women equally. The interests of the conjugal unit increasingly became the interests of the husband, and women were not given space to conceptualise themselves as independent individuals. In this way, Scotland more strongly resembled Germany, where ideals of individualism were reluctantly applied to women, than England.[132] Yet, within these discourses as Nicole Eustace notes for North America, women found space to resist this removal of self, complicating negotiations of power and building identities that operated within the patriarchal system.[133] How these issues affected power relationships within marriage will be the discussion of the rest of this book.

Notes

1 Alan Macfarlane also points to these as key areas in English courtship, see: *Marriage and Love in England: Modes of Reproduction 1300-1840* (Oxford: Basil Blackwood, 1986), especially p. 290; J. Gillis, *For Better, For Worse: British Marriages 1600 to the Present* (Oxford: Oxford University Press, 1985), pp. 4–5.

2 J. Hardwick, *The Practice of Patriarchy: Gender and the Politics of Household Authority in Early Modern France* (University Park: Pennsylvannia State University Press, 1998), p. 52. A similar point is made by Louise Tilly and Joan Scott although referring more widely to control of economic resources, see *Women, Work and the Family* (London: Routledge, 1989).

3 L. Stone, *The Family, Sex and Marriage in England 1500-1800* (London: Weidenfeld and Nicolson, 1977), pp. 270–391; M. Segalen, *Love and Power in the Peasant Family* (Oxford: Blackwell, 1983), pp. 15 and 11–37.

4 For example see M. Spufford, *Small Books and Pleasant Histories: Popular Fiction and its Readership in Seventeenth-Century England* (London: Methuen, 1981), p. 161; D. Cressy, *Birth, Marriage, and Death: Ritual, Religion, and the Life-Cycle in Tudor and Stuart England* (Oxford: Oxford University Press, 1997), p. 235; P. Rushton, 'Property, power and family networks: the problem of disputed marriage in early modern England', *Journal of Family History*, 11 (1986), 211; D. O'Hara, *Courtship and Constraint: Rethinking the Making of Marriage in Tudor England* (Manchester: Manchester University Press, 2000).

5 N. Eustace, '"The cornerstone of a copious work": love and power in eighteenth century courtship', *Journal of Social History*, 34 (2001), 518–45; A. Vickery, *The Gentleman's Daughter: Women's Lives in Georgian England* (London: Yale University Press, 1998).

6 In Scotland, like England, 'friends' was used to refer to people, particularly family members, who had an invested interest in your life, see Chapter 5. The term 'family' was usually used in reference to members of the same household, see N. Tadmor, 'The concept of the household-family in eighteenth century England', *Past and Present*, 151 (1996), 111–140.

7 J. Dalrymple, Viscount of Stair, *The Institutions of the Law of Scotland* (Edinburgh: Edinburgh University Press, 1981), p. 108.

8 R. Perry, *Novel Relations: the Transformation of Kinship in English Relations and Culture, 1748-1818* (Cambridge: Cambridge University Press, 2004).

9 A. Campbell, Marques of Argyll, *Instructions to a Son* (London: Richard Blackwell, 1689), pp. 44–6.

10 K. Brown, *Noble Society in Scotland: Wealth, Family and Culture from Reformation to Revolution* (Edinburgh: Edinburgh University Press, 2000); S. Whyman, *Sociability and Power in Late-Stuart England* (Oxford: Oxford University Press, 1999), p. 120.

11 A. Erickson, 'The marital economy in comparative perspective', in M. Ågren and A. Erickson (eds), *The Marital Economy in Scandanavia and Britain 1400-1900* (Aldershot: Ashgate, 2005), p. 11.

12 Hardwick, *Practice of Patriarchy*, pp. 72–5.

13 D. Purkiss, 'Sounds of silence: fairies and incest in Scottish witchcraft stories', in S. Clark (ed.), *Languages of Witchcraft: Narrative, Ideology and Meaning* (Basingstoke: Macmillan, 2000), pp. 81–99.

14 S. Nenadic, *Laird and Luxury: the Highland Gentry in Eighteenth Century Scotland* (Edinburgh: John Donald, 2007), p. 27.

15 E. Sanderson, *Women and Work in Eighteenth Century Edinburgh* (Basingstoke: Macmillan Press, 1996), p. 131.

16 For further discussion see Chapter 5.

17 P. Jalland, *Women, Marriage and Politics 1860–1914* (Oxford: Clarendon Press, 1986), p. 52; C. Frances, 'Making marriages in early modern England: rethinking the role of family and friends', in Ågren and Erickson, *Marital Economy*, p. 40.

18 S. Tomaselli, 'The enlightenment debate on women', *History Workshop Journal*, 20 (1985), 120.

19 R. Allestree, *The Ladies Calling* (Oxford: Theatre in Oxford, 1700), pp. 184–5; G. Savile, Marquis of Halifax, *The Ladies New-Years Gift: or Advice to a Daughter* (Edinburgh: John Reid, 3rd edn, 1688), p. 110.

20 NAS GD18/5300/2/1 Alexander Mackenzie to John Clerk, 27 March 1729.

21 NAS GD406/1/7422 Duke of Hamilton to Anne, Duchess of Hamilton, 23 January 1693/4.

22 NAS GD406/1/4169 Earl of Arran to Lord Yester, 21 October 1697.

23 NAS GD406/1/6073 Marquis of Atholl to Duke of Hamilton, 24 July 1682.

24 NAS GD18/5173/2 Helen Gray to John Clerk, 6 September 1673.

25 NAS GD406/1/7967 Duke of Atholl to Anne, Duchess of Hamilton, 16 November 1710.

26 NAS GD345/1148/2/7 Archibald Grant to Anna Potts, 14 March 1740.

27 NAS GD26/13/401/1 Margaret Countess of Wemyss to My Lord [?], [1690–98].

28 NAS GD26/13/401/2–4 Various to Margaret Countess of Wemyss [1690–98].

29 The daughter in question was referred to as Nanci, which is presumably Anne. She married David Melville in 1691 and was probably in her mid to late teens. Margaret also had a daughter called Margaret who married Lord Northesk in 1697, aged 21. Lord Northesk and Lord Southesk were cousins, but it is possible that Nanci referred to Margaret and the letter referred to her marriage to Northesk.

30 See NAS GD406/1 for James' numerous courtships that usually fell, and was finally successful, on this condition.

31 NAS GD1/649/3 The Diary of George Home, 16 January to 11 April 1700. The latter condition was considered particularly unreasonable, but appears to have been finally agreed to. Merks were a Scottish coin originally worth 13s 6d but the value rose to 14s in 1681.

32 Whyman, *Sociability and Power*, p. 112.

33 NAS GD406/1/4165 Lord Yester to Earl of Arran, 17 April 1697.

34 S. Nenadic, 'Experience and expectations in the transformation of the Highland gentlewoman, 1680 to 1820', *Scottish Historical Review*, 80 (2001), 213–15.

35 Some good examples of this is the marriage negotiations of Julian Home found in NAS GD1/649/2 The Diary of George Home, 22 September 1698–November 1698; and of William Clerk: NAS GD18/5293 letters re: marriage plans of Mary Clerk and William Clerk, 1717 and NAS GD18/5294 letters re: marriage plans of William Clerk, 1717.

36 NAS GD1/649/3 The Diary of George Home, 13 November 1700–9 April 1701.

37 NAS GD1/649/2 The Diary of George Home, 5 October 1698.

38 NAS GD406/1/6773 Anne, Duchess of Hamilton to Earl of Arran, 8 July 1697.

39 NAS GD1/649/2 The Diary of George Home, 18 January 1698.

40 NAS GD26/13/365 Isobel Hay to Catherine, Lady Melville, 7 November 1682.

41 NAS GD406/1/5890 Duke of Hamilton to Earl of Arran, 27 September 1687.

42 NAS GD406/1/6689 Anne, Duchess of Hamilton to Earl of Arran, 26 November 1695.

43 NAS GD45/14/220 Margaret, Countess of Panmure to James, Earl of Panmure, 26 March 1719.

44 NAS GD1/649/2 The Diary of George Home, 15 October 1697–10 November 1697.

45 S. King, 'Chance encounters? Paths to household formation in early modern England', *International Review of Social History*, 44 (1999), 23–46.

46 Brown, *Noble Society*, pp. 35–7.

47 NAS GD18/5293 letters re: marriage plans of Mary Clerk and William Clerk, 1717; GD18/5294 letters re: marriage plans of William Clerk, 1717; GD18/5253/84 William Clerk to John Clerk, 1 November 1719 and GD18/5253/87 Maxwell of Medlocke to John Clerk, [c. November 1719].

48 Forced marriages were rare after 1650 but there are a couple of famous examples. George Home of Kimmerghame was 'taken out his bed' to marry his kidnapped cousin, the twelve-year-old heiress to a nearby estate, in what was a family power struggle. See: NAS GD1/649/1 The Diary of George Home. The story of the Buccleuch heiresses tells a similar tale, M. Lee, *Heiresses of Buccleuch: Marriage, Money and Politics in Seventeenth Century Britain* (East Linton: Tuckwell Press, 1996).

49 NAS GD1/649/2 The Diary of George Home, 15 October 1697.

50 Perry, *Novel Relations*.

51 M. Darrow, 'Popular concepts of marital choice in eighteenth century France', *Journal of Social History*, 19 (1985), 268.

52 NAS GD45/14/860 Lady Down's death bed letter July 1738. Another similar example is NAS GD18/526/381 Robert Clerk to John Clerk, 15 January 1722.

53 G.J. Barker-Benfield, *The Culture of Sensibility: Sex and Society in Eighteenth Century Britain* (Chicago: Chicago University Press, 1992), p. 326.

54 NAS GD16/34/343 Lord Elibank to Earl of Airlie, 8 January 1743.

55 NAS GD40/9/154 Dorothy Hobart to Lady Suffolk, 1752.

56 NAS GD18/5300/1/24 Colin Mackenzie to John Clerk, 12 October 1731.

57 N. Fix Anderson, 'Cousin marriage in Victorian England', *Journal of Family History*, 11 (1986), 285–301.

58 NAS GD26/13/795 Thomas Macknight to Alexander, Lord Balgonie, 30 October 1797. They were not wrong; it was ten years before Macknight was permitted to marry his sweetheart.

59 C. H. Layman (ed.), *Man of Letters: The Early Life and Love Letters of Robert Chambers* (Edinburgh: Edinburgh University Press, 1990).

60 A. Carlyle (ed.), *The Love Letters of Thomas Carlyle and Jane Welsh* (London: John Lane, 1909), pp. 388–95.

61 Carlyle, *Love Letters*, pp. 60–3.

62 NAS GD172/2584 Ann Robertson to General Robertson, 1779–83.

63 Vickery, *The Gentleman's Daughter*; Jalland, *Women, Marriage*; L. Davidoff, *The Best Circles* (London: The Cresset Library, 1973); J. Perkin, *Women and Marriage in Nineteenth Century England* (London: Routledge, 1989); K. D. Reynolds, *Aristocratic Women and Political Society in Victorian Britain* (Oxford: Clarendon Press, 1998).

64 Gillis, *For Better, For Worse*, p. 74; H. Berry, *Gender, Society and Print Culture in Late-Stuart England* (Aldershot: Ashgate, 2003), p. 78.

65 K. Wrightson, *English Society 1580–1680* (London: Hutchison, 1982), pp. 67–8.

66 King, 'Chance encounters?' 23–46. J. Gillis, '"A triumph of hope over experience": chance and choice in the history of marriage', *International Review of Social History*, 44 (1999), 47–54.

67 Ågren and Erickson, *Marital Economy* gives a good overview of economic resources within marriage from a wider European perspective.

68 W. Ramesay, *The Gentleman's Companion* (London: Rowland Reynolds, 1672), p. 94.

69 Campbell, *Instructions*, pp. 41–3.

70 Ramesay, *Gentleman's Companion*, p. 91 and Campbell, *Instructions*, pp. 41–43.

71 See Glasgow University Library GB 0247 MS Murray 501 William Motherwell, *The Motherwell Collection of Scottish Ballads* c.1820.

72 Whyman, *Sociability and Power*, p. 136; J. Sperling, 'Dowry or inheritance? Kinship, property, and women's agency in Lisbon, Venice, and Florence (1572)', *Journal of Early Modern History*, 11:3 (2007), 206; L. Roper, *Oedipus and the Devil: Witchcraft. Sexuality and Religion in Early Modern Europe* (London: Routledge, 1994), p. 64.

73 A few examples include: NAS GD16/34/326 George Graham to Marchioness of Huntley, [17th century]; and NAS GD18/5300/1/24 Alexander Mackenzie to John Clerk, 12 October 1731.

74 NAS GD1/649/3 The Diary of George Home, 13 November 1700–9 April 1701.

75 NAS GD406/1/6422 Susan Hamilton, Countess of Dundonald to James, Earl of Arran, 18 March 1696/7.

76 NAS GD18/5253/31 John Clerk, snr to William Clerk [April 1713].

77 NAS GD1/649/2 The Diary of George Home, 22 September 1698.

78 For example, see Layman, *Man of Letters*, pp. 146–54 and Carlyle, *The Love Letters*.

79 H. Chapone, *Letters on the Improvement of the Mind* (London: J.F. Dove, 1827), p. 112.

80 S. Pennington, *Advice to her Absent Daughters* (London; J. F. Dove, 1827), pp. 89–99.

81 Carlyle, *The Love Letters*.

82 NAS GD16/34/379/1 David, Earl of Airlie to Clementina, Countess of Airlie, 31 July 1812.

83 There is significant debate surrounding this issue due to the different practices in different regions, see: L. Bonfield, 'Marriage settlements and the "rise of the great estates": the demographic aspect', *Economic History Review*, 32 (1979), 483–93; L. Bonfield, 'Marriage settlements and the "rise of the great estates": a rejoinder', *Economic History Review*, 33 (1980), 559–63; B. English and J. Saville, 'Family settlement and the "rise of the great estates"', *Economic History Review*, 33 (1980), 556–8.

84 NAS GD18/5383/1 Robert Rutherford to John Clerk, 29 November 1731.

85 NAS GD300/30/2 Marriage Contract of George Blaw and Janet Blaw, 17 August 1689.

86 E. Ewan, '"To the longer liver": provisions for the dissolution of the marital economy in Scotland, 1470–1550', in Ågren and Erickson, *Marital Economy*, p. 193.

87 NAS GD1/649/2 The Diary of George Home, 5 October 1698.

88 B. Harris, 'Property, power and personal relations: elite mothers and sons in Yorkist and Early Tudor England', *Signs*, 15 (1990), 606–32.

89 J. Grant (ed.), *Seafield Correspondence from 1685–1708* (Edinburgh: Edinburgh University Press, 1912), Patrick Ogilvie to Countess of Findlater, 9 March 1686.

90 NAS GD16/34/48 Margaret Ogilvy to Earl of Airlie, 7 November 1660.

91 NAS GD300/30/4 Marriage Contract of James Sands of Langside and Jean Wilson, 26 March 1730.

92 Nenadic, *Lairds and Luxury*, pp. 22–8 and 117–18.

93 NAS GD300/30/9 Marriage Contract of Laurence Oliphant and Hannah Johnston, 1801.

94 NAS GD26/13/687 Sir John Wishart to Alexander, Lord Balgonie [1779–1802].

95 S. Staves, *Married Women's Separate Property in England, 1660–1833* (London: Harvard University Press, 1990).

96 NAS GD1/649/3 The Diary of George Home, 26 March 1700; NAS GD172/2584 Ann Robertson to General Robertson [1779–1783].

97 Frances, 'Making marriages', p. 44.

98 NAS GD1/649/3 The Diary of George Home, 13 November 1700–9 April 1701.

99 NAS GD1/649/2 The Diary of George Home, 22 September 1698–November 1698.

100 Nenadic, *Lairds and Luxury*, pp. 24–9.

101 Vickery, *The Gentleman's Daughter*, p. 40; Eustace, 'Copious work', 525–8.

102 Gillis, *For Better, For Worse*; Vickery, *The Gentleman's Daughter*; P. Borschied, 'Romantic love and material interest; choosing partners in nineteenth century Germany', *Journal of Family History*, 11–12 (1986–7), 157–68.

103 Savile, *New-Year's Gift*, p. 110.

104 NAS GD406/1/2983 Mrs C. Poulett to Earl of Arran, 20 October 1679.

105 Grant, *Seafield Correspondence*, James Ogilvie to the Earl of Findlater, 10 March 1686.

106 NAS GD16/34/200 Letters regarding the marriage of the Marchioness of Huntley and the Earl of Airlie, 1668–69.

107 NAS GD18/5236/1 John Clerk, jnr to John Clerk snr [December 1700].

108 NAS GD25/13/557 James, Earl of Wemyss to David, Earl of Leven, 13 September 1720.

109 Gillis, *For Better, For Worse*, pp. 4–5; Vickery, *The Gentleman's Daughter*, p. 39.

110 NAS GD158/2584/1–7 Hugh, Earl of Marchmont to Elizabeth Crompton, 1747.

111 NAS GD158/2584/1–7 Hugh, Earl of Marchmont to Elizabeth Crompton, 1747.

112 N. Cott, 'Passionlessness: an interpretation of Victorian sexual ideology, 1790–1850', *Signs*, 4 (1978), 219–36.

113 Glasgow City Archive [hereafter GCA] TD1073/1/2 Jessie Graham to Walter Crum [September 1825].

114 GCA TD1073/1/2 Jessie Graham to Walter Crum, 2 August 1826.

115 NAS GD16/34/396 Margaret Bruce to the Earl of Airlie, [c.1838].

116 Layman, *Man of Letters*, pp. 146–54.

117 NAS GD192/31 James Balfour to Anne Macintosh, 2 January 1806.

118 Eustace, 'Copious work'.

119 E. Beveridge (ed.), *Fergusson's Scottish Proverbs from the Original Print of 1641* (Edinburgh: William Blackwood, 1924), p. 123; L. Boose, 'Scolding brides and bridling scolds: taming the woman's unruly member', *Shakespeare Quarterly*, 42 (1991), 179–213; Barker-Benfield, *The Culture of Sensibility*, pp. 299–301.

120 R. Sternberg, *Cupid's Arrow: the Course of Love Through Time* (Cambridge: Cambridge University Press, 1998), p. 69.

121 NAS GD1/51/87 Anne Mylne to [? Name torn off, probably J.W. Brown], [c. late 1760s].

122 An interesting discussion of the relationship between love and reason can be found in N. Luhmann, *Love as Passion: the Codification of Intimacy* (Cambridge: Polity Press, 1986), pp. 94–6.

123 I. Brown, 'Domesticity, friendship and feminism: female aristocratic culture and marriage in England, 1660–1760', *Journal of Family History*, 7:4 (1982), 406–24.

124 D. Richie (ed.), *Early Letters of Jane Welsh Carlyle* (London: S. Sonnenschien & Co, 1889), Jane Carlyle to Miss Stodart, 8 March 1821.

125 Ritchie, *Early Letters,* Jane Carlyle to Miss Stodart, 18 January 1825.

126 NAS GD18/5557 Observations on Miss Cathcart's letters to John Houston, no date. The note is anonymous but is likely Sir John Clerk. The identification of Miss Cathcart is almost certainly correct as the source refers to her as Sir John's sister-in-law and discusses her relationship with her grandparents, Sir John Shaw and Lady Shaw. This would date the source to 1744–54, as Elenora married in 1744 and Marie Anne in 1754. Elenora and John's separation for cruelty is discussed in chapter seven.

127 R. B. Yeazell, *Fictions of Modesty: Women and Courtship in the English Novel* (Chicago: Chicago University Press, 1984), p. 51.

128 See H. More, *Strictures on the Modern System of Female Education* (London: T. Cadell Jun. and W. Davies, 1799), pp. 32–9; J. Fordyce, *Sermons to Young Women* (London: A. Millar and T. Caddel, 1766); J. Raven, 'New reading histories, print culture and the identification of change: the case of eighteenth century England', *Social History*, 23 (1998), 268–87.

129 More, *Strictures*, pp. 32–9.

130 Samuel Richardson in Samuel Johnson, *The Rambler*, no.97 (1750), p. 460, quoted in C. Zschirnt, 'Fainting and latency in the eighteenth century's romantic novel of courtship', *Germanic Review*, 74 (1999), 50.

131 Stone, *The Family*, pp. 270–391.

132 J. Wiltenburg, *Disorderly Women and Female Power in the Street Literature of Early Modern England and Germany* (London: Virginia University Press, 1992), p. 266.

133 N. Eustace, *Passion is the Gale: Emotion, Power and the Coming of the American Revolution* (Chapel Hill: University of North Carolina Press, 2008), pp. 107–50.

4

The construction of patriarchy:
love, obligation and obedience

Despite the rise of Romanticism occasionally being mistaken for its invention, the concept of love has existed in most, if not all, cultures throughout history. Yet, what particular people meant by love and how they expressed love is culturally and historically specific.[1] As Michel Foucault noted, 'every sentiment, particularly the noblest and most disinterested has a history'.[2] While cultural historians, such as Irving Singer and Niklas Luhman, have attempted to describe how the meaning of love in Western Europe has changed over time, there is a tendency in such writing to only think about the concept in the abstract.[3] As a result, how different meanings of love affected people's emotional lives and what the implications were for people's relationships has not been uncovered. More seriously for a study of power systems, and despite observations by feminists that Romantic love reinforced patriarchy, there has been little consideration of how different interpretations of love shaped how women and men viewed each other. This chapter explores the various meanings of love within Scottish marriage over the seventeenth to nineteenth centuries, discussing how people used the language of love within their correspondence, and arguing that constructions of love were deeply implicated in the operation of patriarchy.

Loving behaviour: c. 1650–1730

Meanings of love in seventeenth-century Scotland were informed by the model of 'courtly love' common across Europe.[4] Courtly love was manifested in action, where people demonstrated their love through behaviour – sometimes in dramatic gestures of bravery, but equally in the fulfilment of the mundane responsibilities of the everyday. It operated in a society where obligation and duty were a central part of life, reinforcing the rank and social hierarchies ordained by God, and informing broader understandings of how people interacted. As the sixteenth century French philosopher, Etienne de La Boétie, described it: 'Our nature is such that the common duties of friendship consume a good portion of our lives. It is reasonable to love virtue, respect noble deeds, feel gratitude for the boons we have received, and often to diminish our own comfort in order to increase the honor and advantage of the one we love and who is worthy of it.'[5] Courtly love was understood within a rubric of friendship that emphasised actions – virtue, deeds – and physical realities – boons, comfort –, rather than abstract feeling. Yet, this did not mean that it did not take written expression.

Similarly to elite correspondence in Europe and North America, expressions of love and affection were common in seventeenth-century Scotland.[6] Following the courtly model, elite Scots closely associated love with action. Loving behaviour was an important duty within marriage, especially for men. As was discussed in Chapter 2, husbands promised to love their wives within their marital vows and the law and popular culture understood male love to be demonstrated by their provision and protection of their wives. For women, loving behaviour was synonymous with obedience.[7] The marriage troth was a vow of obligation, where like other friend and kinship rituals, such as the oath of god-parent at baptism, love complexly signified both the fulfilment of duty and the emotional import and intimacy that such commitment entailed.[8] Love was manifested in behaviour, which, in turn, was expected to conform to rank-appropriate patriarchal gender norms. As a result, love reinforced male authority and female subordination.

In the seventeenth century, love was reflected in actions and conveyed in messages that closely linked obligation with affection. Couples used concern over welfare and instructions of care in close correspondence with the term love. The instruction by the Earl of Mar to his wife, Margaret, 'as you love me divert your self & go but once to church at most', which combined love with care, was typical of the period.[9] David, Earl of Leven, in 1692, similarly told his wife, 'my dearest lest tis serve to intreat you to be carefull of your selfe if you wold wish me weel and have me belive you love me'.[10] Women used similar language. Anna, Countess of Leven, concluded a letter to her spouse, 'have a cair of your self my sweet thing I'm sure you will if you regard the quite [quiet] or life of you poor daft wife'.[11] Elizabeth Henderson in 1676 wrote to her husband, 'I deisser that as youe have any love to me that ye could haste home'.[12] As behaviour, love could be rewarded. William, Duke of Hamilton in 1650 thanked his wife for her love, noting 'noe hazard shall keip me from letting you know how sensible I am of the great love and kindness you have always had to me'.[13]

People encouraged others to conform to social norms to enable love. David, Earl of Leven noted to his wife in 1692 that his 'mother says in hirs [her letter] that you are as dear to hir as I am so take care to carry so as to deserve and improve this', indicating that love was born of action.[14] The association between love and behaviour continued into the eighteenth century. In 1733, Archibald Campbell wrote to his wife Christine: 'my tender expressions of love, I know they give you pleasure, but I do assure you that I cannot love you more than you deserve, Oh that I had it in my power to put you in circumstances equal to your merit, … You tell me I must not expect you will write to me every week but will my dearest kirsh deny that pleasure when I beg it as a mark of your love towards me'.[15] Archibald Campbell gave his wife love due to her good behaviour and wished to demonstrate his love through the act of provision. The same conduct that caused Archibald to love Christine signified her love towards her husband. Love was marked by outward behaviour. It could be rationally assessed and compared to the values society established as good and loving, rather than being a unique experience for individuals.

The loving behaviour expected within marriage was not just found within the content of the letter, but built into the structure of the letter, and it is here the inequality of power expected within marriage was both created and framed the rest of its content. Strict hierarchical conventions for address and subscription highlighted the social relationship between reader and writer. The use of such form has been used to imply lack of affection in familial relationships, but they indicate that love and patriarchal authority went hand in hand.[16] In the seventeenth century, forms of address, such as 'My Lord' for a superior or 'Dear Sir' for an equal, and subscription, signing off, marked the social relationship of the reader and writer. 'From your lord's most humble servant' was appropriate for a social inferior addressing a superior, while terms such as affectionate friend or brother indicated a more equal relationship.

Internally letters used common phrases and described gestures that reinforced this social relationship. Inferiors described their desire to kiss the hands of their social superior to denote respect. They apologised for any inconvenience caused by the letter and emphasised their love and duty towards the reader. The conventions and form of letters indicated the nature of the power relationship between reader and writer. Letters between husband and wife used letter-writing conventions that revealed how couples understood their social positioning in regard to each other.

While conventions cannot be used as evidence of the 'reality' of the nature of the relationship between husband and wife, they demonstrated what the writer believed was their status in relation to the reader. It is also problematic to disregard such conventions as insincere.

In the seventeenth century, most elite Scottish couples addressed each other with terms of endearment, marking their intimacy and possession of the other.[17] Sweetheart, dear heart, my dearest, my comfort, my dearest heart were common addresses by both men and women. The manner in which couples addressed each other was unique to marriage and suggested that couples understood the relationship between husband and wife as not directly comparable with similar relationships between social superiors and inferiors. Puritan conduct writers in seventeenth century England warned against such familiarity as it indicated equality inappropriate within the marital relationship and there is evidence that this impacted on the Puritan colonies in America, but there was no such advice in Scotland.[18] Despite this, affectionate addresses did not mean that couples believed they were equal. As in colonial America, women were less likely to use their husband's first names than vice versa and it was not uncommon for them to refer to their husbands as 'My Lord' in the body of the text in the seventeenth and early eighteenth centuries.[19]

The subscription of letters also indicated the nature of the relationship between husband and wife and it is here the connection between love and power was often most clearly observed. In the seventeenth century, many wives subscribed their letters with the words 'loving' and 'obedient'. Christian Kilpatrick signed her correspondence to her husband 'I rest your loving obedient wife.'[20] Katherine Hume ended her letters 'my dear your affectionate and obedient wif'.[21] Christian and Katherine's subscriptions were fairly representative of wives of the period, indicating that most women believed that love and obedience were an expected part of their social relationship with their husbands.

Love and obedience were closely connected in the minds of seventeenth century writers. Yet, this relationship was not always expressed without tension, particularly when the hierarchies of rank clashed with those of gender. Marie Gray in 1651 chose to sign her letters 'your loving & obedient friend Marie Gray'. The term friend was usually used between social equals, suggesting that Marie felt that her obligation of obedience did not impact on her social standing via her husband.[22] The single heiress in this period of study who married a social inferior, the Duchess of Hamilton, never signed herself 'obedient', preferring an affectionate *Adieu*.

Men's letters to their spouses in the seventeenth century demonstrated that men had absorbed their prescribed role as 'loving'
husbands. Husbands usually referred to themselves as affectionate and
loving when signing letters. George Hoome signed his letters 'I rest your
very loving husband G. Hoome'.[23] Lord Ogilvie finished his letters 'I am
your affectionate and loving husband Ogilvy' and on one occasion
noted, 'this shall be the ernest stodie of him who is your affectionat and
loving husband to serve you Ogilvie'.[24] Robert Douglas finished his 'my
dearest your most affectionat husband' and William Hamilton signed
himself 'dear hart & your owne'.[25] Men emphasised their love not their
authority, reflecting both their sense of security in their role as masters
and husbands and revealing social understandings of their role in
respect to their wives.

This framework of address and subscription for correspondence
operated to define the social relationship between writer and reader,
establishing formal lines of power and authority and allowing subordinates to highlight their deference at the outset. This set the context for
the remainder of the discussion within the content of the letter. In some
contexts, as in the case of Marie Gray and the Duchess of Hamilton,
unexpected uses of address and subscription highlight that their social
relationship with their spouse was more complex than suggested by
traditional models for husband and wives. For others, it offered an
opportunity to express anger or chastise a spouse (explored in the next
chapter), knowing that such expression was framed within a context of
loving husband and obedient wife. In this sense, the formal structure of
the letter mirrored the model for marriage during the period.[26] The strict
gender and rank hierarchies, which gave meaning to the practice of
marriage, allowed for flexibility and negotiation within it. How individual action was interpreted was informed by whether it was performed by
a loving husband or an obedient wife, ensuring that while the meaning of
patriarchy was negotiable, it could not be escaped.

Sir Archibald Grant of Monymusk and Anna Potts frequently quarrelled over what it meant to be loving within marriage.[27] In 1740, after
Archibald criticised her resentment at his absence, Anna responded:

> Sir Archibald for god sake what do you mean by yours of the 29th of
> Sept in saying you cant imagine how I can pretend to love you and act
> in so inconsistent a way. I for my part should have thought it had been
> a very strong mark of love that I could not see you leave me with a
> seeming indifference at least without upbraiding you a little bit with it
> but as you know my resolution was not to give you any pain if I could
> help it and as much pleasure as was in my power.[28]

Archibald believed that love was reflected in the fulfilment of duties and responsibilities. He believed his absence, in the pursuit of estate business, reflected his love, not his neglect. He described this model for love repeatedly to Anna over the course of their marriage. During one argument, Archibald, addressing Anna in the third person, noted:

> I have many instances gone beyond my circumstances and inclinations to indeavour to convince her of my love and reguard – when she views my conduct impartially she will see, that all my toils and fatigues, are for her comfort and credit in the world, and a thorow conviction in those things, will excite her, to labour a little likewise for my satisfaction, and for our joint ease and happiness ... And let nothing brake in upon our being mutuall consolations and excitements, in and towards our performance of our dueties.[29]

Anna rejected a model for love directly related to action, drawing on a more abstract definition that was to become increasingly important over the eighteenth century (explored below). She argued: 'I must take my word again and beg of you to have a little mercy and compassion on me let it soften your heart a little to think that tho I have not been the frugal wife you could have wished I have been a most affectionate one and you don't know but the want of affection might some weay or other have given you more pain then the want of management'.[30] Love for Anna was more than fulfilling responsibilities. She conceived of love more abstractly, requiring sentiment as well as action. Yet, she continued to appreciate that the fulfilment of responsibilities conveyed love.

Her need to redefine love was in part an act of resistance in a negotiation over household resources. Anna and Archibald's marriage was fraught with financial problems, as the income from the estate could not keep the household at the level required for their social class. Yet, Archibald, who tended to plough the little money they had into his rather tenuous business ventures, felt that their marital problems could be solved by good household management. Anna could not be the frugal wife Archibald desired and maintain the level of gentility that she felt was necessary for their social rank, perhaps reflecting a conflict between her English upbringing and his Scottish thrift. As a result, a model for love that was based on her ability to fulfil her wifely duties as prudent household manager was incompatible with Anna's belief that she was a loving, obedient wife. Negotiations over the meaning of love were more than an adoption of different social discourses, but a reflection that love was intrinsically linked to patriarchal power. When women questioned what it meant to love, they challenged the nature of patriarchal gender relationships. In many respects, it was the ability of women to create such a challenge that necessitated the backlash against women expressing love within courtship later in the century, described in Chapter 3.

Archibald was aware that his conception of love differed from his wife. He explained in one letter that: 'you much mistake my own heart, and cant act for what I always feel, if I don't love you as much as you could desire; try our mutuall regards by the natturall tendency of your conducts and indeavours towards each other, those will best lead to the true spring and motive whence they flow, and whither they tend; the only sure way to judge of the tree is from the fruits'.[31] Yet, while he attempted to explain that he understood love as more than action, Archibald immediately returned to this model, finding it difficult to articulate love as greater than behaviour. Archibald could not endorse Anna's conception of love, even as he acknowledged it, as it would diminish his authority as patriarch. As Anna and Archibald conceived of love differently, the meaning of love became an area of negotiation and discussion within their marriage. Furthermore, in this particular instance, the debate over what love meant was to continue across their thirteen-year marriage as the couple refused to come to a consensus. Anna refused to relinquish one of her central weapons in her negotiation for power, while Archibald could not agree with her without undermining his authority.

More typically, such debates between couples were resolved as individuals sought quick and peaceful resolution to arguments and it was unusual for women to so actively and consistently resist a more restricted model for loving. As shall be discussed further in the following chapter, such negotiations destabilised a patriarchal system that rested on shared discourses and consensual models for gendered behaviour. As Nicole Eustace explores for eighteenth-century North America, the language of love offered a tool for the negotiation of social power.[32] It could be used to provide a framework for social relationships that emphasised affection and care, but provided enough flexibility to negotiate the terms of power within that relationship. This was to continue into the later part of the century, even as models for loving changed.

That love was related to behaviour did not detract from its impact as a felt emotion, or imply that people were cold or calculated in their relationships. While the vocabulary of the culture of sensibility was not yet popular, the tone of letters revealed that love was experienced as a strong emotion. Lord Ogilvy, in 1651, told his wife of his 'longeing desaier to hier from youe'.[33] In 1676, Elizabeth Henderson told her husband that his image was 'ever in my thoughts' and that she desired his return so that they 'may mit [meet] togover in joy'.[34] Ann, Countess of Arran told her husband that she was uneasy without him, longed to be with him and that 'with all the sincerity in the world that whatever you think no body ever loved an other so well as I do you'.[35] David, Earl of Leven wrote to his wife in 1692, 'I love you more then ever I did'.[36]

There was also a precedent within popular culture for a love that sat uneasily within conceptions of duty. Individuals who forsook their responsibilities to friends and family to elope with inappropriate partners were a recurring narrative. This form of love, however, was seen as a form of madness or self-destructive behaviour and was still closely related to duty, being understood in terms of its rejection of proper social conduct. While love was felt as an emotion, seventeenth-century elite Scots had difficulty articulating that emotional experience without reference to behaviour. The army officer, John Blackadder, wrote to his wife in 1705, 'my inclination would lead me to have you always near me, and if both of us had our wills and wishes, we would never be parted at all. But you must consider, it is not by inclinations we are to be held but by duty'.[37] For Blackadder and his contemporaries, love and duty went hand in hand.

Over the course of the eighteenth century, romantic constructions of love became increasingly popular, but the link between love and social behaviour never entirely disappeared. The minister and conduct author, Samuel Stennett, was still arguing in his conduct literature in 1800 that love ensured that men performed their duty to provide and encouraged them to consult their wives' happiness before acting.[38] The nature of the marital relationship, perhaps unlike that of lovers, required that action would always be an aspect of love for married couples. In the nineteenth century, James Balfour reminded his wife 'to take daily exercise' as 'you are complying with the request and duty what you know will be agreeable to one whom you would wish to please', reminding his wife that her love should be marked by her actions.[39] In the 1830s, Walter and Jessie Crum used the act of letter sending to symbolise their love, gently reminding each other of their desire for more letters: 'I do not grudge a postage at any time from my old woman'.[40] Walter also demonstrated his love through his behaviour, noting on one occasion 'wherever I am my dear Jessie I will think of you both on the 24th and 25th and 26th if I am capable of thinking at all'.[41]

Love within marriage was difficult to separate from action, as marriage required both parties to fulfil their prescribed gender roles. These roles evolved over the period, but the power hierarchy between husband and wife remained. As love within marriage was signified by gender-specific loving behaviour that reinforced the social hierarchy between husband and wife, the patriarchal system was reinforced with every act of love. Love and patriarchal power were intricately entwined.

The culture of sensibility: c. 1720–1850

The move from consanguinity to conjugality, underpinned by demographic growth, urbanisation and the changing nature of the Scottish economy explored in Chapters 1 and 3, led to a need to rethink social relationships in Scotland. If family and a close-knit community no longer comprised the basis of social and economic interaction and instead 'strangers' were incorporated into everyday relationships, how should this new society be conceived? This was a central question of Scottish Enlightenment thought, where thinkers like Frances Hutcheson, Adam Smith, and David Hume tried to conceptualise modern society.[42] While different philosophers envisioned the solution to this problem in slightly different ways, the heart of the new Scottish society was agreed to be 'sensibility'.[43] This model envisioned social relationships to be built upon sympathy, where the moral individual was one who could imagine himself in the place of another and act accordingly. The emphasis on sympathy placed the passions at the heart of social relationships, allowing men, and to lesser extent women, greater emotional expression as they displayed their moral self. At the same time, self-control remained central to the new individual as unrestrained passion led to excess and vice.

The 'culture of sensibility', as this new society has been styled by historians, was coupled with the 'rise of the individual'. In the eighteenth century, the 'modern self' came to being, marked by an inner personality that was original and distinct. In contrast, earlier understandings of self saw a person as one of a 'genus', or type, within which category there could be a reasonable degree of variation. Older understandings of self were more malleable and less intrinsic to the individual.[44] For this reason, as highlighted in Chapter 3, people were happy to marry into good families, without considerable knowledge of the personal characteristics of the individual, in the seventeenth and early eighteenth centuries, as it was the 'genus' of family that defined its members. In contrast, as modern understandings of self developed, society became increasingly concerned with the individual, reflected in the greater significance of love before marriage. Yet, as suggested in Chapter 3 and explored below, this new selfhood was gendered.

The rise of the culture of sensibility had a profound impact on the marital relationships of the Scottish elites. It was coupled with the language of 'romantic love', teaching men and women new emotional expressions, and it provided new ways of thinking about social relationships and self, endangering the hierarchies of power that existed within a concept of love based on gendered behaviour alone. Over the course of the eighteenth century, as the elites became increasingly suspicious of empty gestures and rhetoric, letter-writing conventions adapted to reflect new social values, especially within the family.[45]

As in colonial North and South America, the manner of address in letters adapted to reflect new norms of social expression.[46] Following the pattern in Spanish South America but significantly earlier than in the Northern colonies, nicknames became more personalised and direct use of first names became increasingly common. 'My dearest Betty', 'my dear Clem', 'my dear John', 'thou dear bewitching creature' and 'my dearest puddles' were typical examples. Unlike the middling classes discussed by Mary Beth Norton or the South American colonists examined by Rebecca Earle, elite Scottish couples resisted comparing the marital union to other familial relationships. Describing wives as 'sister' or husbands as 'son' is unknown in Scottish letters; while even a paternal 'my child' from husband to wife is unusual before the late nineteenth century, despite large age gaps.[47] This reflected a desire amongst the Scottish elites to understand marriage and the marital union as a discrete, unique and special relationship.

A move towards seeing marriages as distinctive from each other was also reflected in a decline in prescriptive subscriptions, and from around the 1690s, women no longer used the word 'obedient'. Discussions of love expanded beyond duty and behaviour into descriptions of abstract feeling. It became more powerful, able to sway people into foolish behaviour and disrupt sanity. Love appeared to be a force of its own drifting and infecting people (like a disease), rather than something enacted by individuals. This led to difficulties in identifying whether other people were genuinely experiencing particular emotions, and could even cause confusion for individuals over whether their emotional experiences were genuinely their own (problematic in an era where individualism and 'independence' were becoming increasingly important to ideas of self).[48]

Over the course of the eighteenth century, couples increasingly incorporated the language of sensibility into their letters and, unlike in courtship, women engaged in the conversation. Anne Hamilton's correspondence with her husband, Sir Archibald Grant, in 1720, evidenced the increasing influence of these ideals on people's experiences. On one occasion she noted:

> I expected to have got a latter from you yesternight & owning your
> falt for omitting so many ocaisions but was disappointed upon which I
> sad I would write to you no more but that tearant called love who is
> every day engaging my affections to you more & more brakes throw all
> thes resolutions & what ever treatment I receive from yu beds me be
> stal in my deuty which I hope throu god I shall ever be to both our
> satisfactions.[49]

Anne Hamilton was torn between a belief that love should be shown by
the actions of her husband and her feelings towards him. She thought she
should not write to Archibald as she believed he was neglecting her, yet
her love overcame her intentions. Anne's love acted as the impetus for
her writing rather than her husband's actions. At the same, her letter
suggested that she understood love and duty to be related, with love
inspiring her good performance.

A central theme of the culture of sensibility was love as unity or
union between spouses and this became increasingly important within
their writing over the century. Union was central to the Kirk's understanding of marriage. The wedding service prescribed that man and
woman became 'one flesh' upon marriage. Writers of prescriptive literature developed this concept, suggesting that within marriage women
'cleaved' to their husbands and that 'one flesh' implied that women were
subsumed into their husbands. In the seventeenth and early eighteenth
centuries, expressions of union or unity were usually restricted to
expressions of desire to be together. Katherine Hume of Kimmerghame
noted in 1669 to her husband that 'I be very desirous of your company'.[50]
Ann, Countess of Arran noted in the 1680s that 'I hope you will not be
long before you come & make a visit for I don't know what to do with
myself without you, I am sure if you wish for it half so much as I you will
make haste'.[51] In 1716, Lady Erskine wrote to her husband of her longing
to see him and noted that 'my absence from you is the only suffering I
have'.[52] These writers had a sense that being together was an important
aspect of their marriage and expressed their unhappiness at separation,
yet, they did not generally talk about marriage as a union of mind and
body.

As the eighteenth century progressed, this idea became an increasingly important part of the vocabulary of love. Janet Inglis saw marriage
as a romantic union of souls. Her letters to her husband, John Clerk, in
the 1730s indicated she understood love as a spiritual, as well as legal,
partnership:

> my derest lif how much liking I have for you o my dearst life that
> [w]hom I love as min own soul and nothing in a world I value to you

my direst lami [term of affection, i.e. lamb] or if ever I be false to your self I wish that god may send a have cerus [curse] upon me or if ever you live [leave] me as god forbid or that it should plese god to remov you by death the lord forbid it should be seen to god and the world that I should never love enother whill the breth of lif wear in me and my dir lif I wad not leave you abouv all things in a world.[53]

Janet's love for her husband exceeded worldly experience and was unique to them as a couple. She could not and would never love another. Their marriage was both a physical and spiritual union, yet also a temporal one in which Janet chose to remain. Janet's love was not just inspired by her husband's behaviour, but was a merging of souls. Dorothy Hobart used romance to explain her clandestine marriage in 1752, noting to her aunt, 'I can figure but one situation more insupportable than being deprived of the friendship & affection of all my family, which is living without a hope or prospect of marrying him'.[54]

As the period progressed, this discussion of unity became less a merging of two souls, and increasingly the submersion of the female self into that of her spouse. In the early part of the eighteenth century, the newly developing vocabulary of love had allowed women some latitude and a broad range of expression is found within women's letters. After the mid-century, women clearly absorbed a construction of love that required their emotions to be contained by their husbands and increasingly female discussions of love centred on their husbands. The evangelical author Hannah More described the role of wife as 'one who can assist *him* in *his* affairs, lighten *his* cares, sooth *his* sorrows, strengthen *his* principles, and educate *his* children' [my italics].[55] This was quite consistent with the social messages given to women in an earlier period, that it was men's responsibility to love, women's to be loved, but operated in a slightly different fashion. Marion Buchan emphasised her passion and love for her husband's person, when she wrote to him in 1767, 'How happie it is for me, that yoar affaires does not often require yoar absence [...] who is so very dear to me, whose image is very present with me and whose welfare & happiness is dearer than my own'.[56]

In 1785, Mary Graham described how she would adapt and improve herself to ensure her and her husband's happiness:

[I] long impatiently to have you again you accuse me of impatience in every thing, I wish for judge then what it may be in this case I hope & am fully persuaded you think as much of and to have no doubt of our mutual happiness together having our goodness and patience with my many faults & imperfections which with your assistance & all possible painstakes on my side I hope in time to get the better of &

then nothing will interrupt the joy & satisfaction I have in being your affectionate wife MG.[57]

For Mary Graham, love meant improving and adapting herself to her husband's needs and desires. It was quite typical for eighteenth- and nineteenth-century women to use the language of romance to highlight their subordinate role as helpmeets to their husbands. In 1837, Jessie Crum wrote to her absent husband, 'I hope your present society will yield you much pleasure but not so much as not to make you feel very happy at the prospect of the same little group that were so unwilling to part with you – very soon meeting you & welcoming you back with happy faces'.[58] Like many other women of her generation, Jessie's letters suggested that her home and life revolved around the husband she loved.[59] The romantic belief that love could encompass a person's whole being was interpreted by eighteenth- and early-nineteenth-century elite women in Scotland, like middle-class white women in North America, to mean that their husbands' needs and desires would encompass their whole being.[60]

Increasingly, the manner in which women expressed love revealed their subordination to their husband. Women emphasised the power of love to make them fulfil their duty to their spouse, to adapt their behaviour to their spouses' wishes and to place his person at the centre of their lives. Whether the subordination implied in their letters reflected their practice, or even genuine sentiment, is difficult to gauge, but it underlined that women conceived of female love as revolving around their husbands. They understood that loving wives placed men at the centre of their lives. In this sense, women were denied separate identities as individuals, but instead understood themselves in relation to their spouses. Furthermore, as this model became predominant, women found it more difficult to challenge. Negotiations over the meaning of love became less common and, as explored in the following chapters, women had to find alternative ways to negotiate for power.

Men also used this language for loving, but they gained from women's loss of self. Lucia McMahon, in her exploration of nineteenth-century American diaries, argues that romantic discourse allowed people to express a 'true self' that was validated by a loving partner and so created a form of individualism that was given meaning through relationships with others.[61] Similarly, Rosi Carr shows that independent manhood in a Scottish context required involvement in society, as it was through interaction with others that sensibility and man's innate moral sense flourished. This form of individualism could only operate within modern commercial society, where men were able to become independent from other men through trade. Women's 'natural' feminine qualities helped refine men, but male independence, and thus individualism, was assured through their interaction within the male world of commerce. Scottish Enlightenment discourse denied women independence or agency within this model. Women's social position passively signified male progress; they could not affect change. They were denied individuality.[62] This passivity was reflected in romantic relationship amongst the Scottish elites. Women were not individuals, so their relationships with their spouses acted to validate the male self and to subordinate female identities.

Husbands viewed wives as enabling their individuality and supporting their sense of self, but rarely thought of women as individuals with identities beyond their relationship. Indeed, throughout the period, men continued to refer to their wives' behaviour as inspiring love, rather than their person. In 1733, Archibald Campbell described his love for his wife in the context of her good behaviour, noting:

> Thou dear bewitching creature, dost thou think I would not be vastly fond to have so sure a friend & so sweet a companion always along with me? Without complement to either of us, I have too much sense and justice not to perceive & value the endearing qualities with which my charming wife is adorned, & whereby she has made me a happy husband for so many years. You may judge of my tenderness towards my lovely Kirsth, when I tell you this with tears of fondness on my eyes.[63]

Archibald's passion was evident and, in many respects, his letter was marked by an outpouring of love, yet he related his love to his wife's behaviour. Similarly John Sutherland, when heading into battle during the 1745 Jacobite Rebellion, commented 'My heart bleeds at the thoughts of perhaps, parting with my love for ever, God knows how much I prizes her worth'.[64] As Randolph Trumbach comments for England, 'it is likely that as romantic marriage displaced the arranged, regard for the symbolic property conveyed by marriage was heightened in the minds of men who could not think of loving without owning'.[65]

In 1744, Hew Dalrymple wrote to his wife Margaret Sainthill: 'I need not tell you my dearest creature how passionately I love you your constant behaviour to me your reguard to all my friends your attachment to every part of my interest, fully intitle you to all my love, and in return make you the only earthly thing where all my joys centre and where my heart and soull is fixed'.[66] Hew understood love as inspired by his wife's behaviour, but he also engaged with a more abstract conception of love.

His reference to 'heart and soull' suggested the mystical union of romantic love, rather than a love entirely centred upon behaviour. In another letter, Hew commented to his wife:

> love they say make one not only neglect this world but even forget ones self, but my objections against it makes to me the discovery of what I wanted, for by forgetting my self I see my own errors, and by loving of you my dearest my study and pleasures bend all to the sure wish of promoting your happiness, which is this promise is no other way to be attained then by laying a thurrow order and economy in our private affairs as a basis to owr worldly pleasures and happiness.[67]

Hew saw love as a spiritual experience, but it also gave greater clarity to action.

His writings illustrated a romantic conception of love as exceeding human behaviour, but also motivating and explaining it. Love required a performance of duties, but caused the lover to rise above the mundane. Yet, he did not understand love as entirely spiritual, closely relating it to action. Furthermore, whereas female discussions of love revolved around their husbands, despite his claims to the contrary, Hew's discussion revolves around him, his actions and his interest. He realised that he was the patriarch around whom his household revolved. His wife, and his duties towards her, could only be understood within this framework.

Similarly, in 1750, Hugh, Earl of Marchmont wrote to his wife, Elizabeth, of the 'perfect union of minds & unanimous love' that was their marriage.[68] Hugh emphasised the union of souls he expected from marriage, writing, 'I am fully sensible of the happiness she gives me by that entire union of souls & anonymity of opinion she shows on all occasions & that by her sense & love are really one, as I am entirely hers'.[69] Marchmont claimed that he belonged as entirely to his wife as she did to him, yet his pleasure in her 'anonymity of opinion' suggested he conceived of his wife's will as subsumed within his. Furthermore, in a letter addressed to his wife, Marchmont referred to his reader in the third person, which removed her personhood and operated to make her passive within a form of writing where the reader should exert some power. In another letter, Marchmont stressed his belief that union within marriage implied male authority, noting 'my companion for life, whose compliance is as constant a source of ease & union, as her love is of ecstacy'.[70] He assured his wife:

> you reign my Eliza alone in mine (heart), & every sentiment of it, is subservient to you ... as long as you love me, the most endearing word to my thoughts is wife, because it implies my possession & enjoyment

of you whole love for all my life ... I must be first, & superior, in your heart & thoughts, your affection as a parent, must be derived from you love as my wife.[71]

Robert Moncrieff in 1766 similarly commented to his wife, 'happy for me my dr [dear] wife and I are in this mater as in every thing else that I know of – of one mind'.[72] His comment was in reference to his business' success and perhaps he was correct that his wife shared his opinion on this issue. Yet, that Robert assumed his wife would always share his mind suggests that he expected her to conform to his will, although the addition of 'that I know of' may suggest he realised this was only his ideal.

That women were not understood as independent actors did not reduce the force of love as an emotion for men. Patrick Home told his wife in 1782 that 'heaven is my witness my heart is yours – I belive inalterably soe' and 'you may trust my solem declaration that your happiness and quiet is and will always be the chief care and concern of my life– with these sentiments on my part and the honest feelings of your own heart what is there to disturb your peace'.[73] In the same year, James Grant described his wife as 'so dear and near connection', while, in 1814, David, Earl of Airlie showed empathy for his wife's condition, noting 'it has made me quite miserable, that you are unwell and that I am at such a distance from you I can hardly support it'.[74] Some men wrote poetry for their wives. In 1748, after one year of marriage, Hugh, Earl of Marchmont composed for his wife:

Knowst not my love increases at thy sight
Wheneer I view thee all my souls on fire
Transcends all Homer wrote of heavens great fire.
You need no cestus, you no arts demand,
You love sollicitly, you love command.
Your sight inspires more than fond songs express
To think so pains it, were to make it less.[75]

Marchmont's words reinforced that love was a masculine emotion enacted on his wife. In the 1790s, James Grant demonstrated a conception of love as affecting sanity, when he admitted that love caused him to become jealous. He wrote to his wife:

It is always the case my dearest soul, where there is ardent love there will be a thousand imaginary uneasinesses, which have no foundation but in the brain of the person affected by it, & I believe it is often the case with me, for why should I think that so dear and near connection as you whould mistake one another. Yet jeanie you must forgive me I love and adore you.[76]

Men loved their wives, missed them and felt their absence or loss. Yet, this longing was not based on an equal partnership, but a need for the women who validated men's identities and allowed men to reveal their 'true self' through the sacrifice of their own.

As the eighteenth century moved into the nineteenth, the flowery expression of the culture of sensibility declined, reflecting a growing concern with an appearance of self-control over passion and emotion.[77] This was promoted by Enlightenment theorists. Adam Smith noted that 'all serious and strong expressions of it [love] appear ridiculous to a third person; and though a lover can be good company to his mistress, he is to nobody else.'[78] Some men found it increasingly difficult to express emotion. Archibald Lawrie in 1794 noted to his wife that 'I cannot live, I cannot exist without you. I am perfectly miserable in your absence; I will expect you to tea.'[79] In 1828, Walter Crum wrote to his wife:

> Ma tres chere femme, A mode of address more consonant with the feelings of my – than any which my diffidence allows to use in English … I began this letter to you in a manner more affectionate than you have been accustomed to receive from me though I may take this occasion to remark that you must never suppose me cold to you, although sometimes I may express myself without peculiar warmth & I must take care that I do not lose my newly acquired character by any decadence ending it.[80]

Walter found it difficult to communicate his feelings, apologising to his wife for his inability to express himself more effectively. As the culture of sensibility subsided, elaborate expressions of affection became less culturally acceptable for men and were less available within cultural discourse for men to adopt in their correspondence. However, while they were less likely to use flowery expressions, this did not reflect a change in ideas about love. Love continued to subordinate women into their husband's identity, reinforcing the male individual.

The greater use of romantic expressions within letters in the eighteenth and nineteenth centuries corresponded with a declining emphasis on formal addresses and subscriptions in couple's letters.[81] The word obedient disappeared from women's subscriptions, while men were increasingly denoted as 'belonging' to their wives. In the 1730s, Alexander Campbell signed his letters to his wife 'My dearest your own loanely slave', and 'my dearest yours more than my own'.[82] John Sutherland signed one letter in 1746 'I am till my latest breath my dearest angel with boundless affection yours John Sutherland' and another 'my dearest life & love your own unalterably'.[83] In 1766, Robert Scott

Moncrieff finished his letter 'belive me my dearest Jeany's own R Scott'.[84] Hugh, Earl of Marchmont in 1740s signed letters to his wife 'being as entirely & sincerely mine as I am yours' and 'yes love yours & only yours, & all your & ever yours'.[85]

Women increasingly emphasised their affection for their partners, concluding their letters in a similar fashion to men the century before. In the early eighteenth century, Elizabeth Hay subscribed her letters 'how affectionately I am yours', and Mary Campbell ended hers 'my deare yours very affactionetly'.[86] This change in style continued throughout the century, although increasingly subscriptions were abbreviated or standardised. Ann Robertson signed her letters to her spouse in 1781 'I ever am etc', while James Grant in 1800 and David Monro in 1835 concluded their correspondence 'your most affect'.[87] An analogous change occurred in nineteenth century Colonial South America as couples increasingly regarded excessively romantic language as 'tiresome insincerities'.[88] This change in how couples addressed each other may superficially suggest a reversal of power, but while men expanded their language to incorporate terms of deference, there is no evidence that women's subscriptions expanded to include terms of power or authority. The rise of the culture of sensibility did not mark a watershed in women's position within society, but reinforced patriarchal understandings of marriage.

Love was required of men within marriage as it was believed that a loving husband would not tyrannise his wife, but temper his authority. A husband's behaviour was modelled on that of a loving God, whose power was marked by benevolence. In turn, women were not expected to love like men, but to reflect their love and affection through their obedience to their spouses. Female love was to be devoid of authority, marking only their subordination. The act of loving was not disinterested, but distinctly gendered, reinforcing the patriarchal system. Within a seventeenth-century context, love was conceived as directly related to action. Loving behaviour was associated with the fulfilment of ideal models of conduct based upon gender. Men were expected to demonstrate their love through the act of provisioning and protecting their families, while women were to show their love through obedience and the competent management of the household. Men and women who could, or would, not conform to these roles were thought be unloving, an accusation that most strongly resisted. As is described in Chapter 3, even within arranged marriages, love was considered vital by the Scottish elites.

While the meaning of love altered with the rise of the culture of sensibility to emphasise the individual and sentiment, it was still rooted in a gendered conception of love. Like its predecessor, the culture of sensibility conceived of love as a feeling that men bestowed on women and which they demurely accepted. As explored in Chapter 3, women were restricted from expressing love before marriage as it offered them the authority that love had always held. Within marriage, women were allowed to express love, but it was increasingly a form of love that revolved around men and subsumed female identity within the male. Where women, like Anna Potts, tried to utilise more assertive conceptions of love, it was strongly resisted. In many ways, romantic love was more restrictive than a love based on behaviour. Women in the seventeenth century could still hold identities as well-behaved (or disobedient) wives; women, under Enlightenment thought, effectively disappeared. In eighteenth-century conceptions of love, women could only be understood in relation to men. They lost the discourses necessary to create independent identities as loving wives.

The culture of sensibility transformed love into an abstract concept that was considered vital and necessary within marriage and was more difficult to subvert. If a woman wished to be 'in love', she endorsed a model for gender relationships that subsumed her identity under that of her husband. To marry without love was immoral. Women were left with the alternatives of marriage and security, but a loss of selfhood, or the insecurities and economic challenges of singleness. For many elite women, the choice of alternatives was not theirs to make. This, in part, explains the significance of 'romantic friendships' to elite women in the eighteenth and nineteenth centuries, which allowed an outlet for female emotional expression and identity beyond men.[89] It also helped create the tensions that Laura Gowing observes female friendship created when it distracted women from giving their full attention to marriage.[90]

While love has often been discussed as in conflict with, or tempering, the patriarchal system, within the period under study, love was one of its central underpinnings. Conceptions of love and the act of loving reinforced a model for gender that was inherently unequal. The patriarchal system relied on the fact that love was a central and required part of marriage, which people were heavily invested in maintaining. The seductive promise of love allowed it to hide a complex system that enforced male authority and female subordination. While some women tried to resist this model of love, their voices were drowned out by a sea of poetry and romantic expression that, somewhat deceptively, promised to transform human relationships, even as it reinforced their oppression. The act of loving was patriarchy in practice.

Notes

1   C. Stearns and P. Stearns, 'Introducing the history of the emotion', *Psychohistory Review*, 18 (1990), 263–91.

2   M. Foucault, 'Nietzsche, genealogy, history', *Language, Counter-Memory, Practice* (Ithaca: Cornell University Press, 1977), p. 153.

3   N. Luhmann, *Love as Passion: the Codification of Intimacy* (Cambridge: Polity Press, 1986); I. Singer, *The Nature of Love 2: Courtly and Romantic* (Chicago: Chicago University Press, 1984).

4   Luhmann, *Love as Passion*, pp. 94–108; Singer, *The Nature of Love*.

5   Quoted in Y. Castan, 'Politics and private life', in R. Chartier (ed.), *A History of Private Life: Passions of the Renaissance* (London: Harvard University Press, 1989), p. 21.

6   R. Earle, 'Letters and love in colonial Spanish America', *The Americas*, 62:1 (2005), 40.

7   H. Tissari, *Lovescapes: Changes in Prototypical Senses and Cognitive Metaphors since 1500* (Helsinki: Societe Neophilologique, 2003), pp. 274–5.

8   For a discussion of other forms of friend and kinship oath, see A. Bray, *The Friend* (London: Chicago University Press, 2003).

9   NAS GD124/15/231 John, Earl of Mar to Margaret, Countess of Mar, 16 June 1704.

10   NAS GD26/9/23/3 David, Earl of Leven to Anne Wemyss, 8 August [1692].

11   NAS GD26/13/418/1 Anne Wemyss to David, Earl of Leven [c. 1692].

12   NAS GD18/5175/2 Elizabeth Henderson to John Clerk, 11 April 1676.

13   NAS GD406/1/2489 William, Duke of Hamilton to Elizabeth Maxwell, 11 October 1650.

14   NAS GD26/9/23 David, Earl of Leven to Anne Wemyss, 11 August [1692].

15   NAS GD461/14/14 Archibald Campbell to Christina Watson, 10 May 1733.

16   L. Stone, *The Family, Sex and Marriage in England 1500–1800* (London: Weidenfeld and Nicolson, 1977), p. 123 uses this evidence in this manner.

17   L. Maguire, '"Household Kates": Chez Petruchio, Percy and Plantagenet', in S. P. Cerasano and M. Wynne-Davies (eds), *Gloriana's Face: Women, Public and Private in the English Renaissance* (New York: Harvester Wheatsheaf, 1992), pp. 129–36.

18   R. Grassby, *Kinship and Capitalism: Marriage, Family, and Business in the English-Speaking World, 1580–1740* (Cambridge: Cambridge University Press, 2001), p. 90; M. B. Norton, *Liberty's Daughters: The Revolutionary Experience of American Women* (Ithaca: Cornell University Press, 1980), p. 62.

19   Norton, *Liberty's Daughters*, pp. 61–2.

20   For example, NAS GD18/5215 Christian Kilpatrick to John Clerk, 17 September 1698.

21   For example, NAS GD158/2720/1 Katherine Hume to Laird of Kimmerghame, 15 October 1669.

22   NAS GD18/5161 Marie Gray to John Clerk, 18 February 1651.

23   NAS GD158/2712 G. Hoome to Isobel Hoome [c. 1659].

24   NAS GD16/34/23/1 Lord Ogilvy to Helen Ogilvy, 8 May 1651; NAS GD16/34/23/1 Lord Ogilvy to Helen Ogilvy [1653].

25   NAS GD446/40/2 Robert Douglas of Strathenry to Susanna [c. 1694]; NAS GD406/1/2488 William Hamilton to Elizabeth Maxwell, 8 September 1651.

26   A similar point is made in I. H. Tague, 'Love, honour and obedience: fashionable women and the discourse of marriage in the early eighteenth century', *Journal of British Studies*, 40 (2001), 76–106.

27 For an extended discussion of their marriage, see K. Barclay, 'Negotiating patriarchy: the marriage of Anna Potts and Archibald Grant of Monymusk, 1731–1744', *Journal of Scottish Historical Studies*, 28:2 (2008), 83–101.

28 NAS GD345/1146/64 Anna Potts to Archibald Grant, 15 October 1740.

29 NAS GD345/1146/4/8 Archibald Grant to Anna Potts, 15 August [1739?].

30 NAS GD345/1146/74 Anna Potts to Archibald Grant, 28 May 1740.

31 NAS GD345/1146/2/6 Archibald Grant to Anna Potts, 19 April 1740.

32 N. Eustace, *Passion is the Gale: Emotion, Power and the Coming of the American Revolution* (Chapel Hill: University of North Carolina Press, 2008), p. 149.

33 NAS GD16/34/23/1 Lord Ogilvy to Helen Ogilvy, 8 May 1651.

34 NAS GD18/5175 Elizabeth Clerk to John Clerk, 11 April 1676.

35 NAS GD406/1/6990 Ann, Countess of Arran to James, Earl of Arran [c. 1688].

36 NAS GD26/13/420 David, Earl of Leven to Anna, Countess of Leven, 31 July [1692].

37 A. Chricton (ed.), *Life and Diary of Col. John Blackadder* (Edinburgh: H.S. Baynes, 1924), John Blackadder to Elizabeth Callander, 20 May 1705.

38 S. Stennett, *Discourses on Domestic Duties* (Edinburgh: J. Ogle, 1800), p. 136.

39 NAS GD192/29/37 James Balfour to Anne Balfour, 20 October [1807].

40 GCA TD1073/2 Walter Crum to Jessie Crum, 7 August [1832 or 1833].

41 GCA TD1073/2 Walter Crum to Jessie Crum, 23 April 1827.

42 J. Dwyer, 'The construction of community in eighteenth-century Scotland', *History of European Ideas*, 16:4–6 (1993), pp. 943–8.

43 For a detailed discussion see, P. Carter, *Men and Emergence of Polite Society, Britain 1660–1800* (Harlow: Longman, 2001); G.J. Barker-Benfield, *The Culture of Sensibility: Sex and Society in Eighteenth Century Britain* (Chicago: Chicago University Press, 1992); J. Dwyer, *The Age of Passions: an Interpretation of Adam Smith and Scottish Enlightenment Culture* (East Linton: Tuckwell Press, 1998).

44 D. Wahrman, *The Making of the Modern Self: Identity and Culture in Eighteenth Century England* (London: Yale University Press, 2006).

45 A thorough discussion can be found in M. Nevala, *Address in Early English Correspondence: its Forms and Socio-pragmatic Functions* (Helsinki: Societe Neophilologique, 2004). Niklas Luhmann comments on the distrust of rhetoric and empty gestures more widely in society in *Love as Passion*, p. 106.

46 C. Deglar, *At Odds: Women and the Family in America from the Revolution to the Present* (Oxford: Oxford University Press, 1980), pp. 38–40. Earle, 'Letters and love', 40–1.

47 Norton, *Liberty's Daughters*, p. 62; Earle, 'Letters and love'.

48 A. Pinch, *Strange Fits of Passion: Epistemologies of Emotion, Hume to Austen* (Palo Alton: Stanford University Press, 1996), pp. 1–7.

49 NAS GD345/1145/7 Anne Hamilton to Archibald Grant, 22 July 1720.

50 NAS GD158/2720/3 Katherine Hume to the Laird of Kimmerghame, 29 October 1669.

51 NAS GD406/1/6990 Ann, Countess of Arran to James, Earl of Arran [c. 1688].

52 NAS GD1/44/7 Lady Erskine to John Erskine of Alva [March 1716];

53 NAS GD18/5289/4 Janet Inglis to John Clerk [c.1730].

54 NAS GD40/9/154/38 Dorothy Hobart to Lady Suffolk, 25 August 1752.

55 H. More, *Strictures on the Modern System of Female Education* (London: T. Cadell Jun. and W. Davies, 1799), p. 97.

56 NAS GD180/635 Marion Buchan to Robert Cathcart [c. 1767].

57 NLS MS16002 Mary Graham to Thomas Graham [c.1785–6].

58 GCA TD1073/1/8 Jessie to Walter Crum, 12 September 1837.

59 A similar phenomenon is also discussed in H. Wilcox, 'Private writings and public functions: autobiographical texts by Renaissance Englishwomen', in Cerasano and Wynne-Davies, *Gloriana's Face*, pp. 50–1.

60 Norton, *Liberty's Daughters*, p. 62.

61 L. McMahon, '"While our souls together blend": narrating a Romantic readership in the early Republic', in P. Stearns and J. Lewis (eds), *An Emotional History of the United States* (London: New York University Press, 1998), p. 68.

62 R. Carr, 'Gender, national identity and political agency in eighteenth century Scotland' (PhD Dissertation, University of Glasgow, 2008), pp. 141–2.

63 NAS GD461/14/13 Archibald Campbell to Christina Watson, 3 May 1733.

64 NAS GD139/526/1 John Sutherland to Emelia Sutherland [1746].

65 R. Trumbach, *The Rise of the Egalitarian Family* (Oxford: Academic Press, 1978), p. 150.

66 NAS GD110/1084/1 Hew Dalrymple to Margaret Sainthill [July 1744].

67 NAS GD110/1084/4b Hew Dalrymple to Margaret Sainthill, 2 July 1744.

68 NAS GD158/2584/22 Hugh, Earl of Marchmont to Elizabeth Crompton, 26 August, 1750.

69 NAS GD158/2584/17 Hugh, Earl of Marchmont to Elizabeth Crompton, 16 August 1750.

70 NAS GD158/2584/19 Hugh, Earl of Marchmont to Elizabeth Crompton, 21 August 1750.

71 NAS GD158/2584/23 Hugh, Earl of Marchmont to Elizabeth Crompton, 30 August 1750.

72 Underlined in original. NAS GD361/1 Robert Scott Moncrieff to Jean Hogg, 1766.

73 NAS GD267/3/8/4 Patrick Home to Jane Graham [c. 1782]. and GD267/3/8/1 Patrick Home to Jane Graham, 16 March 1782.

74 NAS GD248/515/2 James Grant to Jane Duff [c. 1782]; NAS GD16/34/379/53 David, Earl of Airlie to Clementina, 30 June 1814.

75 NAS GD158/2584/10/2 Hugh, Earl of Marchmont to Elizabeth Crompton [1748].

76 NAS GD248/515/2 James Grant to Jane Duff [c. 1790].

77 J. Fea, 'Presbyterians in love: or the feeling Philip Vickers Fithian', *Common-Place*, 8:2 (2008) [http://www.common-place.org/vol-08/no-02/fea/, accessed 10/02/2009].

78 A. Smith, *The Theory of Moral Sentiments* (London: Henry G. Bohn, 1853), p. 39.

79 NAS GD461/126/8 Archibald Lawrie to Anne Adair, 1794.

80 GCA TD1073/2 Walter Crum to Jessie Crum, 3 October 1828.

81 This is demonstrated within Nevala, *Early English Correspondence*, pp. 245–8.

82 NAS GD128/35/5a Alexander Campbell of Clunes to his wife 'my dearest', 14 June 1737 and 3 May 1737.

83 NAS GD139/256/2 John Sutherland to Emelia Sutherland [1746] and GD139/256/5 John Sutherland to Emelia Sutherland, 18 November 1749.

84 NAS GD361/1 Robert Scott Moncrieff to Jean Hogg [1766].

85 NAS GD158/2584/2 Hugh, Earl of Marchmont to Elizabeth Crompton [c. 1747]; NAS GD158/2584/5 Hugh, Earl of Marchmont to Elizabeth Crompton, 2 January 1748.

86   NAS GD248/561/51/1 Elizabeth Hay to Lord Deskford, 21 November 1714; NAS
      GD112/39/107/4 Mary Campbell to John Campbell, Earl of Breadalbane, 10
      September [early 18th century].
87   NAS GD172/2584/1 Ann Robertson to General Robertson [c. 1781]; NAS GD71/404
      David Monro to Eliza Bennett [c. 1835]; NAS GD248/368/8 James Grant to Jane
      Grant [c.1800].
88   Earle, 'Letters and love', 41.
89   L. Faderman, *Surpassing the Love of Men: Romantic Friendship and Love between
      Women from the Renaissance to the Present* (New York: William Morrow and Co,
      1981), pp. 85–102.
90   L. Gowing, 'The politics of women's friendship in early modern England', in L.
      Gowing, M. Hunter and M. Rubin (eds), *Love, Friendship and Faith in Europe,
      1300–1800* (Basingstoke: Palgrave Macmillan, 2005), pp. 146–7.

5

The negotiation of patriarchy: intimacy, friendship and duty

ntimacy within modern society is increasingly understood to be a mechanism for reducing inequalities of power within romantic relationships. As Theodore Zeldin argues, modern intimacy is about two individuals being able to interest and stimulate each other, enabling them to grow as people, with recognition that they may not be able to fully meet the needs of each other.[1] Anthony Giddens suggests that the democratisation of intimacy is well underway in modern society, with the principle of autonomy as its guiding thread, where individuals relate to each other 'in an egalitarian way'.[2] Intimacy in the modern imagination is meant to dissolve power, which stands in the way of closeness and personal development. It promotes the needs of the individual and so should allow them greater freedom of expression of those needs and of their desires. In many senses, it mirrors classical ideas of higher friendship based on 'equality, choice, complementarity, mutual esteem and the possibility of reciprocal education'.[3]

Yet, intimacy's operation is dependent on historical situation. Rather than being a stable concept with a particular meaning, intimacy is a historical construct and, like love, is enacted differently in various contexts. If it has a unifying concept, it is that it relates to interaction within close, usually interdependent, relationships. For Zeldin, modern intimacy replaced an older model based on romantic ideals where intimacy was marked by the union of two souls, and the individual disappeared rather than flourished. This, in turn, displaced an understanding of intimacy, which was synonymous with domesticity, and marked by touch.[4] These changes were mirrored by transformations in ideas about love, described in the previous chapter, and new understandings of 'self'. Within a patriarchal society, the practice of intimacy was informed by the expected social hierarchies that shaped social relationships, yet, as will be highlighted within this chapter, it also carried democratic potential, as the interdependence of intimate relationships required greater flexibility and negotiation than suggested by prescriptive models. This chapter looks at changing ideas around the nature of the marital relationship, relating to obedience, duty, friendship and finally domesticity, to explore the practice of intimacy within marriage across the seventeenth to nineteenth centuries.

Obedience and duty

Within a seventeenth century framework, the act of marriage created an intimate relationship, which was demonstrated through the fulfilment of duty and obligations determined by gender. A husband's primary duties were to love, provide and protect, while a wife was to obey. The extent to which an intimate relationship was truly 'intimate' was determined by the willingness of people to perform their role, and even to exceed that role through sacrifice or performance in difficult circumstances. As such, an exploration of how women performed obedience is a discussion of how they performed intimacy; just as the discussion of how men performed love in the previous chapter highlighted their place in the intimate relationship of the period. The meaning of wifely obedience, like that of love, was open to negotiation, and it was in that space that women were able to shape the dynamics of power within their marital relationship, reducing the strictures of patriarchy. It was also in that space that early modern intimacy resembled modern conceptions of intimacy that promote sharing of ideas, discussion, and democracy.

In the seventeenth century, intimacy, like love, was performed in a framework of gesture and action, where duty and obligation underpinned social life. Behaviour signified the nature of the broader relationship, hence the importance of bowing and the kissing of rings and hands by social subordinates. The physical body was central to performances of intimacy, where a kiss on the lips or cheek demonstrated friendship, and sleeping together, as is indicated by the shared bed of the Scottish Angus MacDonald and the Irish Earl of Tyrone during alliance negotiations, indicated unity and reciprocal obligation.[5] The shared bed was a particularly important motif of intimacy within marriage, and one that prevailed into the nineteenth century. Elizabeth Hamilton, in 1704, complained to her husband that she could not sleep without him.[6] In the same year, the Earl of Mar asked his wife not to take another bedfellow as he would soon return and 'you'll have one that loves you better than any you can get'.[7] Alexander Campbell complained to his wife in 1737 that 'thinking & wishing hourly for you' prevented him from sleeping, while a century later, Jessie Crum informed her husband that she had taken her daughter to sleep with her as a comfort in his absence.[8] In 1795, Archibald Lawrie informed his wife that 'I have not slept one night since you left me, I cannot live nor exist without you.'[9]

As Alan Bray highlights, the body could operate as a gift of intimacy and could be represented through the giving of 'bodily tokens', such as the kiss, the public embrace and the sharing of bed and table, although not always without ambiguity of meaning.[10] Over distance, the letter hand-written by the giver (as opposed to a scribe or secretary) was symbolic of intimacy and the physical letter acted a relic, representing the absent loved-one, which could be read and reread, held, stored in clothes or private closets, and even wept over.[11] In the seventeenth century, the Scottish elites emphasised that letter writing denoted affection, but also fulfilment of obligation. In a letter to her son shortly after his marriage, Anne, Duchess of Hamilton asked him to tell his new father-in-law:

> I am on[e] that loves to be easie to those I am related to and since I have now the honour to be that to them that they use all freedome with me and whare thare is most of that there is the greatest friendship, I have heard you say my lord presedent does not love to write letters so I desire you may render him from that ceremonial part to me I have so much cause to know his friendship by actions.[12]

In 1717, Anne Hamilton of Monymusk scolded her husband for not writing to her, especially as he had found the time to write to his brother and had missed their wedding anniversary. She noted: 'that you was so busies that you had not time to write a long enough on[e] to me which seemeth to me but a very poor excuse for I should look on my self as worse than an infidel [if] I should find time to write to a brother [but] could not spear non to write to my husband.'[13] As Miriam Slater has noted for love and respect in the seventeenth century England, intimacy could be institutionally created through proscribed behaviour, or a renegotiation of that behaviour.[14]

As suggested in the previous chapter, the seventeenth-century concern with duty and obligation shaped gender relationships within marriage, which in turn affected how intimacy was understood and negotiated between men and women. The central duty of women within marriage was obedience to their husbands, and within modern constructions, it is this duty that is often seen as obstructing intimacy within marriage. As such, it is worth exploring how obedience was understood and interpreted and how it created and hindered intimacy during the period. Obedience was promised from the outset in the marriage vows, and reinforced by understandings of marriage in law and culture. In Scotland, like in other parts of Europe, young women were reminded from childhood of the centrality of obedience to their later lives and they married keenly aware of the implications.[15] Even as late as 1770, one young unmarried woman commented to a single female friend of a wedding she attended, putting a new perspective on weeping women at weddings: 'I found myself quiet melted but especially when he said these words dutifull wife & husband till death just them, I found the tears start in my eyes to think I would certainly draw back at these words with terror as from a dreadfull prejudice or when one thinks it is forever – how it makes us fear every evil that can happen.'[16]

Obedience was an accepted part of wifely duty and most women responded angrily to accusations that they behaved otherwise. Katherine Hamilton resisted any implication of disobedience in a terse exchange with her mother-in-law in 1684. She noted:

> I give yr lady many thanks for the good advice you give me to be an obedient wife which I intend to make my studey & as yet my lord has not tld me that I please him onley in his fidell fadells [little things] & so long as he is <pleased > [above the line] content with me I doe not intend to truble my selfe the others think me an ill wife, & I shall allwise thrive as I have don hererto not to come short of my duty to my lord Marquess & yr ladys[hip] [her in-laws].[17]

Despite this concern, in letters between spouses there was some discomfort with using the term 'obey', outside the reference to 'obedient' wife in subscripts of the late seventeenth and early eighteenth centuries.

Obey was used infrequently in correspondence and when it appeared it was very consciously for effect. In 1669, Katherine Hume apologised to her husband for her lack of news and noted that she wrote to him 'bot to obey you to let you her [hear] we are al wel.'[18] In the 1680s, the Duke of Hamilton used obey playfully when writing to say he had followed his wife's instructions, 'I have obeyed you command in not tutching of them.'[19] The word command was similarly rare. In 1676, Elizabeth Henderson wrote to her husband, only partly in jest, 'I command youe to come home for my mend kan have no rest tell I sei youe.'[20] Couples reluctantly issued commands to each other, expecting cooperation and respect from spouses. When either party wished to place emphasis on a request, they referred to love not obedience as motivation.

While women did not explicitly use words like obey, they did use deferential language. In 1704, Anna, Countess of Leven drew on the model of the deferent wife to persuade her husband to allow her to join him in Edinburgh. She wrote, 'I had the satisfaction of two letters from you this day & I shall be very glade to get another shortly ordering me to come over'. She continued with a lengthy plea for him to send for her, finishing with a request 'not to be angrie with my importuning you to send for me'.[21] Some women, like Margaret Hamilton, Countess of Panmure in the early eighteenth century, talked deferentially to their husbands in their general correspondence so that when they were angry or insistent upon a certain issue, there was a noticeable change in writing style.[22]

Men also adopted patriarchal language, which was especially evident in the paternalistic advice they offered their wives. While awaiting execution in 1650, William, Duke of Hamilton advised his wife on her future conduct. As head of his household, and perhaps following the advice of conduct writers, William felt responsible for advising his family on their religious salvation and behaviour. His advice to his wife was similar to that which he offered the rest of his family. He noted, 'be not too confident of your owne opinions but examine them by the tuchston of Gods word, and refuse not to hear the admonition of his servants'.[23] In the early eighteenth century, Archibald Grant sent his wife numerous passages from sources that described ideal female conduct in his effort to improve their relationship. On one occasion he reminded her 'prudence and good temper can often procure happiness even in forced matches; and a discreet and well timed compliance on the one side can soften and correct the most perverse and obstinate disposition in the other'.[24]

The tone in which most advice was given, however, highlighted that husbands felt that it was beneficial to relate to their wives in terms of mutuality and negotiation, rather than enforcing a strict hierarchy of power. Even when there was a need to discipline wives, men attempted to address problems in terms of a failure of a broader duty that bound them all in society, rather than a direct act of authority from husband to wife. In 1705, John Blackadder, when on campaign in the Netherlands, wrote to his wife, Elizabeth Callander:

> I just now received you letter wherin you beg a thousand pardons for quarrelling with me without reason. I take your submission and pardoned you before you sought it ... I am very thankful to God I have such a wife who need not commands or authority to oblige to duty, and needs no more but to have duty pointed out, and to be advised to it; and I do you but justice to say that I have always found that duty, and sense of duty, pleasantly determines both your judgement and your will.[25]

David, Earl of Leven reproached his wife for being careless with her health, writing 'my dearest, I can abstean no longer from chiding with you, and I shall leve it to your selfe to judge if I have reason'.[26] The act of allowing his wife to determine whether his criticism was valid reduced the harshness of his words, but also pointed to an external measure of duty which both husband and wife could access in negotiations over acceptable behaviour.

While people shared broadly similar ideas about what constituted duty and obligation, in practice it was not always clear what was the best course of action for a household or relationship. This created a place for negotiation within marriage, and it was widely accepted that women could participate in such discussions. Craig Muldrew shows that in the medieval and early modern world, there was significant emphasis on being at peace with one's neighbours that led to an emphasis on interpersonal bargaining.[27] Linda Pollock argues, when discussing conceptions of honour, that for early modern men honour was not about shared opinion, but shared discussion, with compromise preferable to violence. She suggests that men were taught that conflict should be resolved through reconciliation, not imposing will.[28] A similar principle can be seen in operation within marriage. While women used deferential language, this did not mean that they always agreed with their husbands or took criticism without complaint. As Bernard Capp notes, 'it is clear that few women … equated subordination with submissiveness'.[29] Margaret McDonald in 1660 responded with irritation to her husband, James Montgomerie's, suggestion that she did not write frequently, replying, 'indeed I omitted no occasion but to my lord write and never told me till his letters were gon but if I war where I could have as good occasion as you have I should be more trublesom to you with my letters than you ar to me with yours'.[30]

Wives felt free to express their opinions, while husbands were usually content to allow their wives a degree of freedom of expression. In the 1730s, Anna Potts informed her husband that his criticism of her household management was unwarranted, commenting,

> Realy sir Archibald I can [not] tell what you expect from me, I live as frugally as I can and I think my misfortunes great enough, without your constant teasing me with the want of œconomy if want of health renders me incapable of being one of the notable wives, I cant help it, I doe my best and shall continue to do so and if these endeavours don't please I am still the more unfortunate'.[31]

After ten years of marriage and still receiving the same criticism, Anna's response was less subdued. She wrote, 'it is no ill management in me I cant work miracles and must tell you plainly I am vain enough to think my self as capable of governing a house as any of those that finds fault wit me'.[32] Unlike in early modern England, obedience to a husband did not mean suppressing anger or frustration.[33]

Yet, a willingness to listen to wives' opinions did not necessarily equate with equality within marriage. In some relationships, it reflected a desire to be conciliatory, rather than to give equal weight to women's voices. When Christina Watson was angry with her husband in 1724, she informed him that she would no longer write to him. After she relented her husband acknowledged that he was relieved and noted that 'however I say I am glad that you have returned to a way which in my opinion is far more prudent & that much better becomes a kind and affectionate wife'.[34] Archibald did not order his wife to write to him, but allowed her time to calm down. His patronising response suggests he thought her behaviour childlike or 'womanly'. Archibald was happy to allow his wife to speak freely to him and express her opinion, as he was sure in his position of head of house. It was only someone who was insecure in his role that needed to control every aspect of his wife's behaviour. Other men took their wives' criticisms with good humour, but whether they had any intention of acting on them is less clear. Hew Dalrymple relented in an argument in 1749 with his wife after she responded angrily to a criticism. He apologised: 'I own my dearest creature I was in the wrong to attack your gentle nature in so strong terms'.[35]

There were circumstances where women could gain the upper hand in negotiations with their husbands. When women felt that they were lacking in authority, they could resort to manipulation to regain control. In 1704, Elizabeth Hamilton used what authority she had within marriage to persuade her husband to change his mind. She informed her husband that she would not join him in Edinburgh unless he agreed to change doctors, as she was convinced his health was not improving, despite his insistence that it was.[36] In the last decade of the seventeenth century, Anna, Countess of Leven regularly used her ill-health and that of their children to persuade her husband to return home or to send for her. She closely tied her well-being to his and when he was away on campaign with his regiment, she reminded him that if he was injured it 'would very soon make an end of me'.[37] Anna drew on a discourse of husband as protector to give weight to her requests.

Other women held greater authority in marriage due to their wider social position. The copious amount of surviving letters written between

Anne, Duchess of Hamilton and her husband, William, highlights the complexity of negotiating marriage in the late seventeenth century. Anne and William's relationship was more complicated than most couples as Anne held the titles to the estate and as such was head of the family. Despite her gender, Anne never referred to herself as 'obedient', instead emphasising their shared interest and mutuality. As head of the family, she technically had final say on a number of decisions, including large expenditures (like marriage settlements), and the family's political stance. Yet, how the couple negotiated the tension between her role as head of the family and his as patriarch suggested that this was not simply a case of rank overcoming gender. Anne was always respectful and at times deferent and it was clear this was decision on her part to fulfil her wifely duty. Decisions were made through discussion and cooperation, which contrasted sharply with Anne's interaction with her children where she overtly exerted her position as head.

William was regularly away from home, representing Anne's interests at court. Their correspondence highlighted how they conferred and came to a compromise on issues as mundane as the selection of furniture to concerns as significant as seeking posts for their sons from the King. In 1693, the Duke of Hamilton, writing to his wife during an argument over their son's future, noted, 'I must tell you I differ absolutely wit yur opinion that those palaces ar fittest for young noblemen, I think the oldest & of best quality & parts ar the fittest to keep the ordinary lord on some order to take notice what they do, however take out my letter or not as you think fitt'.[38] On another occasion, he informed her that he disagreed with her wish that he ask for the position as commissioner of the assembly, noting that 'things are far otherwise then you can comprehend at distance & I can not inform you this way', yet his tone suggests that he would have otherwise took her advice.[39]

At times, the Duke explicitly sought out his wife's opinion. In 1693, he asked her whether he should ask the King for a post on a 'quorium' of the treasury and what he should to do to serve the King if he is rejected.[40] The trust and respect they showed for each other's judgement was not atypical of the period, but where they differed was that Anne's authority meant that her opinion held considerable weight and at times the final decision was hers to make. In many respects, the dynamics of this marriage perhaps most closely related to a modern conception of equality. Yet, this equality was not based on a general belief that human beings were equal to each other, but on equality created through a balancing of the disadvantages of the female gender with the privileges of rank.

Some women gained authority unexpectedly, especially at times of social upheaval, as has been noted of women in England and North America during times of war.[41] During her husband's exile after the 1715 Jacobite Rebellion, Frances Pierrepont, Countess of Mar, expected her husband to follow her advice, as she was best placed to convey the political situation at home. In a letter to her spouse, she reiterated the importance of following her instructions: 'so as you regard your own interest & my quiet I expect you compliance in this matter & if it were not absolutely necessity you may be assured I wold not ask you to cros your own inclinaton'.[42] In the same circumstances, Margaret Hamilton, Countess of Panmure, wrote angrily to her husband when he refused to follow her advice, which would allow him to return to Scotland. She commented:

> I am both very much grieved and astonish'd to find that you are so nicely scrupulous as to resolve that you will not so much as give security for your peaceable behaviour in time coming … and I hope I may claime that you'l have some regard to the melancholy circumstances of your poor afflicted wife and its seem little do you imagine the anxious and desolate condition I am in when you will not by so small a condescension make my life easie and comfortable.[43]

Margaret directly related her husband's refusal to follow her advice with his disregard for her person, yet despite her strong language she chose to take on the role of the distressed, rather than angry, wife. After five years apart, when Margaret and her husband disagreed on how to proceed, she chose to directly ignore his advice, informing him:

> as to the conveyance I have made in relation to the ten thousand pound bond I take God to witness that I have done it so as I think it will be most conducive to your advantage and as I have been advised by your best friends & tho the method I have settled it in is not according to your directions yet I am perswaided that when you reflect maturely on it you will be of the same opinion with them and me.[44]

Her language was more assertive and less deferent. Time spent apart had given time for Margaret both to consolidate her authority of what remained of the family estates and to recognise what this meant for her social position.

Social conflict also raised a different issue for wives – to whom were they ultimately accountable? Frances Pierrepont complained to her husband that her friends were criticising her for having not informed the government of her husband's plans to overthrow the King. Frances, however, disagreed, responding that she 'never did any thing but was my duty with regard to you.'[45] Yves Castan suggests that the complexities of early modern authority meant that most people limited their homage to their immediate superiors, and that, until the Enlightenment, this was considered a valid interpretation of social order. To ignore an immediate superior to fulfil the orders of another higher up subverted and undermined natural authority.[46] Yet, at the same time, the belief in a broader duty that bound society together, and which husbands and wives referred to in their marital negotiations, highlighted that the lines of power between husband and wife were not entirely linear. Social disorder made the direction of power unclear, disrupting families and hierarchy. This may have been all the more pressing for women whose natal families took a different stance from their conjugal relatives, especially in a seventeenth-century Scottish context where marriage was conceived as the joining of two families, rather than the subsuming of a wife into her marital family. Competing constructions of duty opened up a space for negotiation of power within marriage.

Conceptions of marital intimacy within seventeenth-century Scotland were also informed by models of friendship. As Alan Bray for England and Orest Ranum for France have suggested, friendship was a key vehicle for intimacy, and conversely intimacy in many contexts demonstrated friendship.[47] Friendship, however, was not straightforwardly related to equality, but implied reciprocity and obligation. In seventeenth-century Scotland, 'friend' was used in two main contexts. The first reflected the early modern meaning identified by Naomi Tadmor for England, where a friend was a member of the family broadly defined, and a person who had an interest in another's life and behaviour. A person's 'friends' were not necessarily their social equals, but rather reflected a wide family and kin network based on reciprocity. While 'friend' was used as shorthand for a wide group of people, it did not suggest social levelling within the group.[48] The second usage of friend was in the context of address and subscription and implied a relationship between two equals. It still entailed a complex web of reciprocity and duty, but this form of friendship was closely related to the ideas of classical friendship where power was neutralised through intimacy. In the main, it was used between social equals and notably siblings, except for where the holding of a title brought a distinction of class such as between the heir and his younger brothers and sisters.[49]

In the seventeenth century, unlike in some other European countries, it was unusual for Scottish husbands and wives to refer to themselves as a friend of their spouse and where they did it suggested a subtle democratising of the power relationship. The association between intimacy and friendship during this period has led it to be suggested that intimacy was a same-sex phenomenon associated with homosociability, rather than something experienced within marriage.[50] It is true that some men and women found their strongest and most intimate friendships outside of marriage, but intimacy was a part of married life for the Scottish elites, although not necessarily in a form that implied equality.

Indeed, rather than friendship providing a model for marriage, same-sex friendship was often depicted as a type of marriage. As Alex Shepard shows, in early modern England, a true friend was 'as deere as a good wife', and the intimacy of friendship, with the obligations it entailed as well as the potential for betrayal, was seen to be that found within marriage.[51] The act of being married was recognised in the seventeenth century as implying intimacy, as was seen in the use of wives as intermediaries by those desiring access to their husbands.[52] It is also true that while spouses did not refer to each other as 'friend', they appeared to understand marriage as a form of friendship. After a bout of marital difficulties, Sophia Clerk wrote to her brother that she had barely heard from her husband during his trip to Edinburgh, but 'I know nothing to the contrear but he is on perfect friendship with me'.[53] That friendship and marriage were coterminous meant that the potential for equality that friendship held encroached on understandings of marriage, destabilising the expected gender hierarchy found within it.

Friendship and domesticity

As time moved on, ideas around intimacy changed, reflecting a greater concern with ideas of self, individualism, and a move away from obligation and duty as external drivers of social behaviour to a model of inner self-control.[54] Proximity became less central to conceptions of intimacy as it became related to knowledge of a person's inner mind. In an eighteenth-century context, intimacy involved providing, or pretending to provide, access to a 'private' self that differentiated itself from a 'public' persona. Privacy was a growing concern during the period, reflected in changing architectural concerns, the removal of servants from 'family spaces', and the creation of the home as a 'haven' from the public world, but this sat uneasily alongside the culture of sensibility's concern with hypocrisy and a belief that the public man should be a reflection of the private.[55] The tension between a private, intimate self and the potential for exposure, both as a hypocrite and to the public eye, made one party (usually men) in an intimate relationship vulnerable, while requiring discretion from the other. As a result, it relied on trust, yet intimacy could exist between people where the potential for betrayal was more potent than others, such as between master and servant, and even be an inevitable, but undesirable, consequence of household dynamics.[56]

Over time, explicit references to obedience or commands, even in jest, disappeared. While eighteenth-century society expected women to be subordinate to their husbands, elite Scots distanced themselves from the idea that this subordination was commanded or enforced by men; rather, it became women's natural state, an innate quality of her femininity. Similarly, while duty continued to be a central concept in eighteenth-century thought, people were expected to look inwards to their conscience for their guide to behaviour, rather than to outward rules of deportment, although there was realisation that not all mankind was equipped to do this.[57] This was tied into discussions of female inferiority. Society became less comfortable referring to elite women as 'inferior' to men; instead, they emphasised difference and the perfection of women within their own sphere (although there was a distinct class dimension to this phenomenon).

This change in ideas of womanhood has been observed by a number of authors for the same period in England, while Barbara Lindeman notes its occurrence slightly later in late eighteenth-century Massachusetts.[58] From the 1720s, the nature of authority within marriage became a topic of discussion as obedience moved from a behaviour to a characteristic. Lord President Dundas in a letter to his wife in 1735 suggested that she may have lost her freedom through marriage. He wrote: 'the words loss of liberty I hope you have lost none, I don't think you have lost any, I do but joke you I know we are both pleased with what exchanges we have made'. Yet it was an area of tension which he hoped was resolved 'in the pleasure we have in one another'.[59]

This tension repeatedly appeared across the period c. 1720–70 as couples tried to find a vocabulary to understand how women could be social equals and yet subordinate to their husbands. One model that was explored in this discussion was the rhetoric of friendship. Whereas in the seventeenth century, marriage was understood as a model for friendship; in the eighteenth, friendship became a model for marriage. The minister and conduct author, James Fordyce, wrote of marriage as 'love mellowed in friendship' in 1765, while *The Scots Magazine*, a popular periodical, noted in 1752 that 'Love shall be with friendship joined'.[60] Margaret Robertson of Strowan's upcoming marriage was referred to by her father as 'the greatest friendship' in 1755, while James Balfour suggested to his future wife that their relationship exceeded 'ordinary friendship'.[61] In the 1760s, Miss Mylne was advised by two different correspondents that

marriage required 'love, friendship and esteem' and a 'similarity of opinion' which would enable 'a lasting friendship'.[62] Within marriage, spouses
began to refer to each other as friend. In 1736, Archibald Campbell told
his wife that 'in your absence I always want my friend and companion',
while in the 1770s James Grant referred to his wife as 'My loved friend'
and she in turn signed her letters 'affectionate and faithfull friend'.[63]

This friendship was influenced by the rational friendship popular
in the early part of the eighteenth century in England described by
Irene Brown and which Nancy Cott argued became so influential in
eighteenth-century colonial America.[64] Couples, but especially women,
emphasised that their relationship was built on reason and virtue, where
passion was curbed, but not absent. This model of friendship when
applied to marriage was supposed to encourage greater intimacy and
equality between spouses. Women used the rhetoric of rational friendship to raise their position within marriage and to highlight their expectation that marriage was a partnership. During a debate over Anna Potts'
role within their marriage, she wrote to her husband: 'Cleopatra never
figured her Anthony more agreeable than I do you but besides that what
doe you think of the wanting such a friend is ther anything in life so
rationall as a friend one confides on nay not only so but shares ones grief
feels ones pain and in short every thing that can most sooth and please
frail human nature.'[65]

Archibald was unable to give Anna the intimacy she desired, but he
too used the rhetoric of rational friendship to encourage his wife to do
her duty, as he conceived of it. He wrote to her: 'I sincerely love and
regard you, I know you are able to give delight and satisfaction to every
one about you, and in a particular manner to me, when your conduct
and conversation is ruled by reason without passion; and I thoroughly
believe and think, that no one is more capable to become easily an agreeable friend and companion to me and every one, and a prudent careful
director of a family'.[66] While Anna's construction of friendship aimed at
increasing intimacy and advocated, if not equality, at least unity of
minds, Archibald used the model of rational friendship to control his
wife's behaviour. His failure to properly engage with the true meaning of
rational friendship was common amongst husbands who used the word
friend, but could not conceive of a true partnership with one of the 'fair
sex'. As a result, while the word friend still appeared in the later eighteenth and nineteenth centuries, it did not hold the same potential for
equality and intimacy as it had in the early decades, despite attempts by
a number of social reformers to reintroduce it as a model for marriage
and heterosocial relationships.[67]

The inability of men to conceive of women as friends also became increasingly evident in broader culture, as was the case in North America during the same period.[68] The minister and best-selling author, James Fordyce, in a long discussion of female friendship, argued that, unlike some of his contemporaries, he believed women were capable of friendship with other women, but they had to work considerably harder to have meaningful relationships than men to whom it came naturally. He acknowledged briefly that friendship was a part of marriage, but skirted around what this actually meant, before quoting his contemporary John Gregory, that: 'the fair sex should naturally expect to gain from our conversation, knowledge, wisdom, and sedateness; and they should give us in exchange humanity, politeness, cheerfulness, taste and sentiment'.[69] If friendship was possible between the sexes, it was not one based on equality but complementarity.

The need to apply a model of friendship to the marital relationship, and its later failure, is evidence of an era when understandings of gender were in flux. Discussions of rational friendship almost engaged in an act of historical amnesia as they tried to advocate friendship between the sexes as a novel development whilst ignoring the historical relationship between marriage and friendship. Through doing this, the traditional relationship between marriage and friendship was broken, and at the same time, the meaning of both friendship and marriage was renegotiated, so they were no longer so closely related. Friendship increasingly became associated with men, and conversely marriage became associated primarily with women, but also with men. The marriage/friendship divide came to reflect the private/public divide that caused so much discussion during the period, where the public (civic) sphere was male and the private (domestic) sphere was both male and female.[70] Furthermore, for Scottish Enlightenment thinkers, friendship increasingly became a model for democratic political citizenship; women's inability to form friendships effectively removed their right to participate in the polity.[71]

This gendering of friendship explains the discomfort and inability of male Enlightenment authors to truly conceive of female friendship, without at least requiring women to attempt to exceed the limitations of their sex. Despite their concerns, women had greater faith in their ability to have homosocial friendships, reflected both in the longevity of 'rational friendship' within female relationships and in the attempt by writers such as Mary Wollstonecraft to reclaim friendship, and its concomitant political rights, for women.[72] It is also worth noting, however, that as we move forward into the nineteenth century, it was models of female friendship located firmly in the domestic sphere that came to cultural dominance.[73]

As Irene Brown highlights, rational friendship in the eighteenth century was closely related to the rise of Enlightenment domesticity, where the 'private' or 'domestic' sphere was increasingly idealised as a haven from the corrupting influence of the public world of commercial society.[74] The domestic sphere was not gendered exclusively female as it was essential to the preservation of male virtue, a core part of independent manhood, that they had an escape from the 'world' – an idea heavily influenced by the work of French philosopher Jean-Jacques Rousseau.[75] Yet, it was in the domestic sphere that men interacted with women and benefited from the female influence that ensured men remained 'civilised'.[76] Just like in romantic love, women's role in the domestic sphere was to enable men to become their 'true selves'.[77] While interpretations of male interactions in the commercial sphere were complex, even those (such as Adam Smith) with an optimistic belief that genuine affective (male) friendship arose out of the 'calculation and self-interest' of the commercial world thought that the family remained important as it promoted virtue in men, and through men, in wider society.[78] As Jane Rendall suggests, it was women who were responsible for the education in 'moral sentiments' that lay at the basis of morality in Enlightenment thought.[79] Furthermore, for Smith, while friendship was a rational choice between independent men and founded on mutual need within commercial society, family relationships were 'natural'.[80]

Affection within the family arose 'naturally' out of the intimacy that the close cohabitation of family members created, but was not inevitable, as can be seen amongst siblings brought up separately. It was based on 'physical connection' between family members, which made it inferior to male friendships in civil society that were based on morality, but at the same time it enabled those friendships by allowing men to develop their innate 'natural sympathy'.[81] As the family was a 'natural' phenomenon, relations within in it were not rational and did not require that all parties were equal and independent actors. Furthermore, women were closely associated with the family and the domestic sphere, it being seen as the natural place of women due to their innate sympathies.[82]

The domestic sphere sat outside of the public world of commerce where rational, male and virtuous friendship determined social relations. The affective nature of the household delineated gender relationships within the family quite strictly. Smith rather vaguely argued that 'the general rule is established, that persons related to one another in a certain degree ought always to be affected towards one another in a certain manner, and that there is always the highest impropriety, and sometimes even a sort of impiety, in their being affected in a different manner'.[83] Intimacy, therefore, was not spontaneous, but determined by social rules and situated within the domestic sphere, which was often coterminous with the household, and marked by physical proximity. In this way, eighteenth century models of intimacy did not mark a watershed in family relationships, but drew heavily on older conceptions of marriage, which Smith himself recognised.[84]

This continuity was observed in various aspects of marital life. Nineteenth century husbands continued to engage in paternalistic advice. Walter Crum sent his wife 'a schoolmaster where you will find page 116 an excellent paper on the management of children which and are [sic] to study and apply'. He continued: 'I next send you the much talked of life of William Cobbett' before summarising the main lessons to be learned from the text and finishing 'there are valuable lessons for young people both male and female'.[85] The advice Walter gave was to be taught to his children, rather than learnt by his wife, but he still felt it necessary to give detailed instructions of the text's moral rather than relying on his wife's judgement. Throughout the period, asking wives to be careful of their health, to take exercise and to eat well were common requests by husbands. As protectors of their families, men believed it was their responsibility to ensure their wives' physical, economic and spiritual well-being.

Couples also continued to negotiate the terms of their marriage, with a willingness to seek compromise and resolution. In 1782, Jane Graham had complained of her husband, Patrick Home's, jealousy, bad usage and neglect to a Mr Moor, which 'had encouraged him to make the advances he did'. Chastity was required of women throughout their lives and this extended into restrictions on their behaviour and conversation with men who were not close family members. Expressions of jealousy or concern with their wives' behaviour usually did not imply that husbands believed them to be sexually unchaste, but indiscrete in their expression or action.[86] Infidelity in women was more likely to provoke silence and absolute rejection from their spouse. In the aftermath of this incident, Patrick Home's letter to his wife highlighted his attempts to reconcile his disappointment at her inappropriate behaviour with his feelings of responsibility. He wrote to his wife that:

> you are continually conjuring up chimeras against your own happiness, for which you are much to blame. I never recall the past, but with infinite regret. The impression are still too violent for me, and I turn my mind from them, by every possible means – your taking blame to

yourself, where it is due, I cannot disapprove of … but I am afraid you are now leaning to much to the contrary side – however put your heart at ease. I strive daily to forgive and even to forget the wrongs that have been done me.[87]

Patrick's response wavers between his position as benevolent and forgiving husband, although one who has perhaps neglected his responsibilities, and his role as a partner in a marriage which relied on compromise and reconciliation for its success. His interpretation of the 'wrong' that had been done was informed by broader expectations of appropriate behaviour for women and men, but his need and desire to reconcile with his wife meant that responses to such behaviour had to be flexible and in so doing, undermined their impact. Intimacy continued to create a space for the negotiation of power within marriage. Had the situation been reversed, the double standard applied to sexual fidelity would have limited his wife's response. Unfaithful husbands were disapproved of in Scotland, perhaps more so than amongst the elites in other parts of Europe.[88] The self-control promoted by both Scottish Presbyterianism and Scottish Enlightenment discourses of refined masculinity viewed sexual gratification suspiciously, linking it to excess, effeminacy and corruption.[89] Furthermore, David Stevenson asserts that the provincial nature of Scottish society made heterosexual promiscuity difficult for elite men.[90] In practice, not all men lived up to this standard, but it was expected that they would be discrete and not flaunt their affairs before their wives, sometimes made difficult through the transmission of sexually transmitted disease. Ultimately, however, promiscuity reflected poorly on the man and it was a sin to be hidden from society, rather than a wrong against wives. As a result, husbands sometimes expressed jealousy and mistrust of their wives, but it was unusual within correspondence for women to vocalise anger at their husband's infidelity.[91]

Women continued to show deference in letters, but unlike in the seventeenth and early eighteenth century where this was shown through the correct use of address, polite requests and humble apologies, in the later eighteenth and nineteenth centuries this was shown in the absence of confrontation and attempts to draw attention away from demands upon husbands. Mary and James Stewart Mackenzie's correspondence highlighted this in action. James' frequent absence from home could be an area of tension as the couple tried to negotiate his responsibilities towards his family. Mary frequently insisted that he returned home: 'I do hope my love you will be back on Saturday for indeed there are many things here that require your presence'.[92] When James did not respond to her request, she wrote to him 'tho I am angry with you my naughty naughty Stewart yet this day must not pass over without thanking our almighty father' and finished her note 'adieu my own beloved I am very angry notwithstanding'.[93] He responded 'how could you my dearest Mary even en badinage say on the 9th you were angry with naughty Stewart – my sweet loves know not what this separation costs me ... how can I go away from you?'[94] The language used was playful, yet expressed a genuine negotiation in a manner that did not directly challenge James' authority or damage Mary's self-presentation as a submissive wife.

By the nineteenth century, the significance of the ideals of domesticity shaped how couples corresponded, and letters were marked by lengthy descriptions of domestic life, of children's prattle, family gossip, and household events. It was not that any of these topics were novel to the period, but that letters were crowded with family news to the exclusion of other information, including the lengthy expressions of affection that had been common in earlier years. Jessie Crum in 1837 wrote to her husband: 'I begin to calculate that it is already ten days since you left us and that after enjoying yourself a little longer perhaps a fortnight my picture to the children of their dear papas return will be realised. Alex walked out of the room where he had gone alone with your old hat was very happy calling himself wee Papa.' She continued with a description of their young daughter Maggie escaping from her nurse and of their other daughter Janie getting inoculated, before moving on to give news of wider family and friends.[95] On other occasions, she described daily events, such as 'I heard a piercing cry which took me down just now to the nursery. It was only Papas wee plain lassie getting a dip in a foot bath of cold saltwater.'[96]

The effect was a vivid impression of domesticity in action and its purpose was to create intimacy in the same manner that romantic language had in previous decades. Men engaged in this language similarly to women, although their engagement with the public sphere occasionally gave them a broader range of material to discuss with their wives. The situating of intimacy within the domestic sphere within Enlightenment thought created a situation where the 'creation' of domesticity became the creation of intimacy. Instead of drawing on duty or obligation like in the seventeenth century, or on the vocabulary of love like in the middle decades of the eighteenth century, couples produced images of domestic happiness to establish intimacy over distance. Through doing this, they incorporated the gendered dynamics of domesticity, where wives were located in the private sphere and subordinate to their husbands, into their marital relationships.

While women actively engaged in the language of domesticity, they were not unaware of the implication for their social position. Jane Carlyle recognised the utility of using the models of femininity promoted by the culture of domesticity to smooth her engagement with the wider world. When describing her visit to a lawyer to negotiate the rental contract on her house to her husband, she noted, 'For respectability's sake, I said, in taking leave, that "my husband was out of town, or he would have come himself." In the same letter, she also apologised to her husband for exceeding 'your modest allowance' for decorating.[97] The latter apology might have had greater weight had the use of the word 'modest' not undermined the sentiment. Jane was willing to restrict herself to the confines of domesticity, but this did not mean she could not renegotiate its meaning in her discussions with her spouse. Jane, like other women, was willing to use the language of domesticity to create intimacy, to negotiate the balance of power within her marriage and to allow her access to a world beyond the home. Yet, by doing so, they worked within the patriarchal system rather than dismantling it.

Intimacy was negotiated within a framework for marriage that gave men authority over women. In the seventeenth century, intimacy was created through the fulfilment of duty and obligation, which in turn were determined by gender and rank. In the eighteenth century, the importance of gender and rank continued to define men and women's social role, but intimacy became the 'natural', although not inevitable, product of domestic relationships. This subtly shifted the location of intimate relationships from the public (as conceived in later eighteenth century thought) to the private sphere, although some thinkers continued to believe that intimacy was available to rational, virtuous (elite) men in their relationships with each other.[98] Throughout the period, intimate relationships were built on a framework of male superiority and female inferiority. How intimacy was created therefore reinforced the patriarchal system.

Yet, intimacy also held democratic potential. Intimate relationships required that couples were flexible, that they overlooked breaches of appropriate gendered behaviour, and they responded to individual problems and circumstances in the way that was best for their relationship. It required a working together that gave women a voice within marriage, even if not always on equal grounds with men, and it gave women access to their husband's resources and person that made men vulnerable to exposure and betrayal, which placed women in positions of power. Intimacy opened up spaces to negotiate for power within marriage and through doing so challenged and evolved patriarchy. Intimacy was not an equalising force, but it could be used to complicate power relationships.

Notes

1 T. Zeldin, *An Intimate History of Humanity* (London: Vintage, 1998), pp. 324–5.

2 A. Giddens, *The Transformation of Intimacy: Sexuality, Love and Eroticism in Modern Societies* (Cambridge: Polity Press, 1992), p. 189.

3 R. Abbey and D. J. Den Uyl, 'The chief inducement? The idea of marriage as friendship', *Journal of Applied Philosophy*, 18:1 (2001), 39.

4 Zeldin, *Intimate History*, pp. 324–5.

5 C. Brady, 'The MacDonalds and the provincial strategies of Hugh O'Neill', in W. P. Kelly and J. R. Young (eds), *Scotland and the Ulster Plantations: Explorations in the British Settlements of Stuart Ireland* (Dublin: Four Courts Press, 2009), p. 54.

6 NAS GD406/1/6898 Elizabeth Hamilton to Duke of Hamilton, 16 February, 1704.

7 NAS GD124/15/231 Margaret, Countess of Mar from John Erskine, Earl of Mar [1704].

8 NAS GD128/35/5a Alexander Campbell to his wife, 'my dearest', 3 May 1737; GCA TD1073/1/2 Jessie Crum to Walter Crum [March 1830].

9 NAS GD461/125/15 Archibald Lawrie to Anne Adair [c. 1795].

10 H. Berry, 'Lawful kisses? Sexual ambiguity and platonic friendship in England, c. 1660–1720', in K. Harvey (ed.), *The Kiss in History* (Manchester: Manchester University Press, 2005), pp. 62–79.

11 A. Bray, *The Friend* (Chicago: Chicago University Press, 2003), pp. 140–76.

12 GD406/1/6254 Anne, Duchess of Hamilton to James, Earl of Arran, 20 January 1688.

13 GD345/1145/9 Anne Hamilton to Archibald Grant of Monymusk, 18 April 1717.

14 M. Slater, *Family Life in the Seventeenth Century: the Verneys of Claydon House* (London: Routledge, 1984), p. 29.

15 For a Scottish example of such advice see: GD155/851 Robertson of Strowan to his daughter Margaret Robertson, 23 May 1755.

16 NAS GD1/51/87 H.P. Cleighton to Miss Mylne, 2 March 1770.

17 NAS GD406/1/6121 Katherine Hamilton, Duchess of Atholl to Marchioness of Atholl, 12 March 1683/4.

18 NAS GD158/2720/7 Katherine Hume to the Laird of Kimmerghame, November 1669.

19 NAS GD406/1/8154 William, Duke of Hamilton to Anne, Duchess of Hamilton [c. 1680].

20 NAS GD18/5174A/3 Elizabeth Henderson to John Clerk, 11 May 1676.

21 NAS GD26/13/418/1 Anna Wemyss, Countess of Leven to David, Earl of Leven, 1692.

22 See GD45/14/220 Letters (145) from Margaret Hamilton, Countess of Panmure to James Maule, Earl of Panmure, 1716–1723.

23 NAS GD406/1/2489 William, Duke of Hamilton to Elizabeth Maxwell, 11 October 1650.

24 NAS GD345/1146/5/27 Archibald Grant to Anna Potts, 6 April 1739.

25 A. Chricton (ed.), *Life and Diary of Col. John Blackadder* (Edinburgh: H.S. Baynes, 1924), John Blackadder to Elizabeth Callander, 2 June 1705.

26 NAS GD26/13/418/13 David, Earl of Leven to Anna Wemyss, Countess of Leven, 9 September [c. 1692].

27 C. Muldrew, 'From a "light cloak" to an "iron cage": historical changes in the relation between community and individualism', in A. Shepard and P. Withington (eds), *Communities in Early Modern England* (Manchester: Manchester University Press, 2000), p. 162.

28 L. Pollock, 'Honor, gender and reconciliation in elite culture, 1570–1700', *Journal of British Studies*, 46 (2007), 29.

29 B. Capp, *When Gossips Meet: Women, Family, and Neighbourhood in Early Modern England* (Oxford: Oxford University Press, 2003), p. 72.

30 NAS GD3/5/577 Margaret McDonald to James Montgomerie, 13 August 1660.

31 NAS GD345/1146/49 Anna Potts to Archibald Grant, 7 September 1734.

32 NAS GD345/1146/63 Anna Potts to Archibald Grant [July or August, 1740].

33 L. Pollock, 'Anger and the negotiation of relationships in early modern England', *Historical Journal*, 47 (2004), pp. 578–9.

34 NAS GD461/14/11 Archibald Campbell to Christina Watson [c. 1724].

35 NAS GD110/1084/27 Hew Dalrymple to Margaret Sainthill, 22 September 1749.

36 NAS GD406/1/6896 Elizabeth, Duchess of Hamilton to James, Duke of Hamilton, 11 February 1703/4.

37 NAS GD26/13/418/4 Anne Wemyss, Countess of Leven to David, Earl of Leven, 20 August [c. 1692–1702].

38 NAS GD406/1/7356 William, Duke of Hamilton to Anne, Duchess of Hamilton, 12 December 1693.

39 NAS GD406/1/7424 William, Duke of Hamilton to Anne, Duchess of Hamilton, 27 January 1693/4.

40 NAS GD406/1/7428 William, Duke of Hamilton to Anne Duchess of Hamilton, 6 February 1693/4.

41 Slater, *Family Life,* pp. 66–8; A. Young, 'The woman of Boston: "persons of consequence" in the making of the American Revolution, 1765–76', in H. Applewhite and D. Levy (eds), *Women and Politics in the Age of Democratic Revolution* (Ann Arbor: University of Michigan Press, 1993), pp. 181–226.

42 NAS GD1/44/7 Frances, Countess of Mar to John Erskine, Earl of Mar [1716].

43 NAS GD45/14/220/73 Letters from Margaret Hamilton, Countess of Panmure to James Maule, Earl of Panmure, 18 December 1718.

44 NAS GD45/14/220/147 Letters from Margaret Hamilton, Countess of Panmure to James Maule, Earl of Panmure, 7 March 1723.

45 NAS GD1/44/7 Frances, Countess of Mar to John Erskine, Earl of Mar, 1716.

46 Y. Castan, 'Politics and private life', in R. Chartier (ed.), *A History of Private Life: Passions of the Renaissance* (London: Harvard University Press, 1989), pp. 36–7.

47 Bray, *The Friend*; O. Ranum, 'The refuges of intimacy', in Chartier, *History of Private Life,* pp. 258–9.

48 N. Tadmor, 'The concept of the household-family in eighteenth century England', *Past and Present*, 151 (1996), 111–140.

49 For a discussion of this form of friendship, see Bray, *The Friend*.

50 See Ranum, 'The refuges of intimacy', pp. 258–9.

51 A. Shepard, *Meanings of Manhood in Early Modern England* (Oxford: Oxford University Press, 2003), p. 124.

52 For example see NAS GD16/35/8 Letter to Lady Lauderdale asking her to ask her husband for a favour on the writer's behalf, 3 March 1666.

53 NAS GD18/5250/51 Sophia Clerk to John Clerk, 13 March 1723.

54 Muldrew, 'From a "light cloak"', pp. 156–79.

55 J. Dwyer, *Virtuous Discourse: Sensibility and Community in Eighteenth Century Scotland* (Edinburgh: John Donald, 1987), pp. 95–116; P. Spacks, *Privacy: Concealing the Eighteenth Century Self* (London: University of Chicago Press, 2003), pp. 1–26.

56 An example of the complexity of emotion in master/servant relationships: M. Lamberg, 'Suspicion, rivalry and care: mistresses and maidservants in early modern Stockholm', in Susan Broomhall (ed.), *Emotions in the Household, 1200–1900* (Houndmills: Palgrave Macmillan, 2008), pp. 170–84.

57 A. Smith, *The Theory of Moral Sentiments* (London: Henry G. Bohn, 1853), p. 230.

58 For an English example see M. Legates, 'The cult of womanhood in eighteenth-century thought', *Eighteenth-Century Studies*, 1 (1976), 21–39; B. Lindemann, '"To ravish and carnally know": rape in eighteenth century', *Signs*, 10 (1984), 63–82.

59 NAS GD235/9/2/10 Lord President Dundas to Lady Arniston, 16 January 1735.

60 Quoted in A. Duncan, 'Patronage and presentations of the self: a late eighteenth-century correspondence,' (MSc dissertation, University of Edinburgh, 2007).

61 NAS GD155/851 Robertson of Strowan to his daughter, Margaret Robertson, 23 May 1755; NAS GD192/31 James Balfour to Anne MacIntosh, 2 January 1806.

62 NAS GD1/51/87 H.P. Cligthome[?] to Miss Mylne, 2 March 1770; NAS GD1/51/87 A. Young to Miss Mylne, 19 December 1767.

63 NAS GD461/14/17 Archibald Campbell to Christina Watson, 13 May 1736; NAS GD248/368/8 James Grant to Jane Grant [late 18th century]; NAS GD248/697/5 Jane Grant to James Grant [various].

64 I. Brown, 'Domesticity, friendship and feminism: female aristocratic culture and marriage in England, 1660–1760', *Journal of Family History*, 7:4 (1982), 406–24; N. Cott, 'Passionless: an interpretation of Victorian sexual ideology, 1790–1850', *Signs*, 4:2 (1978), 219–36.

65 NAS GD345/1145/41 Anna Potts to Archibald Grant, 6 May 1739.

66 NAS GD345/1148/2/17 Archibald Grant to Anna Potts [c. 1740].

67 Abbey and Douglas, 'The chief inducement?', 37–52.

68 J. Kross, 'Mansions, men, women, and the creations of multiple publics in eighteenth-century British North America,' *Journal of Social History*, 33:2 (1999), 398–9.

69 J. Fordyce, *Sermons to Young Women* (Philadelphia: M. Carey, 1809), pp. 81–103. In his sermon 'On Love', he doesn't use the term friendship to refer to the relationship between the sexes, J. Fordyce, *Addresses to Young Men* (London: T. Cadell, 1777), pp. 177–222.

70 Dwyer, *Virtuous Discourse*, pp. 95–116.

71 E. Frazer, 'Mary Wollstonecraft on politics and friendship,' *Political Studies*, 56 (2008), 237–56; for a broader discussion on the Enlightenment thinkers and friendship, see: L. Hill and P. McCarthy, 'Hume, Smith and Ferguson: Friendship in Commercial Society', *Critical Review of International Social and Political Philosophy*, 2:4 (1999), 33–49.

72 Frazer, 'Mary Wollstonecraft', 237–56.

73   C. Smith-Rosenberg, 'The female world of love and ritual: relations between women in nineteenth century America', *Signs*, 1 (1975), 1–29; S. Curran, 'Dynamics of female friendship in the later eighteenth century', *Nineteenth-Century Contexts*, 23:2, (2001), 221–39.

74   Brown, 'Domesticity, feminism, and friendship', 406–24.

75   M. Ogrodnick, *Instinct and Intimacy: Political Philosophy and Autobiography in Rousseau* (Toronto: University of Toronto Press, 1999), p. 10.

76   Dwyer, *Virtuous Discourse*, pp. 95–116.

77   See Chapter 4.

78   Hill and McCarthy, 'Hume, Smith and Ferguson', 37l; Smith, *Theory of Moral Sentiments*, pp. 307–45.

79   J. Rendall, 'Virtue and commerce: women in the making of Adam Smith's political economy', in E. Kennedy and S. Mendus (eds), *Women in Western Political Philosophy, Kant to Nietzsche* (New York: St. Martin's Press, 1987), pp. 44–76.

80   Smith, *Theory of Moral Sentiments*, p. 322.

81   Smith, *Theory of Moral Sentiments*, p. 329; see also, S. Nerozzi and P. Nuti, 'Adam Smith and the Family', Working Paper, Università degli Studi di Firenze, April 2008.

82   Nerozzi and Nuti, 'Adam Smith', p. 6.

83   Smith, *Theory of Moral Sentiments*, p. 323.

84   Smith, *Theory of Moral Sentiments*, pp. 326–7.

85   GCA TD1073/2 Walter Crum to Jessie Crum, 4 October [1832].

86   For a discussion see: A. Fletcher, *Gender, Sex and Subordination in England, 1500–1800* (London: Yale University Press, 1995), pp. 386–7.

87   NAS GD267/3/8/1 Patrick Home to Jane Graham, 16 March 1782.

88   Fletcher, *Gender, Sex and Subordination*, pp. 342–43.

89   R. Carr, 'Gender, national identity and political agency in eighteenth century Scotland', (PhD Dissertation, University of Glasgow, 2008), pp. 145–9; J. Fea, 'Presbyterians in love: or the feeling Philip Vickers Fithian', *Common-Place*, 8:2 (2008), www.common-place.org/vol-08/no-02/fea/, accessed 10/02/2009.

90   D. Stevenson, *The Beggars Benison: Sex Clubs of Enlightenment Scotland and their Rituals* (East Linton: Tuckwell, 2001), pp. 81–3 and 132–3.

91   Although this comes out in court cases and letters to female friends when marriages break down.

92   NAS GD46/15/19/25 Mary Stewart Mackenzie to James Mackenzie [May 1819].

93   NAS GD46/15/19/25 Mary Stewart Mackenzie to James Mackenzie [May 1819].

94   NAS GD46/15/19/23 James Mackenzie to Mary Stewart Mackenzie [May 1819].

95   GCA TD1073/1/2 Jessie Crum to Walter Crum, 30 March 1830.

96   GCA TD1073/1/8 Jessie Crum to Walter Crum, 16 August 1837.

97   J. Froude (ed.), *Letters and Memorials of Jane Carlyle*, vol.1 (Charles Scribner's Sons, 1883), p.152, Jane Carlyle to Thomas Carlyle, 18 July 1843.

98   Dwyer, *Virtuous Discourse*, pp. 95–116.

6

The ambiguities of patriarchy:
the marital economy

From the perspective of Scottish law-makers, marriage in the seventeenth to nineteenth centuries was primarily understood as an economic arrangement; an interpretation that reflected the priority of the marital economy in the everyday lives of the Scottish elites. Marriages were built around the marriage contract into the nineteenth century, and unions still failed at this stage, despite disavowal of mercenary motives and the exchange of romantic outpourings. The marital economy, which encompassed not only the management and consumption of the household but the methods of provisioning the household, was a prominent concern in the correspondence of Scottish couples.[1] While the Scottish elites were not free from accusations of aristocratic license and undoubtedly had greater leisure time than many other social groups, the marital economy always figured heavily in their letters.[2] For some couples, it was the primary motivation for writing to each other, while for others the reality that at least part of each day was devoted to managing the household, family consumption and production, ensured it was a central topic for discussion. Throughout the period, the marital economy was understood as a joint effort that required mutual cooperation, if not equality of authority.

The nature of the marital economy and the gendered structures of power within it are complex and debated issues. In Scotland, as is discussed in Chapter 2, a woman's economic role within the household and her right to use its resources were enshrined in law. Yet, equally, the law placed the husband at the head of the household, putting the marital economy under his dominion. While the law laid down the framework for the management of the marital economy, the division of tasks between husband and wife was not clearly defined, creating a space to negotiate for power. This has led some historians to question the nature of power within the household, arguing that male authority was constrained if not removed from the home.[3] Others have challenged the effectiveness of patriarchy in the household more fundamentally.[4] Richard Grassby argues for the English middling classes in the seventeenth century that 'marriages were working partnerships based on reconciliation of differences, not a device to marginalize women or force them to sacrifice their independence and property to men in return for emotional security. For most spouses, inequality and relative power were just not issues.'[5]

Within these discussions, there is a tension between power exercised within the household and that employed beyond the household in wider society. Michelle Rosaldo argues that the application of power by men is socially recognised and legitimate, whereas female power is seen as 'manipulative, disruptive, illegitimate or unimportant'. She suggests that the illegitimate nature of female power ensures that it is limited to the domestic sphere, and cannot affect the world beyond.[6] Similarly Lynn Abrams notes that 'management of the household economy and holding the purse strings does not necessarily translate into status or even respect, and it is rare that women are able to convert their earnings into recognised symbols of power such as property'.[7] Between the seventeenth and nineteenth centuries, this discussion was informed by the shifting meanings of private and public space.

The households of the early modern elite were only with difficulty imagined as private spaces. They not only contained numerous staff, but were often the centre of the local economy, requiring a constant influx of family, visitors, tradesmen, and estate workers. Even, modest homes were subject to prying eyes. With credit networks and household economies closely tied to social reputation, it was often more important to be seen as part of the community and to pass public scrutiny than to maintain a sense of separation from the world.[8] At the same time, as discussed in the previous chapter, most people conceived of self in terms of relationships with family members and the wider community, rather than private, interior individuals, unique and separate from other people, complicating both the practice of, and desire for, privacy.

Over the seventeenth and eighteenth centuries, privacy became increasingly prized and for those with the money to implement it, changes were made to houses, separating the family from servants and often from the trade or business functions of the household.[9] The cash market increasingly impacted on relationships between employer and employee, breaking down patronage networks, where servants were often quite literally family, and making a more mobile workforce (although these developments were neither entirely novel nor straightforward).[10]

The interior self and the private, independent (male) individual became of increasing popular concern, shaping how people understood their relationship with others in the community and their family.

The cult of domesticity, where women were located in the non-productive household as a haven from the commercial world, became increasingly important, giving new meaning to domestic spaces, and was promoted by the Enlightenment writers, such as Adam Smith, who simultaneously made links between the economy and the public sphere. This led to the separation of the work from the home, at least ideologically, although in practice the household's economic functions continued in many families into the twentieth century and beyond, while a constant stream of visitors was an attribute of the Victorian middle-class home, destabilising conceptions of private and public.[11]

The gendering of the private sphere was also complex. Women have long been associated with the household, yet that is not the same as seeing the home as a female sphere. In the early modern period, the household was the centre of most economic activity, a place of work and leisure, and where men and women worked together. In the eighteenth century, as described in the previous chapter, the home was understood as central to allowing men to develop their true selves and to shaping virtuous, independent men that were capable of engaging with the social, public and political world. Similarly, the home remained central to masculinity for many men in the nineteenth century, seen in the Victorian concern surrounding men who chose to spend their leisure time in public houses and clubs, rather than by the fireside.[12] Yet, that men had legitimate alternative spheres of action meant they were never tied to the private sphere in the way that women, and their range of activities, were.

As the nineteenth century developed, women claimed domestic space as their own, using it to nurture female friendships and locating it as a distinct power base for women.[13] While this did not prevent the home from being a central part of masculinity, it created tensions about just what a feminine private sphere offered male identity, with the threat of effeminacy requiring that boys not spend too much time being exclusively socialised in the home.[14] Yet, this was not to say that the domestic remained situated firmly in the household; men could adopt domestic rituals in their homosocial relationships beyond the home.[15]

This evolving framework for interpreting the place of women and men in the world also shaped the nature of the patriarchal system. It impacted on gender roles and how men and women related to each other and so was implicated in the construction of power. This chapter explores how patriarchy was constructed and negotiated within the context of the marital economy, setting out the operation of the marital economy in a Scottish context, and exploring it as a site of negotiation for power both in and beyond the household. It discusses the place of wider family within these negotiations, asking how their interference shaped marital behaviour. Throughout, it emphasises that negotiations for resources and power in the marital economy were informed by the ideas of love and intimacy discussed in earlier chapters.

Negotiating shared interest

The economic basis of the elite household in late seventeenth and early eighteenth-century Scotland was centred on the home and estate.[16] For many elites, most household income came from their estate, where they grew much of their own food and fuel, and had equipment, such as mills, breweries and dairies, to transform crops into consumables. Surplus crops and fuels were traded for goods or sold for cash that was used to buy clothing, furniture and luxury items. Landed families earned a significant part of their income from rents. For families on smaller estates, household incomes were often supplemented by a variety of means. Lairds and other smaller landowners often worked in the law, medicine or in areas such as customs to provide for their families. Merchant families supplemented their business earnings with home-grown crops, selling any surplus. Income from investments also became popular over the period and even those on modest incomes put money into stocks.

The functions of the household were expected to be divided between husband and wife, falling along a division between male gover-nance and female management. For most writers of the period, the distinction between these two roles centred on control of the household budget, rather than the act of provisioning as may have been expected from the duties allocated to a husband in wider culture.[17] The author Richard Allestree in the 1670s believed that the management of the family finances 'is not ordinarily the wives province'.[18] George Savile, Marquis of Halifax, a decade later, presumed when discussing finances that it was the husband's purse, while Archibald Campbell in 1666 referred to male management of the household budget.[19] At the same time, the management of the household was widely recognised as falling to women and her role was considerably broader than that allocated to her husband. Francois Fenelon de Salignac de la Mothe, whilst criticising women for their reluctance to involve themselves in housekeeping, noted in 1687 that: 'if you speak to them of the price of corn, of the till-ing of lands, of the different natures of estates, of the raising of rents, of the other rights of lordship, of the best manner of managing farms, or of settling of receivers; they believe you intend to reduce them to employments quite unworthy of them'.[20] His definition of household encompassed both the maintenance and provision of the home. Even in prescriptive literature, women's broad sphere of management under-mined any sense that money was a uniquely male concern.

Like in other parts of Europe, women were expected to have a work-ing knowledge of all aspects of running the house and any productive operations that were performed within or alongside the home.[21] Men were not as well versed in their wives' functions, perhaps contributing to the higher rates of remarriage amongst widowers.[22] In 1676, while John Clerk was absent on business, his wife, Elizabeth Henderson, took his place as estate manager. She informed her husband that the man he contracted to plaster the house was unable to do the job. She found and contracted another labourer on the same terms.[23] Elizabeth rented out one of the family residences, noting to her husband she was disappointed to only receive 450 merks rent, when she had wanted 500.[24] She also complained that she had only received 300 merks of income since he left, which she had collected from the son of a tenant.[25]

Wives also dealt with business when away from home. Mary, Countess of Caithness performed various estate negotiations while visit-ing family in London in 1690. She reported her success and that she had hired a man to pursue the family interest. Mary emphasised her frugality while away, noting that coal was expensive but that she was using cheap sea coal and only heating one room to save money.[26] She advised her husband that their family could live as cheaply in the city over the winter as in Scotland, detailing the cost of rent, furniture and fuel, before giving him instructions on household furnishings and servants in Scotland.[27] Couples also worked together to get the best deals for their family. Robert Douglas wrote to his wife in 1704 that he had received an offer of '6lb redie money' for their meal and 11s for the pork so that 'ye may send me over ane same unless ye get it sold at home for readie money at 6lb, 6s 8d'.[28]

Spouses often shared the details of their finances or household management decisions. In 1704, the Earl of Mar gave his wife a detailed explanation of their financial situation to justify why he had to remain away on business.[29] In the same year, the Duke and Duchess of Hamilton shared mundane household decisions. On one occasion, the Duke gave his blessing to his wife's choice of housekeeper, but reminded her that she did not have to let the previous servant go until she was certain it was convenient.[30] His father, twenty years earlier, sent his wife detailed lists of goods and prices from London for her to make a selection.[31] Most women had a good grasp of market values and knew at what price to buy and sell. Absent husbands were frequently sent detailed shopping lists for goods that could not be bought locally with recommended prices. Janet Inglis told her husband, around 1715, 'you will remember to look for chairs to the purple room'. Not to be trusted with the decision of tablecloths however, she added that Lady Inglis is 'the fittest hand to buy on [one] of the painted cloaths and one for the side board'.[32]

Shopping was not an exclusively female task. Men not only represented women when purchasing, but made many decisions themselves. During the refurbishment of Hamilton Palace in 1693, the Duke of Hamilton, in his wife's absence, sorted through the existing furniture and made decisions on what to destroy and what to re-upholster. He informed his wife of his choices and what he planned to purchase as replacements. The Duke also made many decisions about the fabric of the building, selecting windows and stonework.[33] His son was similarly involved in the everyday management of the household, sending his wife instructions on the purchase of plate. He directed his wife to pay servants out of the 'family pounde bagge' and to send him butter, clothing, and books from home.[34] Certain purchases were gendered. Just as Janet Inglis did not trust her husband to select tablecloths, men were particularly involved in the purchase of alcohol. In the mid-eighteenth century, John Sutherland instructed his wife to pay for the claret and white wine he had purchased, 'when money comes into your hands'.[35] Hew Dalrymple informed his wife that the Madeira he had ordered was ready and she was to give eight or ten dozen bottles to her father.[36]

Men and women not only cooperated in the management of estates, but in family businesses. As an Edinburgh court judge noted in the eighteenth century, 'there is nothing more common than for married women to be praeapositura in either assisting their husband in carrying out his business or carrying on in business separately from their husbands'.[37] Elizabeth Sanderson's study of women's work in eighteenth-century Edinburgh highlighted that 40% of men received their trading rights through their wives.[38] In 1731, Rachel Husband, the wife of a wealthy Edinburgh merchant, was an active partner in the family business. While her husband was absent, she grew and sold pears, beans, oats and barley. She researched the best price for her crops through discussions with her neighbours and justified the prices to her husband. Rachel offered her husband advice on his business purchases, counselling him not to buy oranges as she had learned they would not last the journey home.[39]

The overlap between a husband and wife's responsibilities, the need for women to be involved in provisioning the household, and that it was often wives who physically received rents or payments for crops (and not necessarily in cash) meant that the distinction between managing the budget and managing the purse was not particularly clear. This was exasperated by the nature of the early modern estate economies, where income was often unpredictable in the wake of good or bad harvests, the ability of tenants and creditors to pay debts, and that not all interactions were performed in cash, or even easily converted into cash. Income often entered the marital economy in small amounts or as consumables, which made saving or planning for the future difficult. While the ability to negotiate marriage contracts and honour jointure payments suggests that most families had a sense of their income, where it would come from and what it would be spent on, the day-to-day functioning of estates suggests that for many the marital economy was reactive and accounting practices 'haphazard'.[40]

Many families operated on a system of debt maintenance, using income to pay off creditors that were immediately pressing, negotiating over what expenditure was most necessary at a particular moment, rather than applying a long-term management strategy. Even some of the early eighteenth-century estate improvers, who looked to the long-term economic stability of their estates, had difficulty transforming their households from reactive to proactive economies.[41] This was highlighted in the chronic complaints from widows and spinster sisters about non-payment of jointures and allowances, as well as the number of elite families who were bankrupted in the eighteenth and nineteenth centuries (although this at least partly was due to families consistently living beyond their means).[42] This is not to say that people were generally irresponsible or unconcerned with the health of marital economy, but that the nature of the credit economy placed limits on how estates were managed, which in turn shaped how couples negotiated over resources.

Despite the opacity of household roles and the high levels of cooperation required between spouses, the distinction between governor and manager held meaning for seventeenth-century Scots and continued to do so into the nineteenth century. This understanding of household roles was often the primary way that men and women interacted with each other in marriage and became the practice of marriage in the everyday. As a result, people were invested in performing their roles within the household effectively as it became a marker of their commitment to their partners. As Kate Fisher and Simon Szreter have shown for twentieth-century England, providing and sharing resources became the central markers of love for married couples; men highlighted their love by providing, and in a twentieth-century context, by not withholding their incomes from their wives. Women showed their love by their prudent management, their ability to stretch resources, and their commitment to the effective running of the household.[43] Similarly, elite Scots closely tied love and intimacy to household roles, so that it becomes difficult to disentangle negotiations over resources from discussions of love, adding emotional charge to what may appear to be minor squabbles over housework. As the philosopher Adam Smith commented, 'a husband is dissatisfied with the most obedient wife when he imagines her conduct is animated by no other principle besides her regard to what the station she stands in requires.'[44]

Within an early modern context, this situation was given greater pressure by the fact that the successful male provider and obedient, prudent wife were social markers to the wider world of the effectual wielding of patriarchal authority, central to male and female identity and the reputation of the household within the broader community.[45] Couples were aware that disputes over household resources undermined not only their intimate relationship with each other, but potentially their broader social status and with it their access to credit networks, patronage and social and political power. In this context, the line between the private and the public could be far from apparent.

In the seventeenth century, the household budget was often flexible and decided not by need or expectation, but by what the estate could afford. The reliance on a successful harvest or the annual profit of a business meant that incomes fluctuated. It was not unusual for wives to negotiate for the proceeds of a particular sale of crops or for husbands to demand that money earned was to be sent to support them in their absence. In 1669 Katherine Hume informed her husband that she had 'nine bols of bear' to go to Berwick for sale and asked whether she was to send him the money. At the same time, she reminded him that the only money she had received in his absence was '25 pund 14 shiling which I got from Pet Brock' for the sale of oats and she was not going to receive any more as he had failed to instruct Pet to sell the remainder of the harvest. Katherine asked whether she was to instruct Pet to sell more oats and where she was to find the money to pay the servants' fee before they left.[46]

The tone of Katherine's letter suggested that she knew where her household income was expected to come from, yet she chose not to interfere in her husband's part of the management. Her husband expected Pet to have sold the oats, and although his response has not survived, Katherine's reply indicated that he was annoyed that it had not happened. Katherine did not feel she had the authority to direct Pet to sell the oats without her husband's permission, but she did not respond meekly to criticism, commenting, 'if ye had bot left the least word with me about selling your otes you should not have the lest ground of anger bot I wret [wrote] in my last the reason whay they were not sold but I have derect pet to sel them thes wicke'.[47] Katherine did not usurp her husband's role or demand the income she needed to run the household. She negotiated with her husband deferentially, giving him place as the master and provider of the household, while she acted as the helpmeet who reminded him of his duties. Yet, as his wife, she was also quick to anger when criticised unfairly, defending her performance in the household and indicating that their squabble was more significant to the couple than just the selling of oats.

Other wives were more assertive. Shortly after their marriage in 1714, twenty-two-year-old Elizabeth Hay took stock of her twenty-five-year-old husband's financial situation as heir to the family estate and informed him, 'I find we shall have need to manage all our affairs after the frugalist way for we are like to have occasion for all your rents will afford as to the servants I design to meddle with none but what are immediately yours for we found the rest here and shall leave them with'. Elizabeth continued with a list of purchases needed for the home, advising him to follow her sister's advice on prices. She added that if his father would pay he could purchase what he wished but 'if you be to pay for them your self I have sent the inclos'd on purpose that you may cause buy nothing else but what is sett down in itt'. In the same letter, she informed him of estate business and that no work could be done due to bad weather.[48]

Despite her brisk instructions, Elizabeth diminished the harshness of her command, by highlighting the primacy of her husband's role in the household. While it was 'our affairs', she referred to 'your rent' and your servants. Elizabeth demarcated between the husband and wife's role, ensuring that she did not undermine her husband's place as head of the marital partnership, even as she took on his role. While instructions on purchases and estate management were a constant feature of her letters, she was careful to demonstrate her obedience and affection, on one occasion noting 'I pray god I may always be enabled to return your true affection with the sincere love which I ought and have for the best of husbands'.[49]

Women could directly appropriate household resources against their husband's wishes. In 1693, the Duke of Hamilton angrily wrote to his wife, Anne, when he discovered their son John had taken a £500 loan in his father's name, despite being explicitly told he was to receive no money. He demanded that his wife investigate how he was given the loan, in particular adding that she should ask the provost of Edinburgh how it happened. While he did not directly accuse Anne of being involved, he did note that 'he knew that she knew' that it was against his wishes for John to receive any money.[50] The Duke's letter implied that he suspected his wife had some knowledge of John's behaviour and that he had expected her to conform to his wishes on this matter, despite her role as head of the family. His unwillingness to directly accuse her of interfering reflected both a wish not to destabilise their intimate relationship, which was built on trust, but perhaps also a need not to make explicit the limits of his own authority in a relationship where his wife held significant power. Yet, the limit of a husband's authority in the wake of his wife's access to economic resources was not a problem restricted to the Hamiltons.

The weak husband and his domineering wife were not just found in fiction. Some women were forced to take charge of their households due to the ill-management of their husbands. In 1731, Margaret Aikman informed her brother that her husband had not been a good financial manager. To compensate she

> dubeld my expence of the hous upon him and saved that and som for buying cloaths for myself and the children which I never did till I got a 100 pound together and then give it him to buy a South Sea bond till at length I gave him five in that nature which he was very thankfull for and after he had a little mind to make a piece of money now that he had a beginning and it was but a lift mind for his mind was such in the nixt world on all occasions ... however he took a little of my advice in his last years and we ventured out that mony on Bottenure bonds which mad more and in all I as I reckon he has left about 16 hundred pounds and if I can mak it mor I will and lords will I shall for I ever did what I could to mak him easie.[51]

Margaret Aikman was aware of her husband's poor financial management and took charge of the household's assets. She saved money and directed their investments to ensure her security as a widow.

Margaret held enough influence over her husband to demand a doubling of expenses, which she seemingly received without discussion. After her husband's death, Margaret used £1000 of her investment as a dowry for her daughter. Her management had ensured her an income as a widow and provided for her offspring. Yet, she did not disclose her role in the household until after her husband's death, ensuring that she did not undermine his masculinity, their marital relationship, or the social reputation of the household. The personality of both husband and wife could shift the balance of power within marriage, but society shunned domineering women and weak men, ensuring that such people kept their relationships from public knowledge.

Some women had the opportunity to turn their economic role within the household into publicly recognised authority.[52] In the early eighteenth century, Margaret Hamilton, Countess of Panmuir, gained significant social power through her successful estate management after her husband, James Maule's, exile. As time passed and it became clear that her husband may not return, she took increasing control of the decision making on the estate. Furthermore, Maule's business associates and family in time dealt exclusively with her, taking her opinion over that of her husband. Her correspondence with her husband highlighted her personal development, increased confidence and self-esteem over the period of his absence.[53]

Margaret excelled as an estate manager and wrote enthusiastically of her progress to her husband, noting, 'I must say (tho in jest) that I deserve a factor fee for I have had some work done on my hand, I heartily wish with al my soul that you were here to take my accompts off my hand and could you make use of wings you would att present see yr cornyard here fuller than ever you saw it, which is some little amusement to me'.[54] As Margaret grew in her role as estate manager, she became more assertive. She began to actively pursue her right to the estate in court as it became clear it would be forfeited. To ensure her financial security, she sued the estate for her jointure and sold all the furniture within her home for cash. When the estate was later forfeited, her servants swore along with her that they had no explanation for the missing furniture.

Over the course of time, the power relationship with her husband altered. While previously Margaret had sought her husband's consent for her decisions, she began to act then inform her husband of her choices. Eventually, as is highlighted in Chapter 5, Margaret disregarded her husband's opinion when she disagreed with him. Her husband's brother Harry Maule also became increasingly confident in Margaret's choices, taking her side over his uncle. James Maule's absence allowed Margaret to utilise her economic resources to gain power beyond the household. She was not unique. Frances, Countess of Mar's relationship with her husband underwent a similar change when he was exiled to France.[55] These women were facing exceptional circumstances not knowing when they would be reconciled with their partners. In both cases, their husbands never returned to Scotland, dying abroad after a number of years. It could be argued that women whose husbands were absent for periods of years, rather than weeks or months, took on the status of widows and the requisite social power.[56] Women whose husbands were gone for shorter periods did not generally appear to gain similar amounts of social power.

Over the course of the eighteenth century, the manner in which couples discussed their role in the marital economy began to alter, reflecting the greater availability of cash, a growing concern with the separation of work and home and the ideology of domesticity. For conduct writers, the expectation that households now operated on a cash-basis allowed them to more clearly define the role between provisioning and management. The best-selling author John Gregory noted a husband 'may give you as much money for your clothes, personal expence [sic], and domestic necessaries, as is suitable to their fortunes',[57] while Hestor Chapone noted, not without some criticism, that 'the settling the general scheme of expences is seldom the wife's province, and that many men do not choose even to acquaint her with the real state of affairs. – Where this is the case, a woman can be answerable for no more than is entrusted to her.'[58]

Despite this clearer distinction between gendered roles, the duties of the wife continued to be extensive, incorporating the supervision of servants, book-keeping and the administration of provisions.[59] Hannah More noted in 1799 that:

> œconomy, such as a woman of fortune is called on to practice, is not merely the petty detail of small daily expences, the shabby curtailments and stinted parsimony of a little mind operating on little concerns; but it is the exercise of a sound judgement exerted in the comprehensive outline of order, of arrangement, of distribution; of regulations by which alone well governed societies, great and small, subsist.[60]

Similarly in 1784, while John Moir's rather ambiguous instructions indicated that men would be knowledgeable of their wives' expenditure, he emphasised that the family economy was under the management of a woman whose 'frugal disposition, attended with activity and diligence, will afford much more solid and substantial content, than a large fortune'.[61] The distancing of women from provisioning activities led to greater concern within the household over the roles of husband and wife, and as Karen Harvey notes, this was not a simple case of the removal of men from the home.[62]

While there was always a sense within correspondence that men and women had different roles within the marital economy, performing a spouse's task in their absence had not been considered to be unusual. From around the mid-eighteenth century, however, people were more likely to emphasise the undesirability and peculiarity of having to take on their spouse's role. In the 1730s, Archibald Campbell, Church of Scotland minister and professor of divinity at the University of St Andrews, noted to his wife in early marriage that he was delayed on business in the hope that he would have a wage for her security.[63] He emphasised that he wished to 'put you in circumstances equal to your merit',[64] and in 1738 commented: 'I most heartily thank you my dr [dear] madam for the compliment with which you begin your letter, and I believe I may venture to assure you that if your husband were so lucky as to make as good a figure in his profession as his wife does in her situation his reputation would become higher & he would be reckoned still more deserving.'[65]

Archibald's understanding of his own role more closely mirrored a model of male breadwinner who brought home an income, than earlier presentations of provisioning masculinity that emphasised good management of resources. He also complemented his wife for her ability in her own distinct sphere, which was described as 'situation', rather than as a 'profession' or 'occupation', which implied work. Yet, this transformation to the world of domesticity and separate spheres was not immediate. In 1740, the laird Alexander Campbell of Clunes requested that his wife return home as 'now the family requires you beyond ordinary' as he was ill, before noting that 'our harvest is farr behind some of our neighbours and this morning we have snow and plenty of rains & high winds in the night time'.[66]

As the period progressed, the idea of the husband as provider and the wife as manager of the purse came to be expressed more explicitly, especially by men. In 1744, the judge Hew Dalrymple warned his wife, Peg, against being too frugal, noting: 'do not let you own blindness to me denie you what you have a just tile to, and what my wife ought to have in pocket money, living and particularly cloaths, I would rather have you dress above our pocket as under it'. He continued that he had left his ledger with 'an account how all our money had been spent and the dates of my bills which inables me to setle accounts with my steward' and another book with his business accounts.[67] Hew's letter suggested that he believed his wife was unaware of their finances or of his business expenditure. He emphasised his role as provider by noting that she was entitled to 'pocket money'.

Yet, while Hew complained of his wife's frugality, it may be that she had a greater awareness of their financial situation than he realised. On one occasion, he wrote her a letter noting that 'economy hither to has been very much neglected by me' and that it was her love that had inspired him to lay a 'thurrow order and economy in our private affairs', before detailing their financial problems.[68] On another occasion, he noted that he had lost heavily playing cards and that he was glad that they had good credit.[69] He continued to complain of her frugality, reminding her that 'it is no pleasure to me to see yu either want ready money or too frugall in dress a trifle on the side of show in dress is often-times better than a penny in pocket, it always looks genteel and gets respect with people, who do not know you'.[70] While Hew was concerned with maintaining his public reputation, and in turn his credit network, Peg's frugality may have been a response to her spendthrift husband, subtly controlling his expenditure through her appearance and so safe-guarding the marital economy.

In 1759, Archibald Cunningham of Cadell apologised to his wife Christian Macredie for asking her to sell the household's meat, noting, 'nothing at present gives me so much uneasiness as that you should be loaded with the whole trouble of everything without doors, when God knows managing things within is a great deal too much'. Yet, he was 'convinced every part of your conduct and management is intirely calculated for our mutal advantage and that of your lovely little ones' and knew that she would get the best bargain possible.[71] Archibald's concern that his wife had to involve herself in estate operations was novel to his period.

As the century passed, women also attempted to rhetorically distance themselves from their role in estate and business affairs, although they did not always seem to be less involved in practice. Marion Buchan noted in 1767 to her absent husband, Robert Cathcart of Genock, that 'they say has rained a good deal which has prevented the corn being carried to the mill but they have it all winnowed & if the morning is good will caray it down early'. Marion's use of 'they say' implied her knowledge of the estate was second hand, rather than because she was actively involved in its management. Her letter contin-ued, 'I wish this bad day may not have prevented yoar getting the trees gathered'. Marion was aware of what was happening on her estate, but discussed it as if it were not her concern. The focus of her letter was how much she missed her husband and the health of her child.[72] Whether she was truly uninterested or whether she did not feel it was appropriate to appear to interfere in estate life is harder to establish.

At the end of the eighteenth century, Anna Peebles informed her husband John, who was in the military, that she had been advised it would take 'fourty shillings worth of fodder' to fatten her cow for May or fifty shillings to be ready in seven weeks. While it was Anna's cow, she separated herself from raising it noting that 'he [Maclean – who offered her the advice] would make her fat in seven weeks'. She asked her husband to make the decision as 'had you been at home your judgement should have directed me', but reminded him that the family needed winter milk.[73] Women remained actively involved in providing for the household, but verbally distanced themselves from activities that classed them as providers. It was not just modesty that caused Anna to dissociate herself from the provider role. In other areas of her home life, she was proud of her successes. In the same letter, she informed her husband that 'we have had a brewing of strong beer which comes on admirably – which I attribute to the place it is in – there is none other so proper about the house – I hope I shall be able to regale you with a drink of good homebrew'd when you return'.

In the nineteenth century, Henrietta Moodie's correspondence highlighted that she not only distanced herself from provisioning and the estate, but understood herself and her role within the household as secondary to her husband's. Henrietta married Mr Heddle, who had purchased her father's estates after he had financial problems. She noted to her friend:

> he won my gratitude and taught me that gratitude is the strongest bond of affection. That his affection for me began from the first meeting which was unexpected appears to me that peculiar providence of God– when I reflect on the various opportunities of going good afforded me by is [this?] situation as possessing large estates in this country and his generous confidence which will put it in my power to be liberal as my prudence will allow I am assured that for this purpose the allotment of affluence and that in a place where I know how to employ it has been made for me.[74]

Henrietta believed that it was through her husband's generosity that she would be able to function as mistress of her estate. Henrietta's situation was complicated by the manner in which she came to be mistress of her childhood home, but she allowed this circumstance to render the role of wife as entirely passive and under the direction of her husband. This interpretation of her circumstances was influenced by broader cultural norms surrounding the role of wife, but it is interesting that she never considered the advantages that an incoming landlord from 'new money' might gain through marrying the daughter of the previous estate owner.

This statement was also made in early marriage and unfortunately evidence does not survive to explore whether her sense of her role in the marital economy changed as her marriage aged.

Men continued to see themselves as providers in the late eighteenth and nineteenth centuries and the expansion of the cash economy often gave them a greater degree of control over their wives' expenditure. In 1774, James Grant sent his wife money to pay her expenses along with detailed instructions for tipping the servants 'to allow her to leave triumphantly', although he added that whether she followed his advice when allocating the money was at her discretion.[75] David, Earl of Airlie, in 1814, wrote to his wife Clementina, that she should not want for any money as 'I wrote to the safe bank in Kirrymuir and you will only have to call at Kenmuir for what you need'.[76] Yet, some relationships continued to show some sense of mutuality in the provisioning of the household. Archibald Lawrie in 1796, when discussing the recent marriage of George, Prince of Wales and Princess Caroline of Brunswick, noted that he thought it was a bad time to marry 'before he had paid his immeasurable debts, I fear he is a sad one & will not be in his power to make his wife, one of the happiest of her kind'.[77] His comment suggested that he believed it was a husband's role to provide for his wife, yet in other letters he asked his wife detailed questions about her estate management, including whether the corn was collected.[78]

In the 1830s, Walter Crum provided cash that his wife used to pay bills and make household purchases, but Jessie Crum's responsibilities as manager of the household were significant. She made decisions about what summerhouse to rent and what purchases to make without consulting her husband. Jessie would ask Walter for money which he provided without debate. When Walter received bills to settle while Jessie was on holiday, he had to send them to her for inspection to ensure he was not defrauded. Walter believed Jessie to be a competent household manager and was unsure how to respond to her mistakes. When Jessie reported her problems renting a summerhouse, Walter gently chided, 'I have received your letter and don't know whether I am more ashamed or disappointed that you should have allowed two excellent houses to escape you for so very low a rent as £17'.[79] His 'shame and disappointment' suggested that Walter saw Jessie's performance as a reflection on him. It indicated that Jessie was not an equal who made her own mistakes, but a subordinate that Walter had, mistakenly on this occasion, trusted. Generally, Jessie's competent management precluded her from criticism and in most areas Walter trusted Jessie's judgement and sought her opinion.[80]

The increasing demarcation between the roles of husband and wife also shaped the nature of negotiation with marriage, although with the rise of the cash economy, women were less likely to be negotiating over sales of crops than their allocated income for household expenses or pocket money. In 1779, Ann Robertson negotiated for £30 annually to spend on 'cards, cloaths etc', yet still accumulated debt. She pleaded with her husband to pay her silversmith's bill, which he agreed after she promised that she was 'perfectly satisfy'd with' her allowance.[81] Her husband was particularly disappointed that she had accrued debts gambling without his knowledge, commenting that 'you soon had access to all my cash & all my credit, bout have used both without reserve but to the full amount of all your desires ... However Im far from wishing to recall my provision or to refuse the allowance'. He continued with a lecture against 'high play and constituting debt' as it would bring remorse and ruin to him and a family of their means.[82]

Ann's role as manager of the household allowed her to amass debt without her husband's permission and, as he warned, to damage his reputation. General James Robertson was aware of the threat that his wife posed to his authority over the household finances and carefully negotiated with his wife to ensure that she had enough resources so that she would not abuse her power or exploit his vulnerability. At the same time, Ann's wrong-doing reduced her authority in her marriage, at least for a time. Her letter was apologetic, more formal than usual and she describes 'the mortification of asking for you to pay them'. Her ability to manage her separate income was clearly a matter of pride. In turn, James' reply was patronising and paternalistic, lecturing her on the importance of good management to credit and reinforcing his authority. While women could exploit their access to household resources, if they did so unsuccessfully or for 'frivolous' ends, they risked damaging the relationship of trust within their marriage and reducing their authority within the home.

Women continued to utilise economic resources for their own interest in the nineteenth century. The marriage of Philadelphia Stuart Monteith and John Francis Erskine (1827–52) was marked by a power struggle over Philadelphia's use of household resources. Philadelphia and John were reasonably wealthy, but even in early marriage John was very frugal and wished to control all Philadelphia's spending. John understood her independent choice in purchasing as a threat to his authority. In a debate over where she bought wine, he argued that she deliberately chose her supplier to undermine his authority (as well as making a subtle criticism of her drinking habits – ardent spirits being an unrespectable drink for women), noting:

The person who supplies you with ardent spirits probably can with wine which will save any insinuation as to quality allowed. And I shall merely have the trouble of paying for it. In this way you will have an opportunity of giving these things at my expense to others; in order that they may be insolent to me. There are persons in this town: (not unknown to you) who supplied sufficiently good wine ... I therefore hope it will be sufficiently good for your purposes.[83]

He was also anxious that his father-in-law was providing Philadelphia with an independent income, despite her repeated denials, 'as to your fears respecting my fathers influence you have no cause as he does not interfere with my affairs'.[84] Philadelphia wished to reassure John that she followed his instructions regarding the household budget, noting, 'I have no wish to oppose you in any thing but wish to be regulated by you in our expenditure'.[85] Yet, she found it difficult to live with a man who was so controlling of the household finances and eventually removed herself from their home, taking residence in a summerhouse.

Her ability to leave her husband was made possible by his legal responsibility to pay her bills. Philadelphia's right and ability to utilise her household's resources gave her enough independence to set up a new home. Her husband repeatedly asked her to return, but she replied by assuring him that she 'only wish[ed] to try the plan of taking house for a short time ... when I go to reside with you I would I have drawn my quartins [? quarterly portion] money I can always return the same to you while under your roof'.[86] John could not force her to return and resorted to emotional blackmail, writing 'Dear Philadelphia, I am dying; surely you will not refuse to come and see me. The chambermaid will tell you I am not outrageous but weak: and have not long to live, if I am to meet with no kindness'.[87] He was not to die for almost thirty years.

The ability to utilise economic resources was clearly seen by John as a threat to his authority and perhaps rightly so. Philadelphia used her role within the marital economy to remove herself from the home and beyond the control of her husband. Yet, that Philadelphia had to leave her husband to regain some power suggested that this was no victory over the patriarchal system. Furthermore, it was only possible because the appearance of marital disharmony, and particularly John's inability to control his wife, was potentially damaging to the family reputation, forcing John to maintain Philadelphia and keep their separation from public eyes.[88]

Women used their access to economic resources to negotiate for power within their personal relationship with their husbands. They could negotiate to ensure the successful operation of their household, to favour children, to gain access to the things or lifestyle they desired, to create a space or identity for themselves within their marriage or to remove themselves from it. While, as Lynn Abrams and Michelle Rosaldo suggests, their access to economic resources only infrequently gave them authority within wider society, it was significant in shaping their relationships within their families and with their spouse. While the nature of the economic resources that were used in negotiation altered over time, within a context where the marital economy was so central to social reputation and credit as well as being tied to intimacy, there usage limited male authority within marriage across the period.

While it has been suggested that elite women's role in the household between the seventeenth and nineteenth centuries became increasingly decorative and unproductive, in a Scottish context, the continued aware-ness by women of how the estate functioned, as well as the expectation that they manage it in a husband's absence, highlights that there was significant continuity over time.[89] Yet, while the operation of the marital economy did not dramatically change for this social group, how they thought about their role within the marital economy did.

While there has always been a nominal distinction between the management of the budget and the management of the purse, in the eighteenth century, this distinction became increasingly central to how people thought about the operation of the household, influencing how they understood and discussed their roles within the marital economy (if having less effect on daily practice). With this shift, the sense of shared interest that was at the heart of the marital economy increasingly became understood as the husband's interest, following broader changes in how the marital relationship was understood, as discussed in previous chapters. His wife, while still managing the household and estates, came to be understood as non-productive and at the same time, her 'domestic' role was given less authority than that allocated to the role of provider, which was located in the husband.

This was reinforced by the increased tie between the economy and the public sphere and the association of the public sphere with political and social power. New models for thinking about the house-hold economy, created by the Scottish Enlightenment literati, ensured that women became increasingly distant from the realm of public power within Scotland. Furthermore, the association of the private sphere with nature in Scottish Enlightenment thought gave it less social legitimacy when compared to the rational, virtuous and for Adam Smith, moral exchanges between elite men in the public sphere.[90] The importance of sociability and friendship to the understanding of the polity in Scottish society, as discussed in the previous chapter, acted to exclude women from the political public sphere, as it did in other contexts such as Revolutionary France and the German states.[91] It was not until the belief that home was a haven from the public world was given religious re-enforcement by the rise of Evangelicalism in the late eighteenth and nineteenth centuries that the moral power of the domestic sphere began to be translated into access into the public sphere by women.[92]

Negotiating with family

The use of economic resources within intimate spousal relationships could be complicated, like other aspects of married life, by the influence of wider family. Margaret Hunt argues that amongst the English middling sorts the role of family could make or break the marital economy. She argues that wives played a significant mediating role in the 'endless negotiations' between kin and highlighted that men whose ambitions were frustrated by their wives' families were often violent toward their spouses. Hunt notes that the quest for money and power was 'pregnant with potential for serious familial conflict'.[93] Yet, for others like Ruth Perry, the move from consanguinity to conjugality displaced wider kin, situating privacy and the domestic sphere within the nuclear family, while wider family were relegated to the edges of this sphere, dangerously close to becoming 'public' visitors.[94] Within the correspondence of Scottish couples, wider family frequently featured, although the role they played depended heavily on individual personality, the place of the couple in the family hierarchy, and their physical proximity to their family.

Wider family was both an ever-present part of married life, often forming the core social circle that people operated within, and a set of relationships with the potential to create tension and trouble. At no historical moment were family relationships particularly smooth or easy as individuals and the marital unit attempted to work out their relationship with kin networks, but amongst the eighteenth-century Scottish elites, the importance of independent manhood as a model of masculinity and the rise of the culture of sensibility with its focus on the couple, created a new set of questions about the relationship between the wider family and the conjugal unit. At the same time, family remained central to the economic success of the family, and as Hunt suggests, to women's authority within the family. The place of family destabilised and complicated ideas of public and private when applied to married life.

In the seventeenth century, women were utilised by their husbands for their access to family networks and to protect their assets, offering them a space in which to hold power. Mary Gray asked Lord Olgilvie in 1661 to speak to Lord Newbrough on her husband's behalf.[95] In 1695, George Home of Kimmerghame was approached by a cousin, 'Dr Irvine's Lady', to seek his influence over his close friend and cousin, Lord Crossrig, who was Lord of Session, on her husband's legal suit. She asked, on behalf of her husband, for a quick judgement and to explain their interest in the matter. The case itself was an example of wider family interest in marriage as Dr Irvine was attempting to have his deceased father's second marriage annulled so that he would inherit his father's entire estate.[96] In 1696, John Bows used his wife's independent status to evade his creditors by disposing of his property to her and their children – a legal loophole that was not closed in Scotland until the nineteenth century.[97]

For others, disputes over economic resources destabilised lines of power. In 1694, George Home was involved in a family conflict over the use of economic resources that lasted several years. As the heir to his estate, he was responsible for paying his sister's annual rent of her portion, the amount of which had been determined by their parents. His sister, Isobel, believed that George underpaid her, while he argued that he did not know how much money she had previously received. Isobel also believed that their brother David was paid more regularly than her. George argued that he was fair to his sister as her portion did not take account of the poor financial state of the estate and he thought that she spent her money frivolously. Isobel eventually requested money from their cousin, spreading the family conflict beyond the immediate circle and using wider family to give weight to her demands.[98] George's poor financial situation had been caused by heavy government fines to his estate due to his own clandestine marriage with his cousin, an heiress under the protection of the Privy Court.

Family feuds placed strain on individual marriages. In 1685, Katherine Hamilton complained to her mother that her mother-in-law, Lady Atholl, 'was in a most extraordinary huff that her son had not come to wait on her'. She noted that: 'all that he or I dos are still reconed crimes how inosent it is I cannot express to your grace how sower she looked on us, I confes it is a lytle troublesome to be raised to pay respect & wait upon those who when we do it looks on us as if we were malefactors'.[99] Katherine and her husband were required to retain ties with his family as he was heir to the estate and relied on his family for their income. There was some indication that this feud had originated from the previous year when Lady Atholl believed that Katherine's father intended to alter the terms of her marriage contract. She reassured her mother-in-law that her father had no such desire.[100] Katherine's brother James had similar difficulties with his mother-in-law in 1704.[101] Even after marriage, the reliance on wider family for economic resources required couples to allow their wider family to interfere in their relationship and affect the balance of power within it. Yet, even in the seventeenth century, as Katherine's letter suggests, couples tended to see unwanted interference from family as an attack on the conjugal unit, rather than taking sides with their natal family against a spouse. Family loyalty was expected to begin with one's partner.

In the eighteenth century, wider family still continued to influence the operation of marital life, but men became increasingly cautious about accessing their in-laws' resources. Alexander Murray wrote to his estranged wife, Grizell Baillie, in 1738, after her father's death, of his suspicions that their marriage breakdown was the fault of her parents as well as her. Murray blamed Grizell's family for supporting her when she left him, and noted that he had hoped if his letter had arrived before her father's death that 'it would have induced him, and you all, to have given me proofs, by your answers of his & your repentance of the many grevious wrongs he and you all have done me'.[102]

The author Mary Leslie's marriage in the 1770s, which ended in separation, was strained by the conflict between her husband, James Walker, and her family. Her husband did not want her family's financial support, but he could not support his family with his own earnings. James believed that taking financial support from his father-in-law would require him to follow the latter's advice on his career, which he refused to do. Yet, he was under pressure from his wife and his mother to make use of the offered resources. The tension caused Mary and James to informally separate, and, eventually, after a long dispute over alimony, James left the country and his wife without any support.[103] Similarly as noted above, in the nineteenth century, John Erskine was concerned that his father-in-law was undermining his authority by offering his wife financial support.[104]

Yet, for others, family continued to offer important resources. In 1735, Archibald Grant borrowed money from his in-laws and then, unsuccessfully, tried to persuade his wife to have her mother forgive the debt. His mother-in-law also lived with his family for a number of years, contributing financially to the household income. She often found herself as the mediator of their marital disputes.[105] In 1773, James Grant's mother-in-law wrote character letters on his behalf to help him professionally and explain his considerable inherited debt. She noted that she had offered to let them stay with her, but 'to my grief that could not be'.[106] It appeared that James was willing to ask his mother-in-law for some forms of help, but wished to retain his independence.

The negotiation of the marital economy by couples was complicated by the role of wider family, especially immediate in-laws. Economic resources offered by wider family gave women authority within their marriage, but it often came with restrictions to the behaviour of both women, as seen in the case of Katherine Hamilton, and men, as with the example of James Walker. As mothers and mothers-in-law, women often acted as intermediaries between their children and their family's resources, offering insight into the degree of authority that many women held within their families, especially as they aged. Yet, that mothers-in-law were more frequently criticised for their interference than their husbands also suggests that their authority was never complete or unquestioned. Family influence could have a detrimental effect on marriage, especially where men felt it undermined their authority within the home. As the eighteenth century progressed, men were increasingly reluctant to allow their wider family to interfere with their role as providers, prizing economic independence as a marker of manhood and as a validation of their place in the polity. Furthermore, even in the seventeenth century, couples clearly distinguished between the conjugal unit and wider family.

Marriage was not just the joining of two family networks, but the creation of new families with a sense of separation and independence from their wider kin. This created different levels of privacy and intimacy within the family, as couples expected to be able to trust their spouse with keeping certain types of information (particularly those that undermined an individual's social reputation) private from their families, and they trusted their families to keep a broader set of information private from the 'public' world. In the eighteenth century, it also led to a focus on privacy as a marker of individualism, creating boundaries that kept out both the public world and the family, and where allowing access to the self reflected greater intimacy within relationships. The border between public and private became blurred as the distinction between the individual, the conjugal unit and wider kin became increasingly distinct.

Broader social constructions of the meaning of 'public' and 'private' and their relationship to production within the marital economy, the concept of work, and gender roles shaped how the Scottish elites understood and performed marriage. As provisioning the household was increasingly associated with men, women were distanced (often more rhetorically than in practice) from the productive functions of the marital economy and the public world to which it was increasingly tied. This was reinforced by social prescriptions that saw women as helpmeet to her husband and which increasingly located women within the domestic sphere. Yet, the relationship between economic resources and power was intimately connected in the seventeenth to nineteenth centuries. The basis of power for the Scottish elites was associated with their ability to access and utilise economic resources, making them anxious over their estate's productive capacity and reinforcing the importance of the display of gentility when they engaged with their tenants and neighbours. The relationship between power and resources filtered through into the marital relationship, creating anxiety in the public imagination around women's role as manager of the household. Female control of economic resources was believed to threaten male authority, yet female management of household and its resources was a vital and indispensable part of the marital economy.

Women often had significant access to economic resources within the home, which belied social prescriptions that reduced them to managers of the purse. Within this sphere women could dominate individual men, escape abuses, hold social power and show their financial and managerial acumen. Their access to resources and their ability to use them, even to the detriment of the family interest, undermined any sense that male authority was complete or invulnerable.[107] It gave women a significant bargaining chip within the marital relationship and, while it did not neutralise power relationships between couples, it gave women a weapon in marital negotiations. Yet, it was difficult to translate this power beyond the household.

In the seventeenth century, popular discourse ridiculed domineering women and society shunned or ritually humiliated families where men were not seen to fully exercise control, ensuring that women, such as Margaret Aikman above, would not reveal their economic role in public. In the later eighteenth century, the separation of production and consumption within the marital economy, and the connection between production and the public sphere, removed the opportunity for women to exercise public power. Even when women had access to significant resources, they were not recognised as having authority as those resources were not associated with the public sphere where power resided (although women increasingly began to find ways to transform their role as consumers into power, as reflected in American women's boycotts on British products during the American War of Independence).[108]

Women who wished to challenge the patriarchal model of male authority and female subordination through utilising economic resources had few discourses on which to draw. Furthermore, marriages were not just economic contracts, but intimate relationships. This ensured that negotiations over and use of resources were not based on simple rational calculations made to give individuals the most power, but were tempered by a need to show support and love for a spouse. These factors culminated to ensure that women's resistance to patriarchal power remained isolated, unique and failed to give them power beyond their individual households. Moreover, as elite women, who held power as estate managers and mistresses, these women had an invested interest in maintaining the status quo.[109]

Notes

1 For a discussion of the term 'marital economy' see A. Erickson, 'The marital economy in comparative perspective', in M. Ågren and A. Erickson (eds), *The Marital Economy in Scandinavia and Britain 1400–1900* (Aldershot: Ashgate, 2005), p. 3.

2 A. Clark, *The Struggle for the Breeches: Gender and the Making of the British Working Class* (Berkley: California University Press, 1995), p. 7.

3 R. Fiebranz, 'Marital conflict over the gender division of labour in agrarian households, Sweden 1750–1850', in Ågren and Erickson, *The Marital Economy*, p. 152; L. Tilly and J. Scott, *Women, Work and the Family* (London: Routledge, 1989), p. 54; J. Hardwick, *The Practice of Patriarchy: Gender and the Politics of Household Authority in Early Modern France* (University Park: Penn. State University Press, 1998), p. 107.

4 B. Capp, *When Gossips Meet: Women, Family, and Neighbourhood in Early Modern England* (Oxford: Oxford University Press, 2003), pp. 78–9.

5 R. Grassby, *Kinship and Capitalism: Marriage, Family and Business in the English-Speaking World, 1580–1740* (Cambridge: Cambridge University Press, 2001), pp. 92–116.

6 M. Rosaldo, 'Women, culture and society: a theoretical overview', in M. Zimbalist Rosaldo and L. Lamphere (eds), *Women, Culture and Society* (Stanford: Stanford University Press, 1974), pp. 17–42.

7 L. Abrams, *Myth and Materiality in a Woman's World: Shetland 1800–2000* (Manchester: Manchester University Press, 2005), p. 199. This conclusion is also supported by Susan Staves, who demonstrates that women who used their 'pin money' to buy property found it belonged to the common stock, not their own, S. Staves, 'Pin money', *Studies in Eighteenth-Century Culture*, 14 (1985), 47–77. Max Weber makes a related point when he argues that a worker's wage claim does not give him power over his employer, see *Economy and Society: an Outline of Interpretive Sociology* (Berkeley: California University Press, 1978), p. 942.

8 C. Muldrew, 'The culture of reconciliation: community and the settlement of economic disputes in early modern England,' *Historical Journal*, 39:4 (1996), 915–42.

9 P. Spacks, *Privacy: Concealing the Eighteenth Century Self* (London: University of Chicago Press, 2003), pp. 1–26.

10 C. Muldrew, 'Interpreting the market: the ethics of credit and community relations in early modern England', *Social History*, 18:2 (1993), pp. 163–83.

11 B. Griffin, L. Delap, and A. Wills, 'Introduction: the politics of domestic authority in Britain since 1800', in B. Griffin, L. Delap and A. Wills (eds), *The Politics of Domestic Authority in Britain since 1800* (Houndmills: Palgrave Macmillan, 2009), pp. 1–26; E. Gordon and G. Nair, *Public Lives: Women, Family and Society in Victorian Britain* (London: Yale University Press, 2003).

12 J. Tosh, *A Man's Place: Masculinity and the Middle Class Home in Victorian England* (New Haven: Yale University Press, 1999), p. 108; Clark, *Struggle for the Breeches*, pp. 248–63.

13 N. Cott, *The Bonds of Womanhood: Woman's Sphere in New England, 1780–1835* (London: Yale University Press, 1981).

14 Tosh, *A Man's Place*, pp. 102–22.

15 K. Harvey, 'Barbarity in a teacup? Punch, domesticity and gender in the eighteenth century', *Journal of Design History*, 21:3 (2008), 205–21; J. Kross, 'Mansions, men, women, and the creations of multiple publics in eighteenth-century British North America', *Journal of Social History*, 33:2 (1999), 398–9.

16 E. Gordon, 'The family', in Lynn Abrams et al. (eds), *Gender in Scottish History since 1700* (Edinburgh: Edinburgh University Press, 2006), p. 238.

17 J. Bailey, *Unquiet Lives: Marriage and Marriage Breakdown in England, 1660–1800* (Cambridge: Cambridge University Press, 2003), p. 71.

18 R. Allestree, *The Ladies Calling* (Oxford: Theatre in Oxford, 1700), p. 204.

19 A. Campbell, Marques of Argyll, *Instructions to a Son* (London: Richard Blackwell, 1689), pp. 79–80.

20 F. Fenelon de Salignac de la Mothe, *Instructions for the Education of Daughters* (Glasgow: R. & A. Foulis, 1750), pp. 146–8.

21 As early as 1405, Christine de Pisan advised women that they should know all their husband's business accounts and estate management so they could run them in times of war or absence, *The Treasure of the City of Ladies* (London: Penguin Books [1405] 1985), pp. 130–1. This is noted for the nineteenth century by Gordon and Nair, *Public Lives*, p. 161.

22 C. Lundh provides a useful discussion of this in 'Remarriages in Sweden in the 18th and 19th centuries', *History of the Family*, 7 (2002), 423–49. See also introduction for the low rates of remarriage among women compared to men in my sample.

23 NAS GD18/5175/1 Elizabeth Henderson to John Clerk, 16 March 1676.

24 NAS GD18/5175/4 Elizabeth Henderson to John Clerk [April 1676].

25 Or 800 merks? NAS GD18/5174A Elizabeth Henderson to John Clerk, 11 May 1676.

26 NAS GD112/39/148/1 Mary, Countess of Caithness to her John Campbell, Earl of Breadalbane, August–October 1690.

27 NAS GD112/39/148/1 Mary, Countess of Caithness to John Campbell, Earl of Breadalbane, 26 August 1690.

28 NAS GD446/40 Robert Douglas to Susanna Balfour [1704–5].

29 NAS GD124/15/231/2 John Erskine, Earl of Mar to Margaret, Countess of Mar, 6 June 1704.

30 NAS GD406/1/5282 James, Duke of Hamilton to Elizabeth, Duchess of Hamilton, 10 March 1704/5.

31 NAS GD406/1/7305 William, Duke of Hamilton to Anne, Duchess of Hamilton, 26 October 1693; NAS GD406/1/6995 William, Duke of Hamilton to Anne, Duchess of Hamilton, 19 March 1688.

32 NAS GD18/5289 Janet Inglis to John Clerk, 7 July [c. 1715].

33 NAS GD406/1/7308 William, Duke of Hamilton to Anne, Duchess of Hamilton, 2 November 1693.

34 NAS GD406/1/7132 James, Duke of Hamilton to Elizabeth, Duchess of Hamilton, 12 March 1702; NAS GD406/1/5285 James, Duke of Hamilton to Elizabeth, Duchess of Hamilton, 27 March 1704/5.

35 NAS GD139/526 John Sutherland to Emelia Sutherland [1746].

36 NAS GD110/1084/1 Hew Dalrymple to his Margaret Sainthill [July 1744].

37 Quoted in D. Simonton, 'Work, trade and commerce', in Abrams et al., *Gender in Scottish History*, p. 208.

38 E. Sanderson, *Women and Work in Eighteenth Century Edinburgh* (Basingstoke: Macmillan Press, 1996), p. 130.

39 NAS RH15/149 Rachel Husband to Francis Husband [February 1731].

40 K. Brown, *Noble Society in Scotland: Wealth, Family and Culture from Reformation to Revolution* (Edinburgh: Edinburgh University Press, 2000), pp. 71–91.

41 T.C. Smout, 'Landowners in Scotland, Ireland and Denmark in the age of improvement', *Scandinavian Journal of History*, 12:1 (1987), 79–97.

42 S. Nenadic, *Laird and Luxury: the Highland Gentry in Eighteenth Century Scotland* (Edinburgh: John Donald, 2007), p. 2.

43 S. Szreter and K. Fisher, 'Love and authority in mid-twentieth-century marriages: sharing and caring', in Delap et al, *Politics of Domestic Authority*, pp. 132–54.

44 A. Smith, *The Theory of Moral Sentiments* (London: Henry G. Bohn, 1853), p. 249.

45 H. Barker, 'Soul, purse and family: middling and lower-class masculinity in eighteenth-century Manchester', *Social History*, 33:1 (2008), 12–35; A. Shepard, 'Manhood, credit and patriarchy in early modern England, c. 1580–1640', *Past and Present*, 167 (2000), 83–7.

46 NAS GD158/2720 Katherine Hume to Laird of Kimmerghame, 8 November 1669

47 NAS GD158/2720 Katherine Hume to Laird of Kimmerghame, 11 November 1669.

48 NAS GD248/561/51 Elizabeth Hay to Lord Deskford [October 1714].

49 NAS GD248/561/17 Elizabeth Hay to Lord Deskford, 26 September 1714.

50 NAS GD406/1/7307 William, Duke of Hamilton to Anne, Duchess of Hamilton, 31 October 1693.

51 NAS GD18/4640 Margaret Aikman to John Clerk, 22 June 1731.

52 E. Chalus, '"To serve my friends": Women and Political Patronage in Eighteenth Century England', in A. Vickery (ed.), *Women, Privilege and Power: British Politics, 1750 to the Present* (Stanford: Stanford, 2001), pp. 57–88.

53 See NAS GD45/14/220 Letters from Margaret Hamilton, Countess of Panmure to James Maule, Earl of Panmure, 1716–23.

54 NAS GD45/14/220/44 Margaret Hamilton, Countess of Panmure to James Maule, Earl of Panmure, 28 October 1717.

55 See NAS GD1/44/7 Letters from Frances, Countess of Mar to John Erskine, Count of Mar, 1716.

56 For discussions on this topic see S. Cavello and L. Warner (eds), *Widowhood in Medieval and Early Modern Europe* (Harlow: Longman, 1999) and M. Ågren, 'Caring for the widowed spouse: the use of wills in northern Sweden during the eighteenth and nineteenth centuries', *Continuity and Change*, 19 (2004), pp. 45–71.

57 J. Gregory, *A Father's Legacy to his Daughters* (Edinburgh: 1774), p. 53.

58 H. Chapone, *Letters on the Improvement of the Mind* (London: J. F. Dove, 1827), p. 151.

59 W. Giles, *The Guide to Domestic Happiness* (London: Whittingham and Rowland for William Button, 10th edn, 1813), p. 155; H. Home, Lord Kames, *Loose Hints on Education* (Edinburgh: John Bell, Geo. Robertson and John Murray, 1782), p. 256; Sarah Pennington, *Advice to her Absent Daughters with an Additional Letter on the Management of Education in Infant Children* (London: J. F. Dove, 1827), p. 164.

60 H. More, *Strictures on the Modern System of Female Education* (London: T.Cadell Jun. and W. Davies, 1799), p. 5.

61 J. Moir, *Female Tuition; or an Address to Mothers on the Education of Daughters* (London: J. Murray, 1784), p. 70.

62 K. Harvey, 'Men making home: masculinity and domesticity in eighteenth-century Britain', *Gender & History*, 21:3 (2009), 520–40.

63 NAS GD461/14/8 Archibald Campbell to Christina Watson, 30 April 1730.

64 NAS GD461/14/14 Archibald Campbell to Christina Watson, 10 May 1733.

65 NAS GD461/14/20 Archibald Campbell to Christina Watson, 27 July 1738.

66 NAS GD128/35/5B Alexander Campbell of Clunes to his wife 'my dearest', 6 October 1740.

67 NAS GD110/1084/1 Hew Dalrymple to Margaret Sainthill [July 1744].

68 NAS GD110/1084/4b Hew Dalrymple to Margaret Sainthill [2 July 1744].

69 NAS GD110/1084/22 & 23 Hew Dalrymple to Margaret Sainthill [c. 1744–7].

70 NAS GD110/1084/28 Hew Dalrymple to Margaret Sainthill [c. 1744–7].

71 NAS GD21/365 Archibald Cunningham to Christian Macredie, 21 June 1759.

72 NAS GD180/635 Marion Buchan to Robert Cathcart [c. 1767].

73 NAS GD21/408/1 Anna Peebles to John Peebles [c. 1797].

74 NAS GD263/162 Henrietta Moodie to Mary Bury, 17 October 1818.

75 NAS GD248/198/3 James Grant to Jean Duff, 9 June 1774.

76 NAS GD16/34/379 David, Earl of Airlie to Clementina, Countess of Airlie, 23 March 1814.

77 NAS GD461/126/2 Archibald Lawrie to Anne Adair, 26 June 1796.

78 NAS GD461/126/9 Archibald Lawrie to Anne Adair, 19 October 1798.

79 GCA TD107/3/2 Walter Crum to Jessie Crum, 5 August 1831.

80 GCA TD107/3/2 Correspondence of Jessie and Walter Crum, 1826–35.

81 NAS GD172/2584/2 Ann Robertson to General Robertson, 8 November [c. 1779].

82 NAS GD172/2584/3 General Robertson to Ann Robertson [c. 1779].

83 NAS GD124/15/1782/20 John Erskine, Earl of Mar to Philadelphia Stuart Menteth, 30 April 1832.

84 NAS GD124/15/1777/15 Philadelphia Stuart Menteth to John Erskine, Earl of Mar, 23 May 1829.

85 NAS GD124/15/1777/15 Philadelphia Stuart Menteth to John Erskine, Earl of Mar, 23 May 1829.

86 NAS GD124/15/1777/11 Philadelphia Stuart Menteth to John Erskine, Earl of Mar, 3 April 1829.

87 NAS GD124/15/1782/7 John Erskine, Earl of Mar to Philadelphia Stuart Menteth, 22 March 1829.

88 For an extended discussion of this marriage see: K. Barclay, 'Intimacy and the Life-cycle in the Marital Relationships of the Scottish Elite during the Long-Eighteenth Century', *Women's History Review* (Forthcoming Spring 2011); L. Carter, 'British masculinities on trial in the Queen Caroline Affair of 1820', *Gender & History*, 20:2 (2008), 248–69.

89 For a review of this argument and a critique, see A. Vickery, 'Women and the world of goods: a Lancashire consumer and her possessions, 1751–1781', in J. Brewer and R. Porter (eds), *Consumption and the World of Goods* (London: Routledge, 1993), pp. 274–304.

90 J. Rendall, 'Virtue and commerce: women in the making of Adam Smith's political economy', in E. Kennedy and S. Mendus (eds), *Women in Western Political Philosophy* (Brighton: Wheatsheaf Press, 1987), pp. 44–76.

91 L. Hunt, *The Family Romance of the French Revolution* (Berkley: University of California Press, 1993) p. 201; I. V. Hull, *Sexuality, State and Civil Society in Germany, 1700–1815* (Ithaca: Cornell University Press, 1997), p. 410.

92 L. Davidoff and C. Hall, *Family Fortunes: Men and Women of the English Middle Class, 1780–1850* (Chicago: Chicago University Press, 1987).

93 M. Hunt, *The Middling Sort: Commerce, Gender and Family in England, 1680–1780* (Berkeley: University of California Press, 1996), pp. 147–60.

94 R. Perry, *Novel Relations: the Transformation of Kinship in English Relations and Culture, 1748–1818* (Cambridge: Cambridge University Press, 2004).

95 NAS GD16/34/73 Mary Gray to Lord Ogilvie, 25 July 1661.

96 NAS GD1/649/1 The Diary of George Home of Kimmerghame, 5 July 1695.

97 NAS GD1/649/1 The Diary of George Home of Kimmerghame, 27 January 1696.

98 NAS GD1/649/1 The Diary of George Home of Kimmerghame, 4 June 1694–25 January 1695.

99 NAS GD406/1/6120 Katherine Hamilton to Anne, Duchess of Hamilton, 7 July 1685.

100 NAS GD406/1/6121 Katherine Hamilton to Marchioness of Atholl, 12 March 1683/4.

101 NAS GD406/1/6892 Elizabeth Hamilton to James, Duke of Hamilton, 3 February 1703/4; GD406/1/6654 Anne, Duchess of Hamilton to James, Duke of Hamilton, 14 November 1698.

102 NAS GD158/2924 Alexander Murray to Grizell Baillie, 19 August 1738. Grizell asked for a formal separation on grounds of cruelty, see Chapter 7.

103 NAS GD26/13/674 Various letters regarding the marriage of Mary Leslie and James Walker, 1777–98.

104 NAS GD124/15/1777/15 Philadelphia Stuart Menteth to John Erskine, Earl of Mar, 23 May 1829.

105 NAS GD345/1146/6 Archibald Grant to Anna Potts, 8 April 1735. See also NAS GD345/1146/74 Archibald Grant to Anna Potts, 4 June 1740.

106 NAS GD248/370/5 Mrs Duff to James Grant and Jane Duff, 15 August 1773.

107 Bailey, *Unquiet Lives*, pp. 61–84; A. Shepard, *Meanings of Manhood in Early Modern England* (Oxford: Oxford University Press, 2003), pp. 195–204.

108 M.B. Norton, *Liberty's Daughters: the Revolutionary Experience of American Women* (Ithaca: Cornell University Press, 1980), pp. 157–61.

109 C. Daniels, 'Intimate violence, now and then', in C. Daniels and M. Kennedy (eds), *Over the Threshold: Intimate Violence in Early America* (London: Routledge, 1999), p. 8. Judith Bennett makes a similar argument, see: *History Matters: Patriarchy and Challenge of Feminism* (Manchester: Manchester University Press, 2006), pp. 56–7.

7

When negotiation fails:
the abuses of patriarchy

I take God to witnes I married with a full resolution and inclination to Love and gratitude, yea too much Love, Because she was the only thing I Loved She was my God and all my duty to my Neighbour For all thoughts of duty whatever were either banished or forgot, and center'd in her ... I truly Lov'd her face, thought (and was not deceived) she had sense, was reasonably perswaded she Loved me, was sensible she preferred me to better worthy offers and made me happy, without her all the world would not have satisfied me at the time (I doe really believe) and therefore it was I valued nothing and no body in any manner of comparison to her, I thought if I gott her I had all I wanted ... my Jealousie has indeed rendered me justly obnoxious to all and many more like Censures from her ... But then she has drove those thoughts of me too far, and by her disrespect, afforded me (in the eyes of the world) an excuse for my madness and within my breast this consideration that I would not have continued as I have been, had she obeyed what I desired at first and all alongst had not repeated or run into the very same or very parallel courses I quarrelled.[1] (Alexander Murray in a letter to his in-laws during his legal separation for cruelty, 1714.)

Alexander Murray's letter to his wife's parents, written whilst his wife Grisell Baillie sued him for a legal separation for cruelty, highlights many of the central themes of this book. His marriage was a relationship built on his love for his wife, who made him happy and satisfied with his place in the world (her happiness is not mentioned). Like other wives, she enabled her husband to become his complete self. But, unlike other marriages, Alexander's love was excessive. Whereas love was to enable men to perform their duty, Alexander's love made him forget his obligations to God and society, making him jealous and 'obnoxious to all'. At the same time, he argued that his wife failed in her duty to him. Instead of overlooking and compensating for his behaviour, she came to disrespect him and refused to obey. In turn, he exerted his authority in the form of violence, attempting to extract by force what he had failed to urge as a duty. And, as he noted, despite his own failings, her refusal to obey opened her to criticism from wider society and justified his actions.

Marital violence happened within a context of love, intimacy, duty and obligation. It was a device within the patriarchal marriage to ensure that husbandly authority was not undermined and that duty, necessary to the good order of society, was fulfilled. Yet, how marital violence was understood within Scottish society was not unchanging over time, adapting to meet the needs of an increasingly commercial, individualised society. At the same time, marital violence was always expected to be limited, constrained to extreme circumstances. What those extreme circumstances were, however, was not particularly clear, opening the use of violence up to debate and question. Similarly, violence itself was used within negotiations, if when other forms of negotiation failed, implicating itself in the continuance of patriarchal power. This chapter will explore the meaning, acceptability and purpose of marital violence in Scottish elite households over the seventeenth to nineteenth centuries using their correspondence and supplemented with evidence from cruelty cases conducted at the Commissary Court in Edinburgh between 1714 and 1830.[2]

Marital violence within Scottish culture

The place of violence within the Scottish household is rarely spoken of explicitly in legal texts or prescriptive writings. Yet, an exploration of legal constructions of liberty and obligation allow us to construct a model for understanding in what context it was considered to be appropriate within marriage. As in early modern England, seventeenth-century legal writers in Scotland understood violence in terms of its legitimacy, which in turn was defined by context.[3] The legal authority, Lord Stair, argued that 'men' were born in to liberty, which entitled them to do as they pleased unless hindered by law or force. Yet liberty was not absolute, but limited by a man's 'obediential obligations' to God and to man through God's ordinance. Obediential obligations were those put upon men 'by the will of God, not by their own wills, so are natural'. As a result, 'men may be restrained or constrained by others, without incroachment upon the law of liberty, in the pursuance of other obediential obligations; as a husband hath power to restrain his wife, from her liberty of going where she will.'[4] Restraint was exercised by imprisonment, captivity or hindrance of the use of things necessary for life; constraint was 'beating, wounding, or the like force upon the body, or the fear of it, whereby any thing is extorted.'[5] A husband's right to exercise 'restraint' or 'constraint' on a wife who failed in her 'obediential obligations' was affirmed by God and law. As is discussed in Chapter 2, a wife's obligation within marriage was vaguely defined as obedience, leaving her vulnerable to punishment in the form of 'beating, wounding or the like force'.

At the same time, the law offered an alternative model for understanding the marriage contract – conditional obligations. Conditional obligations were those created within contracts, where one party agreed to the performance of an obligation on condition of a reciprocal performance. The example Stair used is of the 'tocher', which is promised by a father on condition of marriage with his daughter.[6] While the law clearly defined marriage as an obediential obligation, that marriage required the performance of duties by both spouses, as well as the possibility of separation and divorce, led to many Scots to view it as a conditional contract, influencing responses to marital violence. Furthermore, the law allowed for self-defence in the protection of life and reparation for 'unlawful and private violence'.[7] As the form, limits and justification for marital violence were left undefined, this created a space to contest the role of violence within the household.

In the seventeenth and early eighteenth centuries, as in Antebellum America, the primary discourse for contesting the legitimacy of marital violence was to claim that a husband was mad.[8] Alexander Murray, in the quote beginning this chapter, described his violent behaviour as 'madness'. Similarly, in the 1720s, the Earl of Rosebery's family had him certified as insane due to his violent behaviour towards his wife and children. As discussed in Chapter 5, seventeenth- and eighteenth-century Scots preferred negotiation and discussion when trying to manage their relationships with their spouse, rather than violent force. When such violence was made visible to the wider world, it undermined models of masculinity based on honour, self-control and good management of the household.

This ensured that marital violence was hidden to maintain social reputation. In the seventeenth century, Jane Sanderson, writing to Ann, Duchess of Hamilton, about her husband's cruel treatment, noted: 'I troubled your grace some years since with an account from Bath of the deplorable condition of a friend of mine, allase it was myselfe the unhappy woman mentioned in my letter'.[9] When violence was not hidden, it implied that the household had broken down, opening up men to scrutiny and requiring explanation. 'Madness' both offered an explanation for violent behaviour and allowed the wider community to interfere; as Lord Stair noted, 'we may also without any injury [to lawful liberty] restrain a furious person ... and is done as a duty in us, of love and mercy'.[10]

As the boundaries between acceptable and unacceptable violence were blurry, many families were willing to interfere in violent households, removing daughters and providing them with emotional, economic and legal support. In the 1740s, Robert Dalrymple of Killoch explained to his nephew that he had been preoccupied with his daughter and her violent husband, 'that monster Colli'. After removing his daughter from a violent home, Dalrymple allowed her to return on the condition that her husband would forfeit a bond to the value of £2500 if he maltreated her. His son-in-law once more subjected his daughter to 'cruel usage' and so Dalrymple removed his daughter and sued his son-in-law for the money, which was to be used for a jointure. He also sued separately for a legal separation, which he judged as an additional, unnecessary expense and a reflection of his son-in-law's unreasonableness.[11]

Non-family members were more reluctant to intervene in marital disputes, but would do so if they felt life was endangered. Female witnesses were usually quicker to intervene than men, and many reported they would have helped earlier had their husbands not stopped them.[12] Two servants, acting as witnesses in 1736 for Margaret Drummond, wife of John Home of Kimmerghame, testified that they had sought to intervene in their master and mistress' dispute as they knew there was a pistol in the room. Once they had obtained the pistol they left the room, leaving the couple to go bed. In the morning, they were informed that he had later attempted to slit her throat. The servants were willing to remove weapons that could act as a hazard to life, but left Margaret with her enraged husband.[13]

Families would not knowingly consent to marrying their daughters to violent men. Sophia Clerk's elopement with Gabriel Rankine in 1702 caused great distress to her father due to Gabriel's violent nature. Her father, John Clerk:

> begd her to be ingenous & that I might deliver her from the said affects that wold followe upon her marring a beggar & a mad man, & who had already (as my wife told me she heard from her selfe) upon a small contradicion which she made to some of his assertions in my dyning room given her a boxe upon the face til the fire flow out of her eyes.[14]

As he noted, 'I should be crucified if I consent to my daughters marrieing a mad & a broken man either directly or indirectly'.

John Clerk considered Gabriel's treatment of Sophia before marriage entirely unacceptable, especially within the context of her father's home. His anger arose, in part, because Gabriel did not have the authority to hit Sophia and that it violated John's property in his daughter, yet the strength of his reaction to Sophia's marriage suggested his genuine concern for her welfare. John did not believe a 'small contradicion' merited such behaviour and thought that it reflected the possibility of excessive violence within marriage. Sophia's decision to marry Gabriel without family consent suggested that either she felt that a degree of marital violence was acceptable, or her love blinded her to his behaviour. She repeatedly left him over the course of their marriage due to his abusive, and even life-threatening, behaviour, but returned as she believed he would treat her better in future.[15] Her family arranged a private separation in 1722.

Over the course of the eighteenth century, the model for thinking about violence, especially that against women, evolved. The Scottish Enlightenment literati argued that the progress of civilisation was marked by the position of women within society. The ability of women to live alongside men, provided for without having to labour and protected without the threat of violence, were the cornerstones of a civilised society.[16] This had a class dimension as not all members of society went through the civilising process at the same rate – modernity was the sphere of the social elite. Adam Smith detailed how the truly 'civilised' looked inwards to their conscience (nurtured in the home) for an innate moral guide to behaviour, making elite behaviour moral and natural.

Slightly lower down the social scale were those whose inner guide was not properly developed, but who were able to learn the rules of polite society and generally engage with the elite without causing offence. Their lack of an inner conscience meant their behaviour was never natural, their interactions in polite society often laboured and they were at risk of mis-stepping when encountering uncommon ground. Finally, the lower orders often barely managed to follow social rules, but instead had to be guided by their social betters, and increasingly the State, and punished if need be for the benefit of social order.[17] Similarly to both Germany and England, this class model was highly influential, increasingly shaping how social groups interacted and were treated by society.[18]

In contrast, elite women were viewed as of the civilised class and so violence towards them was less acceptable. As Joanne Bailey notes for England, this was reinforced by changing conceptions of biology, where gender became less fluid, and instead became fixed upon a sexed body.[19] New biologies emphasised that the male body was active and aggressive, in contrast to the female body, which took on women's social characteristics of weakness and passivity. Men became inherently brutal (if also sociable and capable of self-control), while women were always vulnerable.[20]

The threat of male violence became always present as it was ingrained in people's conception of gender, which in turn shaped their understandings of their identity and their relationship with their spouse and the wider world.[21] As the minister James Fordyce noted: 'dread of violence' became a natural part of the female disposition.[22] Furthermore, as the threat became increasingly 'real', acts of violence held greater social significance and so became more traumatic for the victims. Physical violence could be scaled down, particularly in elite circles, as lesser acts of violence became more frightening and by the nineteenth century, emotional violence too was considered harmful. As explored in Chapter 2, this was visible within the Scottish court system, which defined marital violence for the first time in the late eighteenth century, and then allowed the definition to become increasingly broad over the nineteenth century.[23]

Violence against elite women became unacceptable as they easily conformed to the new ideal of passive femininity. As Elizabeth Foyster notes for England, women of the lower orders, whose participation in physical work outside of the home, as well as the experience of poverty that brought the risk of prostitution (the ultimate 'public' woman), found it more difficult to conform to these models.[24] Their 'active' bodies threatened to undermine this gender system and so they were discursively located outside of civilised society and the protection it brought against violence until the nineteenth century, when models of female passivity began to move down the social ladder.[25]

While Scottish Enlightenment thinkers saw elite women as passive and in need of male protection, they also saw the need for violence in certain contexts. As suggested above, most believed in the need for punishment to ensure order within society, especially amongst those that lacked the self-control to discipline themselves. Yet, the role of discipline within family life is remarkably underdeveloped. The issue of punishment or violence within the home is never explicitly discussed in the main texts of the Scottish Enlightenment philosophers or popular authors, such as the Fordyce brothers or John Gregory, who espoused Enlightenment ideas in a prescriptive format for non-academic readers.

Most authors emphasised the centrality of duty to both femininity and masculinity, and the affective relationships of family life, as the driving motivation for good behaviour within the home. If people were socialised properly as children and conformed to expectations of normal behaviour as adults, then violence should not be necessary.[26] Even within the Grant's marriage in the 1730s, where Archibald expressed explicit dissatisfaction with his wife, he offered the writings of conduct authors to motivate change, rather than threats.[27] While this is not evidence of the absence of domestic violence, it demonstrates that the Scottish elites looked to discourse to motivate behaviour, as much as physical force. Having said this, the difference between the two could be blurred. Grissell Baillie in 1714 argued during her court case that her husband used the periodical *The Tatler*, containing a story of a husband who had killed his wife, to threaten her. She argued he had sent it as 'he had a mind to show he was not the only man who had carried violence against his wife to the height of killing, there needed no direct threatening after reading such lecture by way of fables'. She also indicated that this was more threatening than a weapon as it implied deliberation, rather than 'transient passions'.[28]

The use of violence to exercise power within the family indicated a fundamental breakdown in the operation of the household for Enlightenment thinkers, and reflected more than a simple need for discipline. Adam Smith explicitly denounced violence 'when a son seems to want that filial reverence which might be expected to his father ... The sufferer can only complain and the spectator can intermeddle no other way than by advice and persuasion. Upon all such occasions for equals to use force against one another would be thought the highest degree of insolence and presumption.'[29] However, his use of 'equals' suggests that he was not referring to the operation of the newly conjugal, patriarchal household. How authority should be exercised within the household when calls to duty were not effective was not mentioned.

Enlightenment theorists wrote about violence and punishment in the context of ensuring social order more broadly. Punishment was seen as necessary to curb the excesses of those who disrupted social well-being, but it was distinguished from violent behaviour due to self-control. When punishment was exercised by an individual, he should be in control of his passions and violence was often understood as an excess of feeling, rather than a physical action.[30] As Adam Smith noted: 'we ought always to punish with reluctance and more from a sense of the propriety of punishing than from any savage disposition to revenge'.[31] The Scottish novelist, Susan Ferrier, described how this worked in practice in *Marriage*, where a husband found himself trying to manage his new bride's tantrums: 'Provoked by her folly, yet softened by her extreme distress, Douglas was in the utmost state of perplexity – now ready to give way to a paroxysm of rage; then yielding to the natural goodness of his heart, he sought to soothe her into composure.'[32] The inner morality and self-control of the elite man should overcome his instinctual anger.

Due to the difficulty of this in practice, Enlightenment thinkers advocated turning control of punishment over to the State, which could exercise the necessary dispassion required for justice.[33] Abused wives were also directed to seek justice from the State. William Alexander noted that when a husband from 'maliciousness of temper or resentment or any other cause' beats his wife, she could take refuge in the law (although he does not discuss violence as a form of discipline for wives).[34] It was the motive behind physical acts of violence that determined their meaning and their legitimacy into the nineteenth century.[35]

In this sense, the Enlightenment model of discipline had strong continuities with the early modern model for household discipline that emphasised good order and enforcement of obligation. Yet, whereas in the seventeenth century, the lack of clarity over the precise meaning of 'obedience', as well as the ability to contest whether a husband had fulfilled his role, opened up a space to negotiate whether marital violence was appropriate in particular contexts, in the later eighteenth century, marital violence towards elite women had become generally unacceptable, putting the onus on men to justify their behaviour. Enlightenment thinkers never entirely denied the right of men to discipline their wives – always leaving a space for marital violence to occur – but at the same time, they reduced its cultural legitimacy.

This ensured that women continued to hide marital violence from friends and family as they tried not to undermine their marriages. In 1750 Eleanora, daughter of Lord Cathcart, commented during her suit against her husband John Houston, that:

> she was at all times exceedingly carefull to conceal, even from him, how much she was shocked with his behaviour, so she used her utmost endeavour to make the World believe, that his conduct toward her was altogether unexceptionable; and that where differences could not be concealed, she and not he, was to blame, which she then considered as the only chance she had of reclaiming, or bringing him to a Right way of thinking.[36]

Elenora believed that if people knew of her husband's behaviour it would destroy his reputation and any chance of reconciliation. Where it did come to people's attention, she took responsibility, presumably implying that it was appropriate discipline (which in turn highlights that violence within marriage was never entirely socially condemned).[37] Perhaps for similar reasons, Eleanora was reluctant to bring her case before the public eye and that her husband John forced the case to court was given as evidence of his cruelty. One witness noted: 'that there should be a voluntary Separation, and a reasonable Aliment settled, that was duly notified to Sir John by his own Relations, but instead of complying with that very equitable & Just demand, he resolved to stand upon his Defence.'[38]

While the Scottish elites made up roughly a quarter of pursuers in cruelty suits over the period, there were only two cases from the Scottish aristocracy, reflecting the popularity of private separations among the wealthiest families.[39] While Enlightenment thinkers presumed women would turn to the courts for help against abusive husbands, in practice they continued to turn to their families as in past generations. In this way, marital violence was policed within families, hiding elite violence – so problematic to Enlightenment constructions of 'civilised' behaviour – from view, and protecting the self-interest of the ruling class, whose right to govern was based on self-control. Furthermore, as the court system turned marital violence into a direct competition between husband and wife, and created a situation where women were often victorious, turning the 'natural' hierarchy between husband and wife upside down, keeping violence within the family reduced the disruption to the patriarchal social order.[40]

Marital violence within the elite home

Given that marital violence was viewed across the seventeenth to nineteenth centuries as reflecting the breakdown in the good order of the household, the question arises as to what place violence played within the negotiation of power. Did it reflect the failure of negotiation, or part of its process; and what were the underlying reasons for it? This section explores these questions through looking at the contexts in which marital violence occurred. Like in other European countries, male violence was a demonstration of power and a reminder to their wives of their status within the patriarchal marriage, often in a context where that was under threat.[41]

In 1802, Mary Richardson, the wife of the factor to the Earl of Mansfield at Limekilns, argued that her husband's violence originated from her refusal to revoke a trust held in her name. Her servant reported hearing: '"I will horse whip you seven times a day if you don't chuse to do as I order you and wish you". And thereafter he immediately ordered the pursuer to take up the Candle & walk into the bed room adding "I will give you something to make you know that you shall not serve me in that manner".[42] In a campaign of abuse spread over several weeks and intended to force his will, her husband John Patterson locked her in her room, beat her with fists and furniture, turned her out of the gig she was travelling in on the highroad, hit her with a horsewhip, and on two occasions threatened to shoot her with a pair of pistols. She also noted that at one point they had tried using a mediator to reconcile, but he quickly returned to his violent behaviour.

John attempted to use violence to bring his wife into obedience – if a form of obedience that was not socially sanctioned – after negotiation broke down. Yet, at the same time, the purpose of his violence was to bring good order back into the household – it was envisioned as part of the process of ensuring the survival of the patriarchal marriage. In this sense, it was a part of the 'negotiation'. Similarly, as described above, Grissell Baillie's experience of domestic violence followed threats 'disguised' in the form of a newspaper. 'Had she obeyed what I desired', noted her husband Alexander Murray, it would not have happened.

That marital violence was implicated in negotiations for power ensured that it had a close relationship with the control of household resources. As explored in the previous chapter, the ambiguities of the management of the household, alongside women's considerable access to family resources, threatened to undermine patriarchal authority. At the same time, male heads could reduce or remove their wives' access to household resources, limiting their power within the home and ensuring male dominance. This behaviour was an extreme manifestation of normal behaviour, in the same way that physical abuse was an extreme manifestation of the patriarch's right to discipline.

Economic resources were a source of power for both men and women, but the way men and women used economic resources was substantively different due to their social positions. Men used their control of economic resources to shore up their dominance and authority over their wives, while women were restricted to using their economic resources to resist male authority. Theoretically women such as heiresses, who had access to significant, independent resources, should have been able to dominate their spouses. Yet, in practice, with few women having legally separate estates that outstripped their husbands and with authority in marriage being more complex than a simple correlation between wealth and power, women could not use economic resources in a similar manner to men. Even wealthy women were restricted to a position of resistance, rather than dominance, within marriage due to the structures of the patriarchal system that vested authority in the husband.

Women found the removal of household resources particularly unacceptable and it often appeared to be considered as great a violation by many women as extreme acts of physical violence. At its most extreme, this behaviour was a form of psychological and, through the deprivation of necessities, physical cruelty to women. In this respect, it was a form of violence. For the purposes of this chapter, the term economic violence will be used to describe the use or removal of economic resources to cause harm. Economic violence was of particular relevance to the elite classes. Kristin Anderson argues that working class men resort to physical violence as they do not have the resources to construct their masculinity in other ways.[43] Elite men did not have to resort to physical violence as they used their control over economic resources to exert their dominance, although, in many of the examples below, economic violence was closely connected to physical violence.

If violence is defined by the harm caused, it is less easy to categorise women's resistance through the misappropriation of resources as violence. In families with few resources such misappropriation may have caused real suffering, but, amongst the elite, such behaviour by women was often seen as a threat to male authority, but not necessarily to the security or well-being of the household. While husbands could stop their wives from accessing any resources (although not always without difficulty), women generally did not have that level of control over men. Men's wider social power allowed them to effectively counteract their wife's behaviour.

Many women cited in their cruelty suits that their husband used economic as well as physical violence. In 1750, Elenora Cathcart, alongside her evidence of physical violence, claimed that her husband desired 'to make himself master of every shilling his Lady had', including her jewellery. She also noted that although her existing gowns were threadbare, Sir John refused to allow to her to buy one unless he chose it, and then he refused to choose one. He physically removed her from the dining room without cause and did not permit her to return until she sent a submissive message.[44] Sir John used economic violence in a variety of ways. He restricted Elenora's access to his economic resources and attempted to control her independent wealth. He also reinforced the idea that her management of the household was through his sanction by removing her from the dining table where her power as household manager was symbolically manifested.

In an example from late eighteenth-century correspondence, a friend of William Cunningham reported that 'Bounting's wife' had been removed from her marital home by her father as when the latter came to visit, she could not give him meat or tea and sugar as her husband had removed all her economic resources. The writer noted that he was a 'barbarous husband'.[45] Some husbands removed the household management from their wives in its entirety. In 1823, Jane Roberts claimed that her husband, Alexander McDonald, an agent for Leith Bank, stole all her personal property and in an attempt to force her to sign it over to him, removed the management of the household from her and gave it to his daughter. He told his servants not to obey her and allowed his daughter to sit at the head of the table. She added that she was later locked into the bedroom where she was often without food, light or heat. Alexander did not deny that he had removed his wife from household management, but claimed that it was because she was 'unhappily addicted to the undue use of strong Liquors'.[46]

Economic violence was commonly described alongside physical violence in separation for cruelty cases, and in many instances they were closely related. There was a legal basis for their appearance. Women had a right to access the household's economic resources in law and their husband's behaviour infringed on that right. Demonstrating economic violence highlighted that, in addition to their failure to love and protect their wives, husbands restricted their wife's ability to perform their duties. Furthermore, this was a form of madness as it fundamentally undermined the functioning of the household and thus that of the social order.

Yet, as evidence from correspondence highlights, a focus on economic cruelty was not just a legal strategy. Sophia Clerk, who suffered twenty years of violence at the hands of her husband, Gabriel Rankine, was more threatened by his challenge to her authority within the home than his physical violence. After having been apart for several months from her husband due to his behaviour, in 1718 Sophia returned home to find that he was entertaining a servant, Jennet, with mutton and brandy above stairs. Gabriel's reaction to Sophia's entry was to attempt to force her to leave, calling her whore and bitch, before calming down and kissing her. Sophia's anger was not directed at her husband's welcome, but at the servant he had in her place. Sophia 'call'd to her to pack out of her right, being the cause of all the mischief in the family'. The next morning Gabriel behaved as erratically as the night before: 'sometimes he kikt her with his foot next moment he kiss her & then again was at his names of bitch & jade'. Sophia's brother was reluctant to leave her 'being afraid of some sad disaster to fall out there', but she insisted she wished to stay.[47]

Sophia's primary concern was not her husband's physical violence, but his attempt to undermine her authority as mistress of the home. On other occasions, she attempted to hide his violence from servants by taking him into a private room. This conclusion is also supported by Jennet's reaction to Sophia when she dismissed her, at 'which the hussie lifted a great candlestick & threatened to throw it at her mistres's face three several times'. Sophia's reaction to her servant was, in part, caused by her inability to challenge her husband's behaviour. Yet, it was also because economic resources were a central source of power for women. The management of her home was an area that Sophia could retain control of and which offered her some power. This also explains why Sophia's first action when entering the house before she met her husband was to discipline two servants in the hall for swearing (and which in turn was reported by her brother as evidence of Gabriel's mismanagement of the home, highlighting his failure as a man).

The violence against Rachel Erskine, Lady Grange, by her husband in the 1730s, began through restricting her access to economic resources. Rachel had managed her husband's estates for twenty-five years, when her husband decided to remove them from her control, which was partially achieved by locking the door to the estate papers. Rachel was extremely upset, threatening to break down the door and continuing to collect rent from tenants. She also became concerned that her husband was attempting to replace her with a housekeeper. The men around her were disconcerted by her behaviour and her eldest son believed she showed signs of madness, yet her distress could be explained by the reduction of her economic role. Her female family members simply tried to reassure her, commenting that few women had control of the estates for as long as she had. The situation escalated due to the refusal of her husband, a High Court judge, to return home or to answer her letters, other than to ask for a separation. Rachel's unwillingness to accept quietly her removal as manager of the home was a reflection of her realisation that her authority was being usurped.

Her husband responded by having Rachel physically kidnapped and removed to the Isle of St Kilda. Legend says that he reported that she was dead and celebrated her funeral. She later managed to contact her family but was removed to Skye, where she died before a rescue was achieved.[48] Rachel's refusal to submit to her husband's economic violence finally led to physical violence, yet her husband was never present. His ability to undermine her authority over her home, estate and finally her person reflected the power that men had under the patriarchal system in operation during this period. Yet, that Rachel had to be physically removed to eradicate her influence over the household also indicated the power she had within her sphere. Female control of economic resources offered a real threat to male domination and men responded with violence. In some instances that violence was manifested through the abuse of economic resources.

Control of resources was not the only area of marriage that caused tension. As Julie Hardwick notes for France, controlling women's sexuality was often a cause of violence.[49] As highlighted in Chapter 5, jealousy was an aspect of Scottish marriage, although one that most couples recognised was destructive and tried to reconcile through negotiation. Yet, female sexuality was more than just a threat to individual marriages; it was complexly combined with conceptions of femininity more broadly, undermining women's role as passive. In the early modern period, women were thought to be sexually aggressive, desiring sex for health and happiness. Men in turn were expected to sexually satisfy their wives to ensure that women remained faithful within marriage. Sex within marriage operated as one method for constraining women and ensuring household discipline.[50] Female sexuality, when it broke the boundaries of marriage, threatened to undermine male authority and the broader social order.

Over time, as ideas around femininity changed, elite women became inherently pure and chaste, reinforcing a belief in female passivity. As the model of the passive female and active, violent male was at the basis of the Enlightenment gender system, unconstrained female sexuality – an active behaviour – threatened to undermine it. Female sexuality endangered not just male property in the form of female chastity, and in turn a social system based on blood lineage and inheritance, but the basis of the patriarchal system.[51] The fundamental risk that this posed to patriarchal society explains the focus on female chastity as an integral element of female identity throughout the period.[52]

The association between female sexuality and active behaviour threatened male authority, which led men to try to constrain it with violence, but also to associate it with other threats to their masculinity. Almost all reported marital violence was accompanied by highly sexualised verbal abuse. Common insults included bitch, jade, whore bitch, damn'd bitch, Norland [Northern or Highland] whore, barren Norland bitch, and various combinations of the above. It was also related to male jealousy where men constantly berated their wives for imagined infidelity. Sexual insults and accusations of infidelity operated as a language that allowed men to express their frustration with their wives' 'active' behaviour, regardless of the form it took.

At the separation suit of Eleanora Cathcart and Sir John Houston, one witness deponed that John believed: 'tho' a husband was not by Law entitled to beat his wife with a stick of a certain size, he might safely do so with a switch or with his hand, and that he had also the power of locking her up, if he chose it. That though he mortally abhorred lifting his hand to a woman, and had never even beat a whore; yet so much did he abhore the Lady, that he could beat her every day, and be happy in doing it.'[53] The witness's testimony highlighted that being a whore removed a woman's passivity, and so her right not to experience violence. Associating Eleanora's behaviour with extra-marital sex allowed Sir John to justify his domestic violence.

Accusations of sexual infidelity were a shorthand description that allowed men to verbalise their sense of frustration in contexts where women threatened (or were perceived as threatening) male authority, but perhaps in ambiguous ways that did not clearly point to disobedience or misbehaviour. This also explains why women who operated in the public 'active' sphere, such as authors, actresses and market workers, were tainted with the impropriety of sexual misconduct.[54] The insult of 'whore' implied active behaviour beyond the boundaries of acceptable femininity. It was an insult that could only be directed one way. As Lyndal Roper notes, there was no such thing as a cuckolded woman. The cuckold was not just about an unfaithful wife, but the undermining of male authority. Women had no authority to be undermined by an unfaithful husband and the unfaithful husband did not threaten the gender order.[55]

The case of Lord Rosebery in the 1720s intricately connected male violence, female economic power and female sexuality, highlighting the extent to which social discourses about gender were absorbed. Lord Rosebery's violence towards his wife and children was so excessive and uncontrolled that his friends applied to have him confined under house arrest for madness, which was duly sanctioned by the court. Despite this being an intervention by wider family, Lord Rosebery blamed his wife for his situation, believing that she had seized power from him. He wrote to his friend John Clerk, claiming that while held under house arrest:

> she made them use me so ill and caus'd abuse so much that the soldiers were like to sink down with griefe to see such barberitie us'd to me, to name butt one thing, one night at ten o clock, for I was denyed liberty to my servants, paper, pen, ink or to provide my own victuals, I was refus'd one chapin of oil coals or candle; did I with my ears har my lady roseberrie in next room doatting upon her cully [lit. flatterer] Archibald Campbell o Burbank; who was in his bed and feeding him with venison collaps telling him was shure he loved them.

Lord Rosebery maintained that she was trying to drive him insane, inter-fered with the tenants, tried to huddle money away and 'if ever I live at home as master of my affairs she must leave my house'.[56]

Lord Rosebery associated female economic power with violence and sexual infidelity. That his wife was economically active destroyed her passivity linking her to stereotyped behaviours of the active female. His insistence that she leave his house also indicated that he believed that an active woman could never again regain her passivity. The Earl of Rosebery thought that his wife's ability to restrain his violence, and thus his power, was a reflection of her power and a subversion of the patriar-chal system. That marital violence was so closely connected with sexual jealousy and women's use of economic resources was not a coincidence. It was in these areas that women had the ability to undermine the discourses of gender that underpinned the patriarchal social system and so they offered the greatest threat to male domination. Men responded to that threat with violence.

Just as female sexuality threatened to undermine male authority, so did female acts of violence, although this could be more ambiguous earlier in the period. In the early modern period, female violence was not entirely unknown. Cross-dressing women were celebrated for their success within the armed forces in Scotland as elsewhere, suggesting that female violence was acceptable as long as it did not disrupt social hierarchies.[57] For Wiener and Dolan, in the early modern period violent, especially murderous, wives were a much more potent and threatening discourse than the abusive husband, because they undermined natural gender hierarchy.[58] In the eighteenth century, female violence, like female sexuality, was a threat to the discourse that labelled women as passive and men as strong. Women's violence towards men was generally believed to undermine masculinity, while female defiance was a chal-lenge to male authority.[59]

Within the context of the marital relationship, throughout the period, female violence was condemned, but like for men, it may be assumed that not all women followed this prescription. Having said this, within this study, there are no examples of elite women physically abus-ing their husbands or retaliating physically to abuse.[60] The Marquis of Annandale complained that his wife's behaviour was so unreasonable as to be 'a constant rack off torments and vexation', but he did not explicitly note that she was violent. He instead expressed distress at her encour-agement of his 'rebellious obstinant and disobedient son', indicating that it was her undermining of his authority that upset him.[61]

Elite women relied on their passivity to protect them against violence and this may have discouraged them from behaving violently towards their spouse. Successfully obtaining legal protection from a husband required a woman to 'come into Court with clean hands, and be able to show that the sufferings of which she complains are owing to no fault or imprudences on her part'.[62] Like their male counterparts, violent women faced accusations of lack of self-control, which jeopardised their right to be protected from harm and their self-presentation as members of the social elite. It was also unnecessary for men to seek legal separation from wives as they could leave them at any time, as long as they provided alimony, while advertising their wives' violence undermined models of masculinity based on the ability to successfully govern a household, both of which predicate against the survival of historical evidence on female abusers. Furthermore, while men could justify their violence in the name of social order, women had no such excuse.

The tensions between love and duty, obligation and authority opened up spaces to negotiate power within marriage – allowing individuals and families to contest the legitimacy of marital violence in certain contexts, or even at all – but ultimately, patriarchal society vested supremacy in the husband. To reinforce their power, society offered men the right to discipline wives. But power had limits. In the seventeenth century, violence should follow a call to duty and be complemented by fulfilment of husbandly obligations; in the eighteenth century, violence should be unnecessary after appropriate socialisation, but ultimately permitted for the benefit of social order.

Despite the restricted legitimacy given to the exercise of marital violence it continued to be a feature of life for the Scottish elites. It was closely related to disputes over economic resources and female sexuality, reflecting the potential they had to destabilise a patriarchal system based on the passivity of women. A loving marriage was not a violent marriage in the Scottish elite imagination, but at the same time, it was not a marriage of equals. Ideally this inequality was enforced through socialisation, self-control and a desire to fulfil gender-differentiated social roles, but underlying this facade was the threat of violence. Violence reflected the breakdown of the marital relationship, where negotiation and discussion failed, but it was also an attempt to restore the patriarchal marriage – to bring women back under husbands' control and to ensure social order. Marital violence was a necessary tool within patriarchal society.

Notes

1   NAS CC8/5/2/1 Grissell Baillie against Alexander Murray, 5 March 1714.

2   For more on these cases, see L. Leneman, *Alienated Affections: the Scottish Experience of Divorce and Separation, 1684–1830* (Edinburgh: Edinburgh University Press, 1998).

3   S. Amussen, 'Punishment, discipline and power: the social meanings of violence in early modern England', *Journal of British Studies*, 34 (1995), 1–34.

4   J. Dalrymple, Viscount of Stair, *The Institutions of the Law of Scotland* (Edinburgh: Edinburgh University Press [1693] 1981), pp. 19–27, quote p. 20; see also G. Mackenzie, *The Institutions of the Laws of Scotland* (Edinburgh: John Reid, 1684), pp. 217–32.

5   Dalyrmple, *Institutions*, p. 20.

6   Dalyrmple, *Institutions*, pp. 25–7.

7   Dalyrmple, *Institutions*, p. 20.
    Ed Hatton argues that as uncontrolled passion is unmasculine in the eighteenth century, drunkenness or madness were often given as explanations for violence, see E. Hatton, 'He murdered her because he loved her: passion, masculinity and intimate homicide in Antebellum America', in C. Daniels and M. Kennedy (eds), *Over the Threshold: Intimate Violence in Early America* (London: Routledge, 1999), pp. 111–34; NAS GD18/5167/13/11–16 Roseberry/Clerk letters [c. 1725].

9   NAS GD406/1/5238 Jane Sanderson to Anne, Duchess of Hamilton, 15 July 1706.

10 Dalyrmple, *Institutions*, p. 20.

11 NAS GD110/912 Robert Dalrymple to Hew Dalrymple, 10 September 1743.

12 J. Bailey, '"I dye [sic] by inches": locating wife-beating in the concept of a privatisation of marriage and violence in eighteenth century England', *Social History*, 31 (2006), 273–94.

13 NAS CC8/5/4 Margaret Drummond against John Home, 1736.

14 NAS GD18/5249/3 John Clerk to his brother David Forbes, 28 January 1702.

15 The details of her marriage can be found in NAS GD18/5250 Correspondence of John Clerk, snr and jnr, 1702–41; NAS GD18/5293 John Clerk jnr to John Clerk snr, 1716–20.

16 W. Alexander, *The History of Women, from the Earliest Antiquity to the Present Time* (London: C. Dilly 1782); J. Millar, *The Origin of the Distinction of Ranks: or, and Inquiry into the Circumstances which give Rise to the Authority in Different Members of Society* (Edinburgh: William Blackwood [1778] 1806).

17 A. Smith, *The Theory of Moral Sentiments* (London: Henry G. Bohn [1759] 1853), pp. 229–31.

18 L. Abrams, 'Companionship and conflict: the negotiation of marriage relations in the nineteenth century', in L. Abrams and E. Harvey (eds), *Gender and Relations in German History: Power, Agency and Experience from the Sixteenth to the Twentieth Century* (London: UCL Press, 1996), pp. 101–20; A. J. Hammerton, *Cruelty and Companionship: Conflict in Nineteenth Century Married Life* (London: Routledge, 1992), p. 166; E. Foyster, *Marital Violence: An English Family History, 1660–1857* (Cambridge: Cambridge University Press, 2005).

19 For discussions of the developments in medicine and its impact on gender see A. Fletcher, *Gender, Sex and Subordination in England 1500–1800* (London: Yale

University Press, 1995), pp. 33–5; T. Laqueur, 'Orgasm, generation, and the politics of reproductive biology', in R. Shoemaker and M. Vincent (eds), *Gender and History in Western Europe* (London: Arnold, 1998), pp. 111–48; M. Stolberg, 'A women down to her bones: the anatomy of sexual difference in the sixteenth and early seventeenth centuries', *Isis*, 94 (2003), 274–99; J. Bailey, *Unquiet Lives: Marriage and Marriage Breakdown in England, 1660–1800* (Cambridge: Cambridge University Press, 2003), pp. 111–2.

20   An overview of this discourse can be found in C. Helliwell, '"It's only a penis": rape, feminism and difference', *Signs*, 25 (2000), 789–816; M. Wiener argues that increasing intolerance of male violence in the Victorian period was caused by a 'growing sensitivity about attacking the female body'; see M. Wiener, 'Alice Arden to Bill Sikes: changing nightmares of intimate violence in England, 1558–1869', *Journal of British Studies*, 40 (2001), 194.

21   G.J. Barker-Benfield, *The Culture of Sensibility: Sex and Society in Eighteenth Century Britain* (Chicago: Chicago University Press, 1992), p. 350; This can be seen in novels such as Richardson's *Pamela*; see R.B. Yeazell, *Fictions of Modesty: Women and Courtship in the English Novel* (Chicago: Chicago University Press, 1984), pp. 89–91.

22   J. Fordyce, *Sermons to Young Women* (Philadelphia: M. Carey, 1809), p. 117.

23   Foyster, *Marital Violence*.

24   Ibid.

25   Cathy Preston offers an interesting discussion of the tension between female rural worker's sexuality and their potential to become prostitutes, see '"The tying of the Garter": representations of the female rural labourer in 17th, 18th, 19th-century English bawdy songs', *Journal of American Folklore*, 105 (1992), 315–41; L. A. Surridge highlights the representation of lower-class women as passive in *Bleak Houses: Marital Violence in Victorian Fiction* (Athens: Ohio University Press, 2005), p. 18.

26   J. Popiel, *Rousseau's Daughters: Domesticity, Education and Autonomy in Modern France* (London: University of New Hampshire Press, 2008), pp. 89–111.

27   For example, NAS GD345/1146/5/27 Archibald Grant to Anna Potts, 6 April 1739.

28   NAS CC8/5/2 Grissell Baillie against Alexander Murray, 1714.

29   Smith, *Theory of Moral Sentiments*, p. 137.

30   Smith, *Theory of Moral Sentiments*, pp. 63–4.

31   Smith, *Theory of Moral Sentiments*, p. 250.

32   S. Ferrier, *Marriage* (Oxford: Oxford University Press [1818] 1971), p. 11.

33   Smith, *Theory of Moral Sentiments*, pp. 205–6.

34   Alexander, *History of Women*, p. 424.

35   Hammerton, *Cruelty and Companionship*.

36   NAS CC8/5/10 Elenora Cathcart against John Houston, 1750.

37   For another example, see NAS CC8/6/90 Mary McIvor against William Morrison, 1810.

38   NAS CC8/5/10 Elenora Cathcart against John Houston, 1750.

39   There were no suits for cruelty at this court before 1714. Between 1714 and 1830, there were 175 cases, of which 69 were abandoned. L. Leneman, *Alienated Affections*, p. 18.

40   Of the 106 separation for cruelty cases that went to verdict, 87% were successful, although a high number were abandoned. Calculated from Leneman's figures, see L.

Leneman, "'A tyrant and a tormentor": violence against wives in eighteenth and early nineteenth century Scotland', *Continuity and Change*, 12 (1997), 33.

41 Leneman, "'A tyrant and a tormentor"', 39; Foyster, *Marital Violence*, p. 3; J. Hardwick, 'Early modern perspectives on the long history of domestic violence: the case of seventeenth century France', *Journal of Modern History*, 78 (2006), 1–37.

42 NAS CC8/6/72 Mary Richardson against John Paterson, 1802.

43 K. Anderson, 'Gender, status and domestic violence: an integration of feminist and family violence approaches', *Journal of Marriage and the Family*, 59 (1997), 658.

44 NAS CC8/5/10 Elenora Cathcart against John Houston, 1750.

45 GCA T-LX14/64 G. Clyggapus [?] to William Cunningham, 21 October [late eighteenth century].

46 NAS CC8/6/153 Jane Robert against Alexander McDonald, 1823.

47 NAS GD18/5293/19 John Clerk jnr to John Clerk snr, 1 November 1718.

48 NAS GD124/15/1372-1380 Various to Lord Grange, March–April 1730; NAS GD124/15/1506 Rachel Erskine of Grange to friends, 1730s; NAS GD124/15/1524 On Lady Grange's captivity, 1741.

49 Hardwick, 'Early modern perspectives', 1–37.

50 Fletcher, *Gender, Sex, and Subordination*, pp. 44–59.

51 For a discussion of chastity as female property see: K. Thomas, 'The double standard', *Journal of the History of Ideas*, 20 (1959), 195–216. For a critique of the double standard in the context of restrictions on male sexuality see: B. Capp, 'The double standard revisited: plebeian women and male sexual reputation in early modern England', *Past and Present*, 162 (1999), 70–100.

52 N. Cott, 'Passionlessness: an interpretation of Victorian sexual ideology, 1790–1850', *Signs*, 4 (1978), 219–36.

53 NAS CC8/5/10 Elenora Cathcart against John Houston, 1750.

54 S. Lancia,'The actress and eighteenth century ideals of femininity', in I. Baudino, J. Carré and C. Révauger (eds), *The Invisible Woman: Aspects of Women's Work in Eighteenth Century Britain* (Aldershot: Ashgate, 2005), pp. 131–8.

55 L. Roper, *Oedipus and the Devil: Witchcraft. Sexuality and Religion in Early Modern Europe* (London: Routledge, 1994), p. 66.

56 NAS GD18/5167/14 James Primrose, Earl of Rosebery to John Clerk [c. 1720s].

57 F. Easton, 'Gender's two bodies: women warriors, female husbands and plebeian life', *Past and Present*, 180 (2003), 131–74; D. Dugaw, 'Women and popular culture: gender, cultural dynamics, and popular prints', in V. Jones (ed.), *Women and Literature in Britain 1700-1800* (Cambridge: Cambridge University Press, 2000), pp. 263–84, and D. Dugaw, *Warrior Women and Popular Balladry, 1650-1850* (Cambridge: Cambridge University Press, 1989).

58 Wiener, 'Alice Arden to Bill Sikes'; F. Dolan, *Dangerous Familiars: Representations of Domestic Crime in England 1550-1700* (Ithaca: Cornell University Press, 1994).

59 Hammerton, *Cruelty and Companionship*, p. 111.

60 There are some examples of violent women within the Scottish separation cases, but they are for the lower classes. Where women were known to be violent, even in retaliation, it severely diminished their chances of a successful separation.

61 NAS GD406/1/5561 Marquis of Annandale to Duke of Hamilton, 22 November 1709.

62 NAS CC8/6/90 Mary McIvor against William Morrison, 1810.

8

Conclusion: rethinking patriarchy

When Lawrence Stone suggested in the 1970s that the eighteenth century saw a reduction in patriarchal authority within the household of the British elites, he started a long-running debate on the nature of family life across the long eighteenth century. Following a historiography that saw this period as a transitional moment in European history, where not only ideas, society and economy, but people's very sense of self, was transformed, many historians have been happy to emphasise it as a time of change that impacted on marital relationships as much as other areas of life. Others, particularly early modern historians who were uncomfortable with claims that love, intimacy and co-operation between spouses were novel to the period, preferred to emphasise continuity with the past.[1] Within Scotland, the answer is somewhere in between. New models of femininity and masculinity, the increasing importance of individualism, the influence of Enlightenment philosophy, the rise of commercial society and the expansion of the public sphere, all operated to shape new ways of thinking about and expressing emotion as well as negotiating marital relationships. Yet, at the same time, as has been demonstrated, these changes were not always a dramatic break from the past. Intimate relationships were not novel to the period; romantic love built on a foundation of courtly love, and domesticity may have created a new way of talking about gender roles within the home, but the practical management of elite households did not dramatically differ over the period. Similarly, while ideas around domestic violence changed, the violence itself and the justification that it was necessary to maintain social order remained the same. Throughout this process of change, women continued to be subordinate to their husbands and obedience remained central to their role as wives. The patriarchal social order remained unchallenged.

As has been highlighted, the Scottish experience was not particularly unique. Scottish marriage saw increased regulation in line with the European experience, while the influence of the culture of sensibility on love letters, debates over the meaning of friendship within marriage, and the rise of domesticity have been charted across Western Europe and North America. The Scots were not passive in this process. Some of the most influential thinking on family, social, economic and political life came from Scottish Enlightenment thinkers who were themselves members of the Scottish elites. The correspondence of Adam Smith's grandfather, Robert Douglas, a landowner at Strathendry, and his wife Susannah, a daughter of Lord Balfour, a member of the Scottish peerage, was used in this study. Scottish Enlightenment ideas were widely advertised with Scottish authors, such as John Gregory and James Fordyce, being bestsellers into the nineteenth century across Britain. The works they produced are often identified as transforming British, American and European society.[2] Yet, they were quite clearly Scottish products.

It is not surprising that challenges to monarchical authority and the promotion of a homosocial, public sphere came out of Presbyterian Scotland, where absolute authority of any form was resisted, universal education was endorsed and a philosophical tradition of natural rights dated to the sixteenth century (if not earlier).[3] Similarly, the elevation of commercial society and engagement in work, over inherited wealth, was not particularly radical in a country where the social elite had relied on a mixed economy for at least a century, and where heirs and younger sons alike combined trade with land ownership. While Scotland is often pointed to as a country with strong family ties, manifested most clearly in the clan networks, it is also a country that at a legal and religious level consistently promoted the rights of the individual over that of the family, when it came to choice of marriage partner (unlike Scotland's southern neighbour). In this context, a focus on independent manhood as the epitome of masculinity, alongside recognition of the importance of the family in enabling that manhood, makes sense.

While thinkers in France such as Rousseau went further than the Scots in rejecting authority based on rank, that these ideas came from the Scottish elites explains their need to reinforce class boundaries, if through a conceptualisation based on breeding, rather than birth.[4] Privilege is difficult to give up. Furthermore, it is evident that the many aspects of society described by Enlightenment thinkers and modelled as the ideal were already part of Scottish culture before the publication of their writings. The centrality of Scottish thinkers to the creation of modernity in Western Europe ensures that their history cannot be a side-note or outlier in the British and European experience. It was the peculiarities of Scotland and Scottish family life that produced both the thinkers and the thought that contributed so significantly to the shape of modern ideas on gender.[5]

Given this, a study on the patriarchal nature of Scottish marriage raises interesting questions about the relationship between Enlightenment ideas and women's rights. For some historians, the Enlightenment produced the rights-based discourse and individual liberty that would form the basis of liberal feminism in the nineteenth century, leading to the women's movement, suffrage and access for (non-working-class) women to the public world of work and politics. For others, the Enlightenment, through an emphasis on female difference, ensured that women's rights had to be fought for separately from men. It created a situation where unpaid work, notably in the home, had no economic value or recognition, in contrast to an early modern perspective where the household, in which both women and men worked, was the centre of the economy. Furthermore, while early modern conceptions of femininity usually saw female power as disruptive and problematic, Enlightenment thought resisted the idea that women were independent actors. It is argued (and arguable) that the Enlightenment improved women's status, yet respect came with restrictions on behaviour and the reduction in women's spheres of action (or at least, they were not given the right to move with their husbands into the expanding political public sphere). Part of the complexity of this debate is women's place in this process. While a focus on Enlightenment thinkers, particularly in Scotland, leads to a focus on men, it is simplistic to see Scottish society as created by men alone.

The adoption of new conceptions of gender and models for behaviour required female action, especially given the focus on women's self-control and their role in the proper socialisation of men and children.[6] Enlightenment theory became social practice because women, as well as men, adopted and implemented those ideas into their daily lives and taught them to their children. In doing so, as this book demonstrates, women were not just passive recipients of new ideas. They contested and negotiated how discourse was implemented in their marriages; they disputed boundaries and offered challenges to new and old ways of thinking. By the nineteenth century, Scottish women also started contributing to the public debate on the nature of society and social relationships, although their most radical challenges were given limited press.[7] Ultimately, women and men would use these ideas to fight for women's rights. Yet, throughout this process, full equality with men would remain out of reach and even in the twenty-first century, while equality is espoused, gender discrimination, gender violence and gender stereotyping remain a part of everyday life.

For this reason, the concept of a patriarchal system is useful for understanding the evolution of women's role within society. Between 1650 and 1850 Scottish society was patriarchal and thus created and perpetuated patriarchal discourses. The origins of patriarchy cannot be found in this period and it was normalised to the extent that few people felt the need to justify its existence. Scottish marital law and the Kirk favoured the authority of the husband over his wife. They created a framework for marriage where women were subsumed into their husbands' identities, restricting their rights to property and to social power. Obedience was a woman's primary duty within marriage and this was reinforced in law and in her marriage vows. Yet, male power was not without boundaries. Men had the responsibility to provide for and protect their wives. Furthermore, their primary duty was to love their wives, which was to temper male authority and prevent marriage from becoming tyrannical. Popular culture provided a similar discourse on marital relationships to the Scottish church and legislature. Conduct authors promoted male authority and female subordination and they also limited male power by commanding husbands to love their wives. Balladists and playwrights, preoccupied with men's relationships with women, promoted patriarchy as the ideal model for social relationships, reinforcing masculinity through the negative depictions of men who failed to control their wives.

As a system that influenced not only relationships between men and women, but between different social classes and age-groups, patriarchy shaped people's experiences before marriage as well as within it. Courtship practices in Scotland between 1650 and 1850 highlight the importance of family in helping select and vet partners as well as ensuring the economic stability of the match. The role that age, marital status and economic resources played in shaping the power relationship between parents and children when selecting a spouse highlighted patriarchy in operation in different social relationships. Over the eighteenth and nineteenth centuries, family interest declined in favour of the couples' interest, but this did not eradicate the role of family from courtship.

Love became increasingly important before marriage as people incorporated romantic ideals into their understanding of marriage, while economic stability remained an important factor throughout the period. The weakening of family interest was closely linked to the changing role of the household in the national economy, while the rise of romantic love in courtship reflected greater concern with the individual and the couple. This was related to the rise of the waged individual and her or his integration into the family economy. The gendering of these changes, with men identified as the protagonists in love and work, while women were increasingly associated with the home, chastity and passivity, adapted and reinforced the patriarchal system.

Within the patriarchal system, women and men negotiated with each other for power and it was whilst courting that many couples had their first opportunity to affect power within their marriage. In the seventeenth and early eighteenth centuries, the importance of family and kinship networks to social and economic success gave women authority as gatekeepers to their families and may have limited male abuse. While family networks declined in importance over the eighteenth century, women still retained authority as hostesses and because marriage continued to consolidate business, social and political networks. Courtship also offered the opportunity for women and men to negotiate over economic resources that would influence power within their marriages. The terms of the marriage contract established the respect that women would be held in within their marriage and the level of authority men would have over the household.

Once married, couples used patriarchal discourses to negotiate and establish an understanding of marriage that they both found acceptable, although as the examples throughout this book highlighted, this was easier for some couples than others. In the seventeenth and into the eighteenth centuries, love was closely associated with duty and conformance to the patriarchal model for marital relationships. The rise of the culture of sensibility made love an increasingly abstract concept, emphasising unity of the mind and spirit of the couple over behaviour. Romantic ideals influenced the language of love that couples used and altered their expectations of marriage, but this was not linked to increased power for women. New models of loving subsumed the personality of the wife within that of her husband, reducing her agency and using her to reinforce the male individual.

The importance of love to the patriarchal system, both through its close association with female obedience and its ability to temper male authority, meant that it was fraught with power. Couples used love in multiple ways to reduce male authority, enforce obedience, manipulate each other, and as a tool in negotiations. Similarly, the history of marital intimacy is one of a complex negotiation between duty – performance of which was always central to understandings of intimacy – and the fact that intimate relationships required trust and created vulnerability between partners. Performing intimacy required conformance to appropriate patriarchal gender roles for marriage (ideas of which altered over time) and so reinforced the patriarchal system. Yet, at the same time, intimacy offered democratic potential which destabilised lines of power and opened a space for negotiation.

The ambiguity surrounding marital power manifested itself most clearly within the household. The marital economy was at the heart of marriage throughout the period 1650 to 1850. Couples worked together to ensure the economic stability and success of their union, dividing tasks along gendered lines, although there was often overlap between male and female spheres. The success of the marital economy required husband and wife to negotiate and agree over the household's resources. This negotiation was a power struggle where men's social role as head of household was challenged by women's significant knowledge, control of and access to economic resources. Yet, while this offered women authority within the household, they found it difficult to transform this into power outside of the home. Scottish society viewed women's economic power suspiciously and while their economic role gave women influence over their husband's credit and reputation, unless they wished to undermine the household, it simultaneously restricted their influence to the domestic realm. Women were offered power within the home, causing them to identify with the home and be protective of their role within it. This became increasingly important over the eighteenth century with the rise of the ideology of domesticity.

Patriarchal discourses emphasised male authority and underpinned that authority with violence. Over the course of the eighteenth century, violence was incorporated into constructions of the male body, while it was increasingly incompatible with understandings of the female body as passive. Older conceptions of femininity that offered examples of active women, especially in regard to their sexuality, and the ambiguity of power within the household, threatened to undermine the construction of gender upon which the patriarchal system was built. Men reinforced their power against such threats through violence and this ensured that violence against wives was legitimate in certain contexts, although this legitimacy differed across class. That the three main motivations for marital violence – sexual jealousy, control of female labour, and money – were closely related to the main threats women offered to the patriarchal system, uncontrolled sexuality and control of economic resources, was not a coincidence. It was a reflection of the male need to dominate those spaces where women created independent identities that threatened masculinity – their bodies and their homes.

However, men's abuse of their power over women led to legal and social restrictions on male behaviour, which in turn were used by women as a source of power. Women utilised legal protections of their paraphernalia and heritable property to ensure their economic well-being and as resource in marital negotiations. They used family and the court system to protect them from extreme violence and had the possibility of divorce if their husbands were unfaithful or deserted them. Women also had a legal right to manage their household resources, which they defended vigorously. These legal rights gave women protection from their husbands, allowing them some independence from him and providing tools for women in marital negotiations.

The operation of a patriarchal system therefore is not a story of unreserved male power and down-trodden women. Patriarchy is a lived system; it is a framework that people use to justify male superiority over women and it is one that survived through numerous social, cultural and political changes over the last several centuries. Understanding patriarchy as a system for organising gender and social relationships explains women's continued subordination over time, despite historical change in many other areas of life. This study demonstrated how this happened where, despite some radical transformations in how people conceptualised the world around them, women's social status remained unchanged over two centuries. This process was not about unchecked male force or an overt strategy by a group of men to keep women oppressed, but rather that the belief in women's subordination to their husbands was so deeply ingrained within Scottish, and European, culture that people could not conceive of the world differently. This meant that as they encountered new ideas and new experiences, they did so in a way that reconciled them with this belief, rather than using them to undermine it. This was not always straightforward, but the space for negotiation allowed within this system meant that people found room to adapt. Negotiation was essential to the patriarchal system as it allowed people to relieve tensions and reconcile new experiences with patriarchal values. It was through negotiation that patriarchy adapted and survived, ensuring that challenges to the belief in women's subordination were resisted, and that full equality between men and women remained elusive.

Notes

1   For a review of this literature, see Chapter 1.
2   C. Davidson, *Revolution and the Word: the Rise of the Novel in America* (Oxford: Oxford University Press, 2004), p. 204.

3 A. Broadie, *The Tradition of Scottish Philosophy: A New Perspective on the Enlightenment* (Edinburgh: Polygon, 1990).

4 J.-J. Rousseau, *Discourse on Inequality* (Oxford: Oxford University Press, 1994).

5 A. Herman, *The Scottish Enlightenment: The Scots Invention of the Modern World* (London: Fourth Estate, 2002), pp. 70 and 303–4.

6 J. Popiel, *Rousseau's Daughters: Domesticity, Education and Autonomy in Modern France* (London: University of New Hampshire Press, 2008).

7 J. Rendall, 'Bluestockings and reviewers: gender, culture and power in Britain, c. 1800–1830', *Nineteenth-Century Contexts*, 26:4 (2004), 355–74.

Select bibliography

Archival sources

NATIONAL ARCHIVES OF SCOTLAND (NAS)
CC8 Series Records of the Commissary Court, Edinburgh 1684–1830.
GD1/31 Series Papers of the Maxwell Family of Williamwood, Renfrewshire.
GD1/44/7 Series Letters of Lord and Lady Erskine of Alva.
GD1/51 Series Mylne Papers.
GD1/649 Series The Diary of George Home of Kimmerghame, 1694–1701.
GD3/5 Series Correspondence of Montgomerie Family, Earls of Eglinton.
GD16 Series Papers of the Earls of Airlie.
GD18 Series Papers of the Clerks of Penicuik.
GD21 Series Papers of the Cuninghame Family of Thorntoun.
GD25 Series Papers of the Kennedy Family, Earls of Cassillis.
GD26 Series Papers of the Leslie Family, Earls of Leslie and Melville.
GD32 Series Papers of the Viscounts and Barons of Elibank.
GD40 Series Paper of the Kerr Family, Marquises of Lothian.
GD44 Series Papers of the Gordon Family, Dukes of Gordon.
GD45 Series Papers of the Maule Family, Earls of Dalhousie.
GD46 Series Papers of the Mackenzie Family, Earls of Seaforth.
GD71 Series Papers of the Monro Family of Allan.
GD105 Series Papers of the Duff Family of Fetteresso.
GD110 Series Papers of Hamilton-Dalrymple Family of North Berwick.
GD112 Series Papers of the Campbell Family, Earls of Breadalbane.
GD113 Series Papers of the Innes family of Stow, Peeblesshire
GD124 Series Papers of the Erskine Family, Earls of Mar and Kellie.
GD128 Series Fraser-Mackintosh Collection.
GD137 Series Papers of Scrymgeour Wedderburn of Wedderburn Family, Earls of Dundee.
GD139 Series Papers of the Sutherland Family of Forse, Sutherland.
GD158 Series Papers of Hume of Polworth, Earls of Marchmont.
GD172 Series Papers of the Henderson Family of Fordell.
GD180 Series Papers of the Cathcart Family of Genoch and Knockdolian.

GD190 Series Papers of the Smythe Family of Methven, Perthshire.

GD192 Series Papers of the Balfour Family of Pilrig, Midlothian.

GD193 Series Papers of the Steel Maitland Family.

GD220 Series Papers of the Graham Family, Dukes of Montrose.

GD235 Series Papers of Bonar, Mackenzie and Kermack, WS, Lawyers in Edinburgh.

GD245 Series Papers of Mackenzie, Innes and Logan, WS.

GD248 Series Papers of the Ogilvy Family, Earls of Seafield.

GD263 Series Papers of the Heddle Family of Melsetter, Orkney.

GD267 Series Papers of the Home-Robertson Family of Paxton, Berwickshire.

GD268 Series Papers of the Loch Family of Drylaw.

GD297/1 Series Papers of Hastings (Hamilton Fitzgerald) Family.

GD300 Series Papers of Johnston of Sands.

GD345 Series Papers of the Grant Family of Monymusk, Aberdeenshire.

GD361 Series Papers of the Scott Moncrieff Family.

GD406 Series Papers of the Dukes of Hamilton.

GD446 Series Papers of the Douglas of Strathendy, Fife.

GD461 Series Papers of the Lawrie Family.

RH15/1 Series Papers of Gordon of Carnoustie.

RH15/149 Series Papers of Francis Husband, Merchant at Stockton (Leith).

National Library of Scotland (NLS)

MS.3628 Lyndoch Papers.

MS.16001 Lyndoch Papers.

MS.16002 Lyndoch Papers.

University of Glasgow (GUL)

Acts of the Parliaments of Scotland.

GB 0247 MS. Murray 501 William Motherwell. *The Motherwell collection of Scottish ballads.* c. 1820.

Glasgow City Archives (GCA)

TD219 Series Papers of Campbell of Succouth and Garscube Family.

TD263 Series Papers of Houston Family of Johnstone.

TD589 Series Papers of Hamilton of Barns.

TD1073 Series Papers of Crum Family.

TD1318 Series Papers of Speirs Family of Elderslie.

T-ARD Series Papers of Shaw Stewart Family of Ardgowan.

T-CL Series Papers of Colquhoun of Luss.

T-LX Series Papers of Lennox of Woodhead.

T-PM Series Papers of Maxwell of Pollock.

T-SK Series Papers of Stirling of Keir.

Printed primary sources

An Account of the Most Remarkable Trials and Executions which took place in Scotland for above 300 years (1826).

Answers and Duplies for Mrs Anna Muir, to the Replies given to the Lord's Commissars of Edinburgh, by Walter Nisbet of Craigintinnie (1726).

The Book of Common Order for the Church of Scotland (Edinburgh: William Blackwood and Sons, 1901).

A Fully True, and Particular Account of that Awful Bloody Battle for the Breeks! (Edinburgh: A. Turnbull [c. 1825]).

Report of the General Register's Office of Scotland, 2002, Appendix 1, Table 1, 'Population and vital events Scotland 1855–2001.

The Trial of Divorce at the instance of Peter Williamson printer in Edinburgh, against Jean Wilson, daughter of John Wilson, bookseller in Edinburgh, his Spouse (The booksellers of Edinburgh: 1789).

Alexander, W., *The History of Women, from the Earliest Antiquity to the Present Time* (London: C. Dilly, 1782).

Allestree, R., *The Whole Duty of Man* (London: R. Norton for Robert Pawlet, 1675).

Allestree, R., *The Ladies Calling* (Oxford: Theatre in Oxford, 1700).

Bell, G., *Principles of the Law of Scotland* (Edinburgh: Thomas Clark, 4th edn, 1839).

Beveridge, E. (ed.), *Fergusson's Scottish Proverbs from the Original Print of 1641* (Edinburgh: William Blackwood, 1924).

Campbell, A., Marques of Argyll, *Instructions to a Son* (London: Richard Blackwell, 1689).

Carlyle, A. (ed.), *The Love Letters of Thomas Carlyle and Jane Welsh* (London: John Lane, 1909), pp. 388–95.

Chapone, H. *Letters on the Improvement of the Mind* (London: J. F. Dove, 1827).

Chricton, A. (ed.) *Life and Diary of Col. John Blackadder* (Edinburgh: H. S. Baynes, 1924).

Clive, E. M., *The Law of Husband and Wife in Scotland* (Edinburgh: W. Green, 3rd edn, 1992).

Dalrymple, J., Viscount of Stair, *The Institutions of the Law of Scotland* (Edinburgh: Edinburgh University Press, [1693] 1981).

Erskine, J., *An Institute of the Law of Scotland* (Edinburgh: The Law Society of Scotland, 8th edn [1871] 1989).

Erskine, R., *The Best Match; or the Incomparable Marriage between the Creator and the Creature* (Glasgow: William Smith, 1771).

Fenelon de Salignac de la Mothe, F., *Instructions for the Education of Daughters* (Glasgow: R. & A. Foulis, 1750).

Ferrier, S., *Marriage* (Oxford: Oxford University Press [1818] 1971).

Fordyce, J., *Sermons to Young Women* (London: A. Millar and T. Caddel, 1766).

Fordyce, J., *Addresses to Young Men* (London: T. Cadell, 1777).

Forrester, J., *The Polite Philosopher* (Edinburgh: Robert Freebairn, 1734).

Fraser, P., *Treatise of the Laws of Scotland as Applicable to the Personal and Domestic Relations* (Edinburgh: 1846).

Froude, J. (ed.), *Letters and Memorials of Jane Carlyle*, vol. 1 (Charles Scribner's Sons, 1883).

Giles, W., *The Guide to Domestic Happiness* (London: Whittingham and Rowland for William Button, 10th edn, 1813).

Grant, J. (ed.), *Seafield Correspondence from 1685–1708* (Edinburgh: Edinburgh University Press, 1912).

Gregory, J., *A Father's Legacy to his Daughters* (Edinburgh: 1774).

Home, H., Lord Kames, *Elucidations respecting the Common and Statute Law of Scotland* (London: Routledge [1777] 1993).

Home, H., Lord Kames, *Loose Hints on Education* (Edinburgh: John Bell, Geo. Robertson and John Murray, 1782).

Layman, C. H. (ed.), *Man of Letters: The Early Life and Love Letters of Robert Chambers* (Edinburgh: Edinburgh University Press, 1990).

Mackenzie, G., *The Institutions of the Laws of Scotland* (Edinburgh: John Reid, 1684), pp. 217–32.

MacKenzie, G., *Moral Gallantry* (London: 1821).

McDouall, A., *An Institute of the Laws of Scotland in Civil Rights* (Edinburgh: A. Kincaid and A. Donaldson, 1713).

Millar, J., *The Origin of the Distinction of Ranks* (Edinburgh: William Blackwood [1779] 1806).

Moir, J., *Female Tuition; or an Address to Mothers on the Education of Daughters* (London: J. Murray, 1784).

More, H., *Strictures on the Modern System of Female Education* (London: T.Cadell Jun. and W. Davies, 1799).

Otway, T., *The Orphan or the Unhappy Marriage: A Tragedy* (London: J. Darby, 1726).

Pennington, S., 'Unfortunate mother's advice to her absent daughters', *The Young Lady's Parental Monitor* (Hartford: 1792).

Ramesay, W., *The Gentleman's Companion* (London: E. Okes for Rowland Reynolds, 1672).

Richie, D. (ed.), *Early Letters of Jane Welsh Carlyle* (London: S. Sonnenschien & Co, 1889).

Rousseau, J.-J., *Discourse on Inequality* (Oxford: Oxford University Press, 1994).

Savile, G., Marquis of Halifax, *The Ladies New-Years Gift* (Edinburgh: Matt. Gillyflower and James Partridge, 1688).

Secker, W., *A Wedding Ring Fit for the Finger or the Salve of Divinity on the Sore of Humanity* (Edinburgh: James Watson, c. 1715).

Smith, A., *The Theory of Moral Sentiments* (London: Henry G. Bohn, 1853).

Stennett, S., *Discourses on Domestic Duties* (Edinburgh: J. Ritchie for J. Ogle, 1800).

Walton, F. P., *A Handbook of Husband and Wife according to the Law of Scotland* (Edinburgh: W. Green, 1893).

Whitefield, G., *The Marriage of Cana; a Sermon Preached at Black-heath* (Edinburgh: James Beugo, 1739), pp. 10–11.

[Wilson, A.], *Watty and Meg, or the Wife Reformed* [1790–1810].

Secondary sources

Abbey, R. and D.J. Den Uyl, 'The chief inducement? The idea of marriage as friendship', *Journal of Applied Philosophy*, 18:1 (2001), 37–52.

Abrams, L., *Myth and Materiality in a Woman's World: Shetland 1800-2000* (Manchester: Manchester University Press, 2005).

Ågren, M. and A. Erickson (eds), *The Marital Economy in Scandanavia and Britain 1400-1900* (Aldershot: Ashgate, 2005).

Amussen, S., *An Ordered Society: Gender and Class in Early Modern England* (Oxford: Basil Blackwell, 1988).

Anderson, K., 'Gender, status and domestic violence: an integration of feminist and family violence approaches', *Journal of Marriage and the Family*, 59 (1997), 655–69.

Bailey, J., *Unquiet Lives: Marriage and Marriage Breakdown in England, 1660-1800* (Cambridge: Cambridge University Press, 2003).

Barclay, K., 'Scottish Marriage Texts 1650–1750 (MPhil Dissertation, University of Glasgow, 2004).

Barclay, K., '"I rest your loving obedient wife": marital relationships in Scotland, 1650-1850' (PhD dissertation, University of Glasgow, 2007).

Barclay, K., 'Negotiating patriarchy: the marriage of Anna Potts and Archibald Grant of Monymusk, 1731-1744', *Journal of Scottish Historical Studies*, 28:2 (2008), 83–101.

Barker-Benfield, G. J., *The Culture of Sensibility: Sex and Society in Eighteenth Century Britain* (London: Chicago University Press, 1992).

Bennett, J., 'Feminism and history', *Gender and History*, 3 (1989), 251–72.

Bennett, J., *History Matters: Patriarchy and the Challenge of Feminism* (Manchester: Manchester University Press, 2006).

Berry, H., *Gender, Society and Print Culture in Late-Stuart England* (Aldershot: Ashgate, 2003).

Borschied, P., 'Romantic love and material interest; choosing partners in nine-teenth century Germany', *Journal of Family History*, 11–12 (1986–7), 157–68.

Bossis, M. and K. McPherson, 'Methodological journeys through correspon-dences', *Yale French Studies*, 71 (1986), 63–75.

Bourdieu, P., *Outline of a Theory of Practice* (Cambridge: Cambridge University Press, 1972).

Boyd, K., *Scottish Church Attitudes to Sex, Marriage and the Family 1850-1914* (Edinburgh: John Donald, 1980).

Bray, A., *The Friend* (London: Chicago University Press, 2003).

Brown, I., 'Domesticity, friendship and feminism: female aristocratic culture and marriage in England, 1660–1760', *Journal of Family History*, 7:4 (1982), 406–24.

Brown, K., *Noble Society in Scotland: Wealth, Family and Culture from Reformation to Revolution* (Edinburgh: Edinburgh University Press, 2000).

Capp, B., *When Gossips Meet: Women, Family, and Neighbourhood in Early Modern England* (Oxford: Oxford University Press, 2003).

Carr, R., 'Gender, national identity and political agency in eighteenth century Scotland' (PhD Dissertation, University of Glasgow, 2008).

Carter, L., 'British masculinities on trial in the Queen Caroline Affair of 1820', *Gender and History*, 20 (2008), 248–69.

Carter, P., *Men and Emergence of Polite Society, Britain 1660–1800* (Harlow: Pearson Education, 2001).

Cathcart, A., *Kinship and Clientage: Highland Clanship, 1451–1609* (Leiden: Brill, 2006).

Chartier, R. (ed.), *A History of Private Life: Passions of the Renaissance* (London: Harvard University Press, 1989).

Clark, A., *The Struggle for the Breeches* (Berkeley: University of California, 1995).

Cott, N., *The Bonds of Womanhood: Woman's Sphere in New England, 1780–1835* (London: Yale University Press, 1981).

Cressy, D., *Birth, Marriage, and Death: Ritual, Religion, and the Life-Cycle in Tudor and Stuart England* (Oxford: Oxford University Press, 1997).

Daniels, C., and M. Kennedy (eds), *Over the Threshold: Intimate Violence in Early America* (London: Routledge, 1999).

Darrow, M., 'Popular concepts of marital choice in eighteenth century France', *Journal of Social History*, 19 (1985), 261–72.

Davidoff, L. and C. Hall, *Family Fortunes: Men and Women of the English Middle Class, 1780–1850* (Chicago: Chicago University Press, 1987).

Deglar, C., *At Odds: Women and the Family in America from the Revolution to the Present* (Oxford: Oxford University Press, 1980).

Dolan, F., *Dangerous Familiars: Representations of Domestic Crime in England 1550–1700* (Ithaca: Cornell University Press, 1994).

Duncan, A., 'Patronage and presentations of the self: a late eighteenth-century correspondence' (MSc dissertation, University of Edinburgh, 2007).

Dwyer, J., *Virtuous Discourse: Sensibility and Community in Late Eighteenth-Century Scotland* (Edinburgh: John Donald, 1987).

Dwyer, J., *The Age of Passions: an Interpretation of Adam Smith and Scottish Enlightenment Culture* (East Linton: Tuckwell Press, 1998).

Earle, R., 'Letters and love in colonial Spanish America', *The Americas*, 62:1 (2005), 17–46.

Erickson, A., *Women and Property in Early Modern England* (London: Routledge, 1993).

Eustace, N., '"The cornerstone of a copious work": love and power in eighteenth century courtship', *Journal of Social History*, 34 (2001), 518–45.

Eustace, N., *Passion is the Gale: Emotion, Power and the Coming of the American Revolution* (Chapel Hill: University of North Carolina Press, 2008).

Ewan, E., and M. Meikle, *Women in Scotland, c.1100–c.1750* (East Linton: Tuckwell Press, 1999).

Ewan, E., and J. Nugent (eds), *Finding the Family in Medieval and Early Modern Scotland* (Aldershot: Ashgate, 2008).

Ezell, M., *The Patriarch's Wife: Literary Evidence and the History of the Family* (London: North Carolina University Press, 1987).

Fletcher, A., *Gender, Sex and Subordination in England 1500–1800* (London: Yale University Press, 1995).

Forte, A. D. M., 'Some aspects of the law of marriage in Scotland: 1500–1700', in E. M. Craik (ed.), *Marriage and Property* (Aberdeen: Aberdeen University Press, 1984), pp. 104–18.

Foucault, M., *The Will to Knowledge: the History of Sexuality*, vol. 1 (London: Penguin Books, 1998).

Foyster, E., *Marital Violence: an English Family History, 1660–1857* (Cambridge: Cambridge University Press, 2005).

Frazer, E., 'Mary Wollstonecraft on politics and friendship', *Political Studies,* 56 (2008), 237–56.

Giddens, A., *The Transformation of Intimacy: Sexuality, Love and Eroticism in Modern Societies* (Cambridge: Polity Press, 1992).

Gillis, J., *For Better, For Worse: British Marriages 1600 to the Present* (Oxford: Oxford University Press, 1985).

Gordon, E. and G. Nair, *Public Lives: Women, Family and Society in Victorian Britain* (London: Yale University Press, 2003).

Gowing, L., M. Hunter and M. Rubin (eds), *Love, Friendship and Faith in Europe, 1300–1800* (Basingstoke: Palgrave Macmillan, 2005), pp. 131–49.

Graham, M., *The Uses of Reform: "Godly Discipline" and Popular Behaviour in Scotland and France, 1560–1610* (Leiden: Brill, 1996).

Grassby, R., *Kinship and Capitalism: Marriage, Family, and Business in the English- Speaking World, 1580–1740* (Cambridge: Cambridge University Press, 2001).

Griffin, B., L. Delap, and A. Wills (eds), *The Politics of Domestic Authority in Britain since 1800* (Houndmills: Palgrave Macmillan, 2009).

Hammerton, A. J., *Cruelty and Companionship: Conflict in Nineteenth Century Married Life* (London: Routledge, 1992).

Hardwick, J., *The Practice of Patriarchy: Gender and the Politics of Household Authority in Early Modern France* (University Park: Pennsylvania State University Press, 1998).

Harris, B., 'Power, profit and passion: Mary Tudor, Charles Brandon, and arranged marriage in early Tudor England', *Feminist Studies,* 15 (1989), 59–88.

Harris, B., 'Property, power and personal relations: elite mothers and sons in Yorkist and Early Tudor England', *Signs,* 15 (1990), 606–32.

Hartman, M., *The Household and the Making of History: a Subversive View of the Western Past* (Cambridge: Cambridge University Press, 2004).

Harvey, K. (ed.), *The Kiss in History* (Manchester: Manchester University Press, 2005).

Harvey, K., 'Men making home: masculinity and domesticity in eighteenth-century Britain', *Gender & History*, 21:3 (2009), 520–40.

Hull, I.V., *Sexuality, State and Civil Society in Germany, 1700–1815* (Ithaca: Cornell University Press, 1997).

Hunt, L., *The Family Romance of the French Revolution* (Berkley: University of California Press, 1993).

Hunt, M., *The Middling Sort: Commerce, Gender and Family in England, 1680–1780* (Berkeley: University of California Press, 1996).

Ingram, M., *Church Courts, Sex and Marriage in England, 1570–1640* (Cambridge: Cambridge University Press, 1987).

Kandiyoti, D., 'Bargaining with patriarchy', *Gender and Society*, 2 (1988), 274–90.

Kelsall, H., *Scottish Life 300 Years Ago: New Light on Edinburgh and Border Families* (Edinburgh: John Donald, 1986).

King, S., 'Chance encounters? Paths to household formation in early modern England', *International Review of Social History*, 44 (1999), 23–46.

Kugler, A., 'Constructing wifely identity: prescription and practice in the life of Lady Sarah Cowper', *Journal of British Studies*, 40 (2001), 291–323.

Legates, M., 'The cult of womanhood in eighteenth-century thought', *Eighteenth-Century Studies*, 1 (1976), 21–39.

Leites, E., 'The duty of desire: love, friendship, and sexuality in some Puritan theories of marriage', *Journal of Social History*, 15 (1982), 383–408.

Leneman, L., *Alienated Affections: The Scottish Experience of Divorce and Separation, 1684–1830* (Edinburgh: Edinburgh University Press, 1998).

Leneman, L. and R. Mitchison, *Sexuality and Social Control: Scotland 1660–1780* (Oxford: Basil Blackwell, 1989).

Levine, D., '"For their own reasons": individual marriage decisions and family life', *Journal of Family History*, 7 (1982), 255–64.

Luhmann, N., *Love as Passion: the Codification of Intimacy* (Cambridge: Polity Press, 1986).

Lyons, M., 'Love letters and writing practices: on ecritures intimes in the nineteenth century', *Journal of Family History*, 24 (1999), 232–9.

MacFarlane, A., *Marriage and Love in England: Modes of Reproduction 1300–1840* (Oxford: Basil Blackwell, 1986).

Marshall, R., *Virgins and Viragos: A History of Women in Scotland from 1080 to 1980* (London: Collins, 1983).

Mullen, D. G., *Women's Life Writing in Early Modern Scotland* (Aldershot: Ashgate, 2003).

Nenadic, S., *Laird and Luxury: the Highland Gentry in Eighteenth Century Scotland* (Edinburgh: John Donald, 2007).

Norton, M. B., *Liberty's Daughters: The Revolutionary Experience of American Women* (Ithaca: Cornell University Press, 1980).

O'Hara, D., *Courtship and Constraint: Rethinking the Making of Marriage in Tudor England* (Manchester: Manchester University Press, 2000).

Outhwaite R. B. (ed.), *Marriage and Society: Studies in the Social History of Marriage* (London: Europa, 1981).

Perkin, J., *Women and Marriage in Nineteenth Century England* (London: Routledge, 1989).

Perry, R., *Novel Relations: the Transformation of Kinship in English Relations and Culture, 1748–1818* (Cambridge: Cambridge University Press, 2004).

Pinch, A., *Strange Fits of Passion: Epistemologies of Emotion, Hume to Austen* (Palo Alton: Stanford University Press, 1996).

Pollock, L., 'Rethinking patriarchy and the family in the seventeenth-century England', *Journal of Family History*, 23 (1998), 3–27.

Pollock, L., 'Anger and the negotiation of relationships in early modern England', *Historical Journal*, 47 (2004), 567–90.

Pollock, L., 'Honor, gender and reconciliation in elite culture, 1570–1700', *Journal of British Studies*, 46 (2007), 3–29.

Popiel, J., *Rousseau's Daughters: Domesticity, Education and Autonomy in Modern France* (London: University of New Hampshire Press, 2008).

Rendall, J., 'Virtue and commerce: women in the making of Adam Smith's political economy', in E. Kennedy and S. Mendus (eds), *Women in Western Political Philosophy, Kant to Nietzsche* (New York: St. Martin's Press, 1987), pp. 44–76.

Rendall, J., 'Bluestockings and reviewers: gender, culture and power in Britain, c. 1800–1830', *Nineteenth-Century Contexts*, 26:4 (2004), 355–74.

Reynolds, K. D., *Aristocratic Women and Political Society in Victorian Britain* (Oxford: Clarendon Press, 1998).

Rosaldo, M. Z. and L. Lamphere (eds), *Women, Culture and Society* (Stanford: Stanford University Press, 1974), pp. 17–42.

Rushton, P., 'Property, power and family networks: the problem of disputed marriage in early modern England', *Journal of Family History*, 11 (1986), 205–19.

Sabean, D., *Property, Production, and Family in Neckarhausen, 1700–1870* (Cambridge: Cambridge University Press, 1990).

Sanderson, E., *Women and Work in Eighteenth Century Edinburgh* (Basingstoke: Macmillan Press, 1996).

Scott, J., 'Gender: a useful category of historical analysis', *American Historical Review*, 91 (1986), 1053–75.

Shepard, A., *Meanings of Manhood in Early Modern England* (Oxford: Oxford University Press, 2003).

Shorter, E., *The Making of the Modern Family* (London: Collins, 1976).

Singer, I., *The Nature of Love 2: Courtly and Romantic* (Chicago: Chicago University Press, 1984).

Slater, M., 'The weightiest business: marriage in an upper-gentry family in seventeenth century England', *Past and Present*, 72 (1976), 25–54.

Slater, M., *Family Life in the Seventeenth Century: the Verneys of Claydon House* (London: Routledge, 1984).

Smart, C., *The Ties that Bind: Law, Marriage and the Reproduction of Patriarchal Relations* (London: Routledge, 1984).

Smith-Rosenberg, C., 'The female world of love and ritual: relations between women in nineteenth century America', *Signs*, 1 (1975), 1–29.

Smout, T. C., *A History of the Scottish People, 1560–1830* (London: Fontana Press, 1985).

Spacks, P., *Privacy: Concealing the Eighteenth Century Self* (London: University of Chicago Press, 2003).

Sperling, J., 'Marriage at the time of the council of Trent (1560–70): clandestine marriages, kinship prohibitions, and dowry exchange in European comparison', *Journal of Early Modern History*, 8:1/2 (2004), 67–108.

Staves, S., *Married Women's Separate Property in England, 1660–1833* (London, Harvard University Press, 1990).

Stearns, P. and J. Lewis (eds), *An Emotional History of the United States* (London: New York University Press, 1998).

Stearns, C. and P. Stearns, 'Introducing the history of the emotion', *Psychohistory Review*, 18 (1990), 263–91.

Stone, L., *The Family, Sex and Marriage in England 1500–1800* (London: Weidenfeld and Nicolson, 1977).

Summerfield, P., 'Culture and composure: creating narratives of the gendered self in oral history interviews', *Cultural and Social History*, 1 (2004), 65–93.

Tadmor, N., 'The concept of the household-family in eighteenth century England', *Past and Present*, 151 (1996), 111–40.

Tague, I., 'Love, honour and obedience: fashionable women and the discourse of marriage in the early eighteenth century', *Journal of British Studies*, 40 (2001), 76–106.

Tague, I., *Women of Quality: Accepting and Contesting Ideals of Femininity in England, 1690–1760* (Woodbridge: Boydell Press, 2002).

Taylor, B., 'Feminists versus gallants: manners and morals in Enlightenment Britain', in S. Knott and B. Taylor (eds), *Women, Gender and Enlightenment* (Houndmills: Palgrave, 2005), pp. 30–52.

Thomas, K., 'The double standard', *Journal of the History of Ideas*, 20 (1959), 195–216.

Tilly, L. and J. Scott, *Women, Work and the Family* (London: Routledge, 1989).

Tissari, H., *Lovescapes: Changes in Prototypical Senses and Cognitive Metaphors since 1500* (Helsinki: Societe Neophilologique, 2003).

Tomaselli, S., 'The enlightenment debate on women', *History Workshop Journal*, 20 (1985), 101–24.

Tosh, J., *A Man's Place: Masculinity and the Middle Class Home in Victorian England* (New Haven: Yale University Press, 1999).

Trumbach, R., *The Rise of the Egalitarian Family* (Oxford: Academic Press, 1978).

Vickery, A., *The Gentleman's Daughter: Women's Lives in Georgian England* (London: Yale University Press, 1998).

Wahrman, D., *The Making of the Modern Self: Identity and Culture in Eighteenth Century England* (London: Yale University Press, 2006).

Walby, S., *Theorising Patriarchy* (Oxford: Blackwell, 1990).

Watt, J., *The Making of Modern Marriage: Matrimonial Control and the Rise of Sentiment in Neuchâtel, 1550–1800* (London: Cornell University Press, 1992).

Whyman, S., *Sociability and Power in Late-Stuart England* (Oxford: Oxford University Press, 1999).

Wrightson, K., *English Society 1580–1680* (London: Hutchison, 1982).

Yeazell, R. B., *Fictions of Modesty: Women and Courtship in the English Novel* (Chicago: Chicago University Press, 1984).

Zeldin, T., *An Intimate History of Humanity* (London: Vintage, 1998).

Index

Lightning Source UK Ltd.
Milton Keynes UK
UKHW051442080622
404125UK00014B/276